SEX TALK

HOW BIOLOGICAL SEX INFLUENCES GENDER COMMUNICATION DIFFERENCES THROUGHOUT LIFE'S STAGES

DR. STEPHEN A. FURLICH

Copyright © 2021 by Stephen A. Furlich
All rights reserved, including reproduction of this book or portions in any form whatsoever except brief quotations within research articles and reviews.

This book is not intended to substitute for professional medical treatment. Consulting with a medical professional is recommended for any problems addressed in this book that one may have. The author is not responsible for outcomes from any treatments attempted based upon information from this book.

Dr. Stephen A. Furlich
Communication Studies Program
Texas A&M University-Commerce

Paperback ISBN: 978-1-7366406-0-9
eBook ISBN: 978-1-7366406-1-6

I would like to thank my parents, Charles and Mary Furlich, for their love and support through the years. They have inspired me to help others through my work.

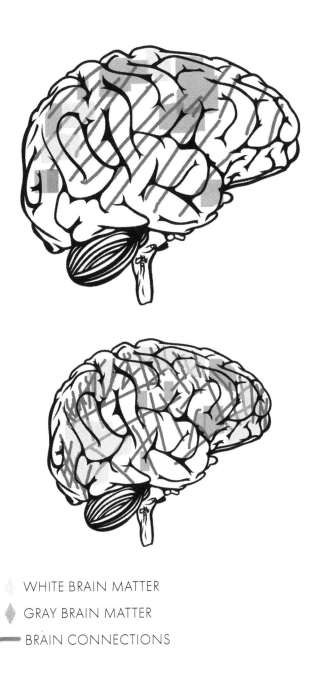

♦ WHITE BRAIN MATTER
♦ GRAY BRAIN MATTER
━━ BRAIN CONNECTIONS

After reading this book, you should be able to identify 5 differences between these examples of the male and female brains. You should also be able to explain how those distinctions are associated with gender communication differences.

TABLE OF CONTENTS

Introduction	xv
PART 1: THE BACKDROP OF GENDER COMMUNICATION.	1
Chapter 1: Are Humans Difficult to Live With or Live Without?	3
- Basic Need of Touch	4
- Later Years	5
- Amount of Touch	6
- Conclusion	7
Chapter 2: History of Gender Communication Research	8
- Gender Communication Information	9
- Gender Communication Research Methodology	10
- Biological Science Research	12
- Gender Communication Research Critiques	12
- Gender Communication Classes	13
- Conclusion	14
Chapter 3: Communibiology History and Research Methods	15
- Gender Communication Academic Research	15
- Biology and Communication	16
- Biological Research Linking Communication	19
- Early Research in Communibiology	20
- fMRI	20
- EEG	23
- Hormone Research	24
- Conclusion	25
PART 2: BIOLOGICAL UNDERPINNINGS OF GENDER COMMUNICATION.	27
Chapter 4: Where to Begin?	29
- Sex Differences Beginnings	29
- Brain Sex Differences	30
- Brain Sex Differences Controversies	32
- Sex Hormones and Development	34
- Sex Hormone Effects	35
- Fetal Sex Survival	37
- Conclusion	38
Chapter 5: Processing Information	39
- Sex Hormones	39
- Performance Sex Differences	40
- Sex Structural Brain Differences	42
- Sex Structural Performance Differences	46
- Activation Sex Differences	46
- Conclusion	48

PART 3: OH HOW WE DIFFER, COMMUNICATIVELY TOO!   49

Chapter 6: Talking about Gender Communication   51
- Biological Basis of Gender Communication   51
- Hippocampus   53
- Gray Matter, White Matter   54
- Corpus Callosum   55
- Language Social Understanding   56
- Blood Flow   58
- Language Differences Evidence   59
- Spatial Communication   64
- Conclusion   65

Chapter 7: She Figured He Understood; Literally He Did Not   66
- Sex Brain Connections   66
- Empathy   67
- Evolutionary Explanations   69
- Conclusion   70

Chapter 8: He Answers Only Questions Asked; She Answers Unasked Questions   71
- Body System Sex Differences   72
- Conversational Gender Differences   73
- Conclusion   74

Chapter 9: He Forgets our Last Conversation, How Previous Conversations Relate to the Current one, Weekend Plans, How She Feels About...   75
- Sex Physiology and Recall   75
- Conversation Topic Recall   76
- Improving Conversational Recall   77
- Conclusion   79

PART 4: FEELS SO GOOD.   81

Chapter 10: How do you Feel?   83
- Sex Hormones and Emotions   83
- Depression Gender Differences   84
- Males and Emotions   84
- Females and Emotions   85
- Brain Sex Differences   85
- Negative Emotional Sex Differences   86
- Serotonin Sex Differences   87
- Stress Gender Differences   89
- Conclusion   91

Chapter 11: Chill, Don't Stress   93
- Affectionate Communication and Stress   93
- Stress Gender Brain Differences   93
- Stress and Gender Social Awareness   95
- Stress and Gender Reaction Differences   96
- Sex Hormones and Stress   98
- Conclusion   100

PART 5: DO YOU UNDERSTAND? — 101

Chapter 12: Women's 6th Sense — 103
- Female Brain 6th Sense — 103
- Empathy — 104
- Insula — 106
- Oxytocin — 107
- Bio evolution — 107
- Senses — 108
  - Smell and Taste — 108
  - Touch — 109
  - Hearing — 109
  - Sight — 110
    - Mirror Neurons — 110
    - Color — 111
- Conclusion — 112

Chapter 13: The Man Trance — 113
- Resting Males — 113
- Resting Females — 114
- Sex Hormones and Rest — 114
- Resting Activity Gender Differences — 114
- Conclusion — 115

PART 6: NAVIGATING GENDER COMMUNICATION. — 117

Chapter 14: Evolution and Problem Solving — 119
- From the Beginning — 119
- Epigenetics — 120
- Male Biological Traits — 121
- Female Biological Traits — 124
- Conclusion — 127

PART 7: RELATIONSHIPS AND INTIMACY. — 129

Chapter 15: Sexual Intimacy, the Double Standard? — 131
- Gender and Offspring Uncertainty — 131
- Infidelity Problems — 132
- Gender Mating Differences — 133
- Sexual Desire & Functioning — 134
  - Attention — 134
  - Arousal — 135
  - Orgasm — 137
- Biological Sexual Differences — 140
- Conclusion — 141

Chapter 16: Should we Date, Procreate? — 142
- Evolutionary Mate Selecting — 142
- Male Attractiveness — 143
- Female Attractiveness — 144
- Applying Evolutionary Attraction — 146
- Body Hair — 147
- Unconscious Attraction — 148
- Conclusion — 150

Chapter 17: Relationship Needs 152
- Relationship Physiology 152
- Sexual Desire and Hormones 152
- Sexual Readiness 154
- Oxytocin, the Bonding Chemical 155
- Synchrony and Mimicry 156
- Love Physiology 157
- Relationship Maintenance 159
- Conclusion 161

Chapter 18: She Demands, He Withdraws 163
- Demand and Withdraw 163
- Conflict Management Styles 165
- Helpful Solutions 167
- Conclusion 168

Chapter 19: Difficult Relationship Conversations 169
- Uncertainty Reductions Theory 169
- Gender Timing for Criticism 171
- How to Criticize 172
- Relationship Perception 173
- Empathy 174
- Deception 174
- Conclusion 176

PART 8: GENERAL ISSUES AND TOPICS. 177

Chapter 20: Her Hobbies, His Hobbies 179
- Early Childhood Hobby Differences 179
- Adult Hobby Differences 181
- Sex Hormones and Hobbies 182
- Conclusion 183

Chapter 21: I Want a Baby, and Another... 184
- Evolutionary Baby Desires 184
- Pregnancy 185
- Post-Pregnancy 187
- Depression 191
- Conclusion 192

Chapter 22: the Family 194
- Children & Gender 194
- Boys 194
- Girls 196
- Family Unit 197
- Clothing 199
- Later Years 200
- Conclusion 201

Chapter 23: Let's Eat	202
- Gender Food Perceptions	202
- Insula Sex Differences and Food	203
- Sex Hormone Food Differences	203
- Eating Disorders and Gender	204
- Conclusion	204
Chapter 24: Workplace	205
- Gender Pay Gap	205
- Gender Discrimination	206
- Basic Biological Workplace Influences	206
- Biological Environmental Responses	208
- Language Career Skills	210
- Gender Communication Applied in the Workplace	211
- Gender Specific Advantages and Disadvantages	212
- Conclusion	214
Chapter 25: Where do we go From Here?	215
- Hormone Therapy	215
- Women	216
- Men	217
- Psychological Effects	219
- Conclusion	219
Chapter 26: '10 Life Lessons'	220
References	221
Index	257
About the author	271

INTRODUCTION

I have taught communication classes for over twenty years at the university level consisting of at least fifteen different course subjects. My time here has led me to find a tremendous need for both communication research and communication classes taught for practical and specific information that can be used in everyday life.

Often, the most admired research and classes taught in communication and related fields are comprised of information that is difficult to apply both professionally and personally. The information is too theoretical and abstract to be applied, or has too many variables in one study to deduce any practical use. It may also be true that the world is seen as too complex to make any generalizations from specific information. Another major issue is research in social sciences and related fields often lacking scientific rigor.

I have taught a gender communication class at the university level for many years and have found these aforementioned problems and many more. The lack of diversity of perspectives in research regarding gender communication has left a void for understanding the subject. The lack of diversity of thought is one reason for this shortcoming in gender communication research.

My personal experiences with teaching gender communication classes over the years has lead me to write this book. I became frustrated by the limited different perspectives on the topic within the social sciences.

I would come across the same research narratives over and over: that any differences in gender communication can be accounted for by social influences.

I would then have to use other research from the sciences, such as biology and neuroscience, to bring other perspectives to the topic. Therefore, I would use several different research approaches in class, one from the social sciences and others from the sciences of biology and neurosciences. I would have to bring these different research tracks together for a more comprehensive understanding of gender communication.

The students taking my gender communication classes over the years have clearly expressed a shared sentiment. They overwhelmingly were not aware of biological influences with gender communication, but often noticed the biological gender communication differences in their everyday lives. They expressed their deep appreciation for my covering of biological influences with gender communication, which they could use to understand and communicate more effectively with others after taking this class.

I have found a third element lacking with the study of gender communication, even after bringing together the social sciences and sciences involving biology and neuroscience from everyday life: More information and perspectives on gender communication are needed, not less. This is what has brought me to write this book; I aim to bring together the social sciences, sciences of biology and neuroscience, and to tie this information together into a practical guide for everyday life, both personally and professionally.

This book combines social science research with biological science research stemming from rigorous scientific research investigations. It precisely tracks how gender communication differences change as one's biology and physiology changes, and how these changes occur throughout different stages of life. This text provides easy-to-understand scientific information for better understanding of oneself and others. It teaches one how to strategically communicate more effectively, and even to change biological physiology of oneself and others through simple-to-understand recommendations. This book can benefit all readers from teens to senior citizens in their personal lives, as well as advancing their careers through strategic communication. A reader can start reading any chapter and gain valuable insight. Overwhelming scientific research evidence proves, with absolute 100% certainty, that biological sex influences gender communication differences!

PART 1

THE BACKDROP OF GENDER COMMUNICATION

CHAPTER 1

ARE HUMANS DIFFICULT TO LIVE WITH OR LIVE WITHOUT?

Humans are a complex species. These complexities range from the way we think, feel, communicate, relate with others, and survive to mention a few areas. These should not be thought of as separate areas, but rather as interrelated. They are interdependent and influence the whole person. To add to the complexity, it is often a delicate balance to maintain a healthy person. Too much or too little attention or focus in one area can lead to overstimulation in that area and neglect for other areas of life. An underlining theme for these areas and humans as a whole is communication.

Communication is essential in order to survive.[207] For the most part, humans rely upon others for their own survival. This can come in the form of basic needs such as food, water, shelter, and in modern society employment and money. Furthermore, humans have a necessity for connecting with others and building different forms of relationships.

Evidence of this is present prior to birth. Human fetuses look toward three dots that resemble a human face but do not look toward three dots that do not resemble a human face.[549] Oved (2017) contends that the need for love and belongingness is more crucial to human survival than was originally set forth in Maslow's hierarchy of needs. This viewpoint is taken because love and belongingness is a prerequisite to feeling safe. The security that comes from forming interpersonal relationships is especially vital to society's continuation. Humans have a need to build and maintain relationships with other people. Of course, in order to do this, communication is key. However, the more pressing question to ask involves the parameters of this need.

BASIC NEED OF TOUCH

Let's first begin by understanding the importance of touch. Evidence has shown that this physical and psychological need to connect with others greatly influences our physical health.[211] Harlow and Zimmerman (1958) had one of the first studies showing the need monkeys have to connect through touch for psychological and physical development and health, even if the touch and connection is with an inanimate object. Recent research has also found similar results.[616] This same essential need for touch can also be found with humans.

Haney (2018) describes the extreme side effects of solitary confinement in incarceration facilities. When a person is isolated for over twenty-four hours, it takes a serious toll on their psychological health. They can begin to lose sense of time; their senses become much more fragile; hallucination becomes frequent, and the person exhibits dangerously unhealthy behaviors. These lead to psychological damage, which influences the individual's physical health as well. This includes appetite, sleep, behavioral routines, and self-mutilation.

The human need for connecting through touch begins early on in everyone's lives. The health and well-being of newborns is dependent upon connecting with other humans, especially through the use of touch. Infants having contact with caregivers is necessary because it provides necessary comfort and stress relief.[643] There was an institution years ago that had infants. A serious problem started to occur with development among the newborns. It was perplexing because the newborn babies had all of their physical needs met, such as food, water, shelter, and sleep. However, one key component was missing: connecting and bonding with other humans. The babies were not touched except during feeding times. This led to developmental problems from what some have called, informally, a broken heart. Once the institution began to incorporate holding the infants into protocol, it did not take long to see improved health results.[98] Touch plays an important role in an infant's life because the infant takes on the emotional state of the caregiver through touch.[690]

Recently, orphanages have seen even greater positive psychological and mental health outcomes in orphanages with intentional healthy touch. Knowing that someone cares is one such outcome. The Buds to Blossom organization has utilized affective touch learned through massage therapy training for children in orphanages. Affective touch communicates compassion and caring to the children, and positively affects physiological as well as psychological development that boosts the immune system.[448] The importance of touch is further illustrated by breastfeeding mothers, who are more cognitively sensitive to their infant's crying needs than mothers who do not breastfeed.[342]

LATER YEARS

In our later years, the need for connecting with others and touch is not much different. Pressman and Sheldon (2005) found social support linked to physiological health of residents in senior living. Residents who had more social relationships with others had healthier physiological states. Lubkin and Larson (2013) describe the negative impact on mental and physical health of people living in isolation, such as in senior living facilities. Their findings of senior living facilities resemble those of Menehan's (2012) findings related to children living in orphanages.

Senior living facilities have realized this need for contact with other people and have made adjustments to meet the needs of their residents. Facilities now build social support systems between the residents living in the facility, and train employees to socially engage with residents.[576, 601] Time has not changed the need for touch. Now, some senior living facilities even have robotic assistants with which their senior residents may interact.[520]

AMOUNT OF TOUCH

Now that it has been established that touch and connecting with others is important psychologically and physically, one can conclude the more touch the better. Wrong; too much touch or crowdedness can be detrimental to one's psychological and physical health.[518] Walk down any major sidewalk or take public transportation in any big city and observe the effects of overcrowding. People tend to view other people less individually, empathize less, make less eye contact, and display fewer socially polite behaviors. These are the result of stress caused by too much crowding. Numerous studies have found negative effects of too many animals living in the same area. One of the major outcomes is disease.[374]

A classic study is Christian's (1963) study of the effects of overcrowding with deer. The deer had plenty of food, water, and shelter to meet their basic needs. However, they began to die off regardless. The one commonality for this was the stress caused by overcrowding of too many animals in one place. The psychological stress from overcrowding led to a weakened immune system. As a result, the deer became less healthy and more vulnerable to dying off.

Humans need some connection with others and to exchange touch; two people living together in a relationship must be ideal. The answer is not that simple. If it were, then the excessively stated statistic that half of marriages end in divorce would not be consistently found.[21] Digging beyond a simple number of how many people should live together, it is the lack of communication and also arguing that are in the top-five popular reasons for divorce according to several studies covering years of data collection.[387]

Again, our needs for survival come back to communication. If it were true that males and females are so similar to each other and communicate the same way, then the divorce rate would not stem from arguing and conflict as the top reasons for divorce. Scientific evidence suggests gender communication differences, such as females being more sensitive to touch. They can sense touch more acutely and experience more pain than what a male will feel from the same touch.[322] Hence, relating to others is important and touch plays a vital role, but males and females have different sensitivities and experiences with touch.

CONCLUSION

Humans have a basic need to have social interactions with others. This has been found early on in life and carries throughout one's life. However, it is complex in terms of the amount of interaction and the circumstances of the interactions. If a vital component of a relationship such as touch can have gender communication differences then perhaps other areas of communication essential in relationships can differ as well.

It is the intention of this book to explore these other areas of communication that may differ between males and females, and how they influence how we communicate and understand each other. Specifically, the rest of this book aims to better understand how our biological sex influences how we communicate and interpret other people throughout our lives. To ignore biological sex as a factor influencing communication is detrimental to forming and maintaining healthy relationships, both personally and professionally.

CHAPTER 2

HISTORY OF GENDER COMMUNICATION RESEARCH

What we know about a topic is often dependent upon the available information. Gender communication is no different. What we know about gender communication is dependent upon the researchers producing it and the publishers publishing it.

Before diving deeper into the research that is responsible for the majority of available information on gender communication, let's identify a few basic definitions. Often, the general public uses the words sex and gender interchangeably, but they are not the same. Sex refers to one's biological makeup characteristics of male or female.[21] Sex involves chromosome pairing usually of XX or XY, genetic coding, reproductive organs, and body chemical composition to mention a few areas. These inner sex characteristics often influence the outward appearance of individuals.

Gender, on the other hand, is a social construct involving how one communicates, behaves, and one's outward appearance.[21] As one can observe from the definition of gender, it is studied and understood from a social perspective compared to sex that is understood and studied from a biological science approach.

GENDER COMMUNICATION INFORMATION

Much of the available information that we have about gender communication studies gender as a social construct while ignoring the role of biological sex. The vast majority of research about gender communication approaches gender as a separate construct from biological sex. This approach limits the amount of perspectives and information available addressing gender communication. Often, having fewer perspectives and ideas is detrimental to holistically understanding a given area of study.

How did understanding gender communication reach this point of limited perspectives and approaches? It begins at a basic level and grows from there. Tannen (1990) has a central piece addressing gender communication. She takes the position that there are language gender communication differences between males and females. This argument comes from a sociolinguistic approach. Essentially, from this perspective, society creates these gender communication differences. This occurs because boys and girls grow up in two different cultures, according to Tannen. Assumptions are made as to how males and females should communicate, and society reinforces these assumptions. Those who abide by these standards are rewarded, and those who do not abide often experience repercussions. Gender communication classes are taught mostly from this sociolinguistic perspective. This approach does not recognize biological sex as playing a part with influencing one's communication, but rather the way culture structures the communication for that particular sex.

Biological sex does not fit the sociolinguistic narrative on gender communication. To think that gender communication differences are entirely derived from society is unequivocally incorrect. Societies change, social norms change, and social structures change, but some of the same gender communication differences persist regardless.[97]

It is rather easy to understand how the study of gender communication arrived to this point. The instructors teaching gender communication classes tend to come from the sociolinguistic paradigm embracing the different cultures approach, with Tannen's (1990) book as a major contributor. Universities hire individuals that fit this line of thinking, which match those already teaching gender communication. Instructors teach their classes accordingly. This involves biology as a non-factor of influence with gender communication.

The instructors only account for part of the lack of diversity of perspectives on gender communication. The textbooks are written based on previous research, which is often conducted by these same individuals with similar viewpoints on gender communication. Therefore, students get a double exposure to the same set of ideals—one from the instructor, and the other from course materials all reinforcing the same topics and narratives about gender communication, often from a sociolinguistics approach.

GENDER COMMUNICATION RESEARCH METHODOLOGY

The research process resembles that of the teaching process for gender communication. It often involves submitting manuscripts to academic journals. The review process involves one person who is deemed an expert on the topic serving as a journal editor. The journal editor receives the manuscript and sends it out to two or three reviewers, who are also deemed experts on the subject. The reviewers give their feedback about manuscripts to the editor, who then decides which manuscripts get published in academic journals and which do not.

These academic journal articles are the ones used for course material in classes taught, such as synthesizing them together for a class textbook. As is the case with gender communication research, the journal editor often has similar perspectives as the journal reviewers of articles. Therefore, the same ideas and perspectives get accepted and those that differ often do not. Frequently the gender communication editor and reviewers have a sociolinguistic approach to gender communication.

Diversity of thought is lacking in the study of gender communication, especially regarding the influence of biological sex. To sum up available gender communication information: you have people with similar ideas, values, and perspectives, in charge of hiring the instructors, teaching the classes, conducting the research, and influencing what research gets published and which does not. That is the system that controls the available information about gender communication.

This book differs from Tannen's (1990) sociolinguistics approach to gender communication. This book takes the position that rather than society, different cultures, and language structure influencing gender communication differences, gender communication differences are a reflection of biological differences in the areas responsible for communication. These areas include the human brain and sex hormones. The human brain is a major contributing factor to all human communication. Furthermore, analyzing brain characteristics can distinguish biological sex with over 90% accuracy.[22]

The research methods often employed in gender communication research vary. Issues can arise about the objectivity of the research design of popular gender communication research data collection techniques.[404] Gender communication research often relies upon the researcher's interpretations of data to determine results of a study.[619] The research methods can range from theoretical pieces, television viewing data, textbook language use, pictures in books, and mass media portrayals to mention a few of the interpretive methods of data collecting.[171, 403, 517, 533, 546, 633]

When reading these articles, it is difficult to understand the level of objective certainty when statistical analyses do not represent the data. In other words, it is upon the researchers to determine the major themes to infer from a study rather than relying upon statistical analysis to determine the conclusions. Often, these data-gathering techniques do not have a predetermined criteria threshold of requiring statistical 95% certainty that their findings are a result of their data and not from other factors. This is important because that is the criteria for biological research to be deemed statistically credible.

In order for research in biology to credibly claim that there is a significant contributing variable for a particular finding, they have to be at least 95% certain that it is that particular variable's contribution and no more than 5% uncertain that it may be from some other variable. Otherwise, the biological scientific research finding is considered nonsignificant.

BIOLOGICAL SCIENCE RESEARCH

The biological sciences conduct research in highly controlled environments, such as labs that enable them to isolate other distracting variables and focus only on the variables of interest. The statistical analyses in biological research is also rigorous. One approach involves using statistical analyses to compare the results of two sample groups, such as male scores and female scores for a particular gender communication variable.[249, 416] Another methodological approach in biological science is to statistically test whether there is a significant correlational relationship between two variables, as one variable changes then another is likely to change as well.[722]

These controlled experiments help to control the research environment, reduce researcher biases, and have statistics that support findings. Some of the research about biological sex influencing gender communication comes from the highest quality neuroscience research programs, psychology programs, medical schools, and psychiatry clinics at the most highest prestigious universities and private practices in the world. It is this type of research that is used throughout this book.

GENDER COMMUNICATION RESEARCH CRITIQUES

Soderlund and Madison (2017) investigated whether gender studies and closely related fields of study in the social sciences had research considered to be less objective when compared with other research areas in the social sciences. They examined journal articles in gender studies and related fields consisting of over 2,800 statements. The objective was to examine whether these articles lacked objectivity in the areas of bias, normativity, or political activism and also explanations for behaviors in the areas of biology/ genetics, individual/ group differences, environmental/ culture, and societal institutions. The conclusion was that gender studies research did express more bias and normativity compared with other social science research.

Furthermore, gender studies research emphasized much more cultural, environmental, social, and societal realms for influencing gender. It allowed for considerably less biological and individual differences when compared with other social science research. This study illustrates a lack of diverse thought when approaching gender studies research.

A follow-up study addressing research quality in gender areas was conducted. Madison and Soderlund (2018) compared different types of articles regarding scientific quality and to what degree they emphasized gender as a major perspective. Their research concluded that the more a gender perspective was emphasized, the lower the scientific quality of the research article. As a result, Madison and Soderlund suggest that areas of study involving gender should implement research methods strategies that are more scientific, such as those found in other disciplines.

Jaschik (2017) writes about an article published on the topic of gender studies that called the male penis conceptual and not a male organ. The article Jaschik addressed was an intentional hoax by Lindsay and Boyle (2017). Jaschik writes that Lindsay and Boyle published the article as an intentional hoax to call the quality of gender studies research into question. The article by Lindsay and Boyle lays out the argument that the male penis is not a physical organ but rather is created through society as a construct. This article was initially submitted to NORMA: International Journal for Masculinity Studies and was rejected.

NORMA is published by a well-known company of Taylor and Francis. However, the journal, owned by Taylor and Francis, did recommend submitting it to another journal of theirs called Cogent Social Sciences. Lindsay and Boyle did ultimately get this article published with ease in Cogent Social Sciences, while also emphasizing masculinity as being responsible for global warming.

GENDER COMMUNICATION CLASSES

Classes about gender communication often focus on historical data and information to maintain their current positions. While it may be important to remember this information, it becomes questionable whether statistics from fifty years ago are relevant to decisions made in today's drastically different world.[119] For example, life expectancies change, the number of women pursuing advanced degrees changes, and types of careers change.

These are general topics that classes addressing gender communication often cover while overlooking ways to understand the role of gender communication during interpersonal communication interactions. Here are some of the gender studies courses found at universities: Women Writers, Women Gender Lit. Culture, Feminist Media Studies, Women and Art, Women and Gender in European History, Women Politics Public Policy, Women in Post-War America, Feminist Theory, Women Gender & Sexuality in the United States.

One can see from this list that understanding communication by recognizing biological sex as a variable with gender communication is negated. Also overlooked are the many issues men struggle with in our society on a daily basis.

CONCLUSION

Our understanding of gender communication is limited by the available information on the topic. The system in place that produces the research and teaches the classes on gender communication has flaws. More diversity of thought and scientific rigor is needed in order to more comprehensively understand gender communication. Biological science has great potential to increase the knowledge base of gender communication.

CHAPTER 3

COMMUNIBIOLOGY HISTORY AND RESEARCH METHODS

GENDER COMMUNICATION ACADEMIC RESEARCH

Academic areas that study gender communication have often been in biological denial. There has been a long lasting debate of nature versus nurture; gender communication research has chosen nurture when referring to society's influence on gender communication. The use of self-reported data in gender communication has missed the nuance causes for communication that biology offers.[694] Furthermore, the use of self-reported data lacks objectivity and accuracy because it is not in real-time, has difficulties accessing the subconscious, relies upon recall of participants, and does not focus on precise physiological attributes and functions that can give great insight into communication.[453]

Conversely, all communication has always been influenced by biology.[207] All communication is greatly influenced by the brain.[22] It is not a question of whether biology exists and influences communication, but whether we accept decades of overwhelming biological evidence that finds biology influential with communication, or whether we discount that evidence entirely.[610] The National Institute of Health now requires grant applications to account for biological sex as a variable when studying vertebrate animals.

There is compelling evidence to suggest that neuroscience research should accept this same policy.[607] A simplistic understanding of the communication process clearly shows an interconnection between the physical body and communication performing together. The sender of a message encodes the electrochemical signal in their brain that is conveyed for the receiver to decode. Both the sender and receiver of the message create a mental image of what the message represents. Verbal communication uses vocal cord movements to create sounds that have language meaning, which the receiver will distinguish through their auditory system.[693] It is the aim of this book to settle the debate with 100% certainty that some of what is observed in society regarding gender communication behavioral differences are a reflection of biological sex.

BIOLOGY AND COMMUNICATION

Let's first begin by overviewing the role of biology with communication. It is not a new concept to suggest biology influences our communication. Darwin (1872) suggested biological influences on communication behaviors. He suggested that our genes influence our traits and communication behaviors, usually in order to survive. Ekman and Friesen (1975) overviewed six universal emotional expressions in the face that are still recognized today regarding nonverbal communication. If most people around the world from different cultures are expressing emotions similarly, then these cultural differences are too many to attribute socialization as the constant contributing factor. On the other hand, biology is likely influencing emotion expressions of people around different parts of the world in a similar way.

Beatty and McCroskey (1998) were among the first researchers to use statistics to link biological influences on communication with more advanced scientific research designs and methodology. They defined this area of study as communibiology that focuses on neurobiological fundamentals of human communication behaviors. They focused some of their early research on how one's biology influences one's communication anxiety. In other words, the level of anxiousness that one feels when one communicates—such as giving a speech—is influenced to some degree from their biological makeup. They derived this connection from researching and teaching public speaking classes. Some students did not change their level of anxiety even after specialized treatment for communication apprehension.[168]

McCroskey created treatment sessions for those students with high levels of communication apprehension. He found these treatment sessions could not entirely alleviate communication apprehension. He and his research team considered that if treatment with communication apprehension is limited with its potential, then there may be a permanent biological variable at play. Furthermore, having consistent communication behaviors by an individual in various contexts illustrates a lesser influence from these environmental factors and more so from biological traits.

These observations illustrate the limitation of social learning, while providing more predictable results from neurobiology.[50] Beatty, McCroskey, and Heisel (1998) created the area of communibiology as a result. They focused on studying neurology to help understand communication apprehension. Beatty and McCroskey (2000) quantified biological influences on communication. They take the position that communication is influenced by biology ranging from 60-80%, such as communication apprehension is 80% influenced by biology and 20% by social factors. The neurobiological system responsible for some of our communication behaviors is mainly a result from biology, and is not influenced by social learning.

McCroskey's communibiological approach to communication helped grow the study of communication with a scientific research approach from top universities in the world using the 95% statistical significant threshold in order to accept a research claim about a particular variable's contributing effect, while only 5% uncertainty that the research finding is from some other factor not accounted for. If scientific researchers are not at least 95% certain about the claims they make, then those claims are deemed insignificant and cannot be ruled as a contributing factor.

Often, biological research uses highly controlled experiments that help remove researcher bias. An example of this is a placebo-controlled, double blind, between subjects experiment.[419] This experimental design allows researchers to objectively study the differences between groups of people that differ on a particular variable.

McCroskey and Beatty, along with others, take the position that the more people have in common biologically, the more similarly they will communicate. The body, mind, and communication are not inseparable. Floyd (2014) specifically calls for more research in communication from a biological understanding. Communication research too often ignores biology, while other research focused on biological influences with communication is derived from disciplines that do not focus primarily on communication research, such as neuroscience.

The crux of culture, media, and other components of human society have biology preceding all of these social influences for thousands of years. It is a far stretch to think that influences of modern society, or even the past few hundred years, can unravel what has kept the human species sustainable. There are behaviors that were necessary for survival that have been refined and improved upon over thousands of years that are still used today.

This book is written with a monism paradigm. The brain influences psychological states and processes, which influences and is influenced by the peripheral nervous system, endocrine system, and immune system.[453] The brain is not merely activated in a reactionary function to stimuli but rather makes predictions about social situations from the stimuli evidence that is present and then proceeds with what is thought as appropriate behaviors or communication to engage.[615] Therefore, the more a group of people have biological similarities and likely predictive behaviors, the more likely they are to communicate in a similar fashion. If the brain and body chemicals play an important part in one's communication and differences have been found between males and females regarding these areas, then the focus of this book is to examine how these differences between the sexes can influence gender communication.

BIOLOGICAL RESEARCH LINKING COMMUNICATION

Communication and related areas of study have not adequately addressed biological influences on communication. These fields of study that research social behaviors, such as gender communication, often rely upon survey data, observations, interviews, historical data, and societal observations to mention a few. All of these approaches have major flaws. They are not able to adequately isolate individual variables to remove other possible explanations.

Researcher bias can influence questions asked, answers received, and conclusions drawn. Often, conclusions drawn from the results are open to interpretations of the researchers. For example, researchers interview participants in their study of gender communication and then draw the conclusions of the themes they identify from the interview material. Social observational studies might only provide a small snapshot of social interactions but often general conclusions are drawn from limited data.

Historical data can be outdated and no longer relevant. Humans are complex and so is language. It is beneficial to the advancement of understanding and predicting communication theory with greater accuracy when it is testable, measures nuances, and have a multidimensional approach such as combining brain imaging activity, self-reports, content analytics, and communication behavioral measurements.[694]

It is the position of this book that biological anatomy and physiology, which functions to understand others and communicate with others, can be studied to better understand communication. If a particular part of a male's body influences communication differently from the same part in a female's body, then gender communication differences are likely to be found.

Communibiology research can have various research designs to collect data. Some of the more popular ones that this book will use to better understand gender communication are fMRI, EEG, and body hormone levels. These scientific research approaches are almost exclusively conducted outside of the area of communication and related fields. This research is often performed in disciplines such as biology, neuroscience, psychiatry, and within medical schools. These studies are often able to isolate and measure specific precise variables to better understand their role with gender communication. The data provides visibly observable results of gender communication influences. The brain is the core element for communication creation and understanding, which can provide great insight into better predicting communication.[693]

EARLY RESEARCH IN COMMUNIBIOLOGY

Earlier research in communibiology used research methods that relied heavily on correlational variable reactions. For example, some of the initial communibiological research involved the central nervous system, such as chemical reactions of brain activity in response to studies involving drug effects.[51] Other studies involved the peripheral nervous system, such as communication between the brain and the rest of the body through sensor and motor neurons.

Information that can be deemed from the peripheral nervous system is heart rate, skin conductance, skin amplitude, and facial electromyography.[453] For example, skin conductance can be used to better understand affect and cognition during communication.[529] While these early studies helped to better understand the role of biology with communication, they were limited regarding how well they could exclude other variables as possible causes. The brain is a main starting point for communication and these early methods were further removed from the starting point source of the brain.

fMRI

The initial fMRI studies began in the early 1990's.[433] An fMRI scanner produces an image of the brain and neural activity from neurovascular coupling mechanisms having combinations of physiological and chemical components. The images produced by the scans show hemodynamic changes companioned with neural activity.[6]

Functional magnetic reasoning imaging (fMRI) can be used to show how brain imaging visual displays can enable neural predictions of communication behaviors.[187] This research approach is more popular recently in communibiological research because it hones in on the starting block of communication: the brain. It enables physiological and neurological reactions to become building blocks for communication models and theories that have predictive abilities. These communication models and theories can expand from the individual neuron level to population generalizations.[694] As time goes on, more studies are using fMRI technologies to better understand communication and contribute to communication theory.[695]

Weber, Mangus, and Huskey (2015) offer several pieces of advice to consider when evaluating conclusions of fMRI studies. First they stress the importance of localization and dissociable focuses of the study. Studies using fMRI should concentrate on one particular area of the brain that can be independently analyzed as to high activity during a particular task and not observing high activity during other unrelated tasks that contradict the premise of the relationship between that area of the brain and communication behaviors.

A more precise understanding can occur when isolating a particular area of the brain for one specific emotion communicated and that same area observed as less active or not at all when opposite emotions are communicated. Secondly, they recommend linking this localized finding to communication task outcomes.

Communication behaviors should align with the localized findings. What is found and concluded from the fMRI study should be observable communication behaviors. For example, a specific part of the brain that is activated when someone receives positive communicaiton should have a similar activation when that individual communicates positively to others. Thirdly, the brain should have consistent brain activity localizations when performing different communication tasks involving the same variables of interest. For example, to better understand brain activity and aggression by observing the same brain areas activated when watching a violent movie as when playing a violent video game.

Weber, Mangus, and Huskey (2015) describe the physiological and visual depiction of using an fMRI to better understand communication.

The session usually begins with an initial scan of the participant's brain. This helps to align the scanner and the participant's brain. Then, functional scans are taken with the participant performing a particular communicative task. These separate three-dimensional scans are taken at different time periods, usually seconds apart, and then converted into an image. The brain is comprised of interconnected neurons that work as a system using electrochemical means to send messages to other parts of the system.

The fMRI measures the blood flow and oxygen levels in the form of glucose when neurons fire. Neuron activity corresponds with oxygen consumption. The changes in oxygen levels in the blood change magnetic properties of that particular area of the brain. Neural activity picks up when this occurs from the higher amount of oxygen provided. Magnetic fields and radio-frequency pulses are detected by the fMRI for these oxygen and brain activity changes. The differences between oxygenated and deoxygenated areas are called BOLD contrast.[6]

The fMRI studies can be set up in different ways. Turner, Huskey, and Weber (2018) describe three prominent ways that almost all fMRI studies involving communication can be used. One way is the functional brain activity. This approach is used to identify where brain activity is located and even sometimes when it occurs. This approach is structured from a linear model, such as that the presence of a stimuli can compare brain activity with removing that stimuli. The same participant can be exposed to a particular stimuli of interest and then at a different time exposed to a neutral stimuli. To understand the area of the brain activated with emotion, the participant may watch a film about a math equation and then a separate film from a romance movie. The brain images of activation would then be compared.

Functional connectivity is another methodological approach that is employed with fMRI research. This method is not only focused on understanding where brain activity occurs, but how it is related to other areas of the brain. This approach considers the brain as an interconnected system in that each part influences other parts.

A third approach would be the synthetic analysis methods. This approach takes into consideration the findings from the previous approaches and makes useful applications from those findings. It goes a step further than merely finding a particular location on the brain of activity or identifying interrelationships between different brain areas. It can be quite useful for communication scholars to apply fMRI findings to better predict future communication behaviors.

The above approach often uses correlational relationships to better understand the brain with communication. A stimuli can be introduced—such as watching a film—and a correlation can be constructed between the relationship of the activity area of the brain when watching the film and the area of the brain activated when not watching the film. Correlations between different areas of the brain can also be performed. When a stimuli is present or communication behaviors performed, correlations of different areas of the brain can observe synchrony of brain activity from the areas of the brain having similar or dissimilar changes together. Correlations can also be made to predict which communication behaviors are likely to be displayed when a stimuli activates a particular area of the brain.[694]

EEG

Another approach to studying the connection between biology and communication is through the use of Electroencephalography (EEG). There are advantages and disadvantages of using an EEG rather than fMRI. Morey (2018) describes advantages and disadvantages between EEG and fMRI and also describes the processes involved with using EEG. An advantage is that the EEG can record much shorter time periods of brain processes, milliseconds in comparison to the fMRI that can take up to several seconds.

On the other hand, the fMRI has a better resolution than the EEG, which enables it to give more precise detailed information. The EEG begins with securing anywhere from 4 to 256 electrodes on the scalp of the participant to monitor electric signals given by cortical neurons. The activities are recorded by the strength of the summed electrical signals along with the location as determined by the electrode location. As with fMRI, the EEG focuses on learning more about communication from the brain.

Neurons are the foundation of the nervous system responsible for information sending, receiving, and synthesizing. Small gaps between neurons are connected to one another through synapsis. This complex system enables communication within the brain and between the brain and the rest of the body system through neural messages transferred through chemical and electrical signals that influence our thoughts, feelings, and behaviors. Positive and negative ions moving inside and outside of the cell are related with activation of the neuron. Neurons that are in close proximity to each other can experience similar reoccurring activations that create interrelated networks. These networks, working in unison of synaptic activity, can then sum up electric activity that makes it to the surface of the scalp.

Two different types of information can be done through the use of EEG. One is event-related potentials, which monitors bursts or spikes of electric activity as related to events such as perceptual, cognitive, emotional, sensory, or motor. The intensity, magnitude, and amount of activity are recorded. The second type of use for EEG is neural oscillators, which monitors the synchronous firing of the neurons. The frequency of the electric oscillator activity can give insight into different cognitive processes depending upon the pace of the oscillator. The strength of the activity can give insight into communication outcomes such as memory, emotions, and complexity of mental processes.

HORMONE RESEARCH

As will be covered more extensively later in this book, biological influences on gender communication differences are not confined to the functioning of the brain. Hormones also play a pivotal role with influencing gender communication differences. There are numerous ways through which researchers investigate hormonal influences.

One way that researchers can study the influence of sex hormones on development of humans and subsequently later with gender communication is by analyzing the embryonic fluid of the fetus in the mother's womb. This can be done by extracting amniotic fluid with a diethyl ether.[37] There are other ways to measure hormone levels of a fetus, such as through the use of hyphenated mass spectrometric tools and also through the testes in vitro.[486]

Another way to measure hormone levels is through blood-testing participants in the experiment to understand how hormone levels are related with brain functioning.[291, 620] Blood sampling can also be used along with ultrasounds to measure fetal sex-specific development associated with hormones.[43, 212] Extracting fluids is not the only way to measure hormone levels; breast tissue can be another option.[154]

To understand the effects of a hormone, participants are often randomly assigned for one group to receive the hormone, while the other group does not receive the hormone treatment. The interested outcomes between both groups are compared.[245] One common approach to expose participants to a given hormone is through intranasal administration.[416] Another approach is to measure each participant's natural levels and determine whether certain levels are related with particular communication behaviors.

Various types of hormone levels can also be measured through saliva.[26, 164] The skin can be another valuable means to gather hormone levels without medically extracting body fluids. An absorbent paper technique can be placed on a person's skin to absorb follicles in its micro-cavities as early as twenty-four hours after birth.[296]

Documents are yet another avenue to understand the role of hormones. Self-reported data can be an effective way to measure the impact of hormone levels.[212, 689, 726] Another approach using reports are the medical record history of participants in a study concerning their hormone levels.[186]

CONCLUSION

The advancement of science has opened possibilities to better understand gender communication differences by enabling researchers to more objectively study specific variable influences of gender communication differences. Precision of research has improved greatly with these scientific technologies. It is imperative that a multiple of measurement techniques be used to more comprehensively study gender communication. These improvements in studying biology have put to rest any doubt that biology does indeed influence communication. This book will use research findings that implemented these different research approaches just covered to study biology and gender communication.

PART 2

BIOLOGICAL UNDERPINNINGS OF GENDER COMMUNICATION.

CHAPTER 4

WHERE TO BEGIN?

SEX DIFFERENCES BEGINNINGS

Approximately 95% of similarities exist between the genomes of males and females, but there are some gene, protein, and molecular sex differences.[31] It is the position of Arnold (2017) that sex-specific chromosomal differences start sex differences between males and females at conception, before sex hormonal influences take place. Irreversible and lifelong cell and tissue sex differences occur at conception.

There are two X chromosomes for females, whereas males have a Y chromosome to accompany their single X chromosome. According to Arnold (2017), these sex chromosomal differences in expression are the originating source for differing males from females in development and throughout adulthood. The sex difference of XY chromosome combination from XX leads to the expression of different sex characteristics by promoting and suppressing different attributes in XY humans from XX humans that are present in the entire body. After the chromosomal differences are in place, the gonads of male or female are developed that then express certain sex-specific hormones. It is the masculinization from the Y chromosome that creates sex differences in biological expressions. These create effect differences throughout the entire life of the male both in body and behavior. There are functional differences for cells that have two Xs compared with cells only having one X.

Two X chromosomes means that one of them will activate the RNA Xist, differentiating all cells from those with only one X chromosome.[31] Sunwoo, Colognori, Froberg, Jeon, and Lee (2017) agree that this differentiation occurs from silencing one of the two X chromosomes in XX, but this process does not occur with XY. This inactivation has XX cells that are vastly different from XY cells and creates a large sexual attribute difference.

Those cells with both XX activation have a stronger presence than those cells with only one X activated. Those X cells that escape deactivation are expressed at higher levels with two XX than those with XY. Sex chromosomes have a direct effect on brain sex differences.[32]

BRAIN SEX DIFFERENCES

The brain has a major influence on all of our behaviors. To understand brain sex differences is to understand gender communication differences.[22] The nervous system entails the central nervous system of the neurons within the spinal cord and skull and the peripheral nervous system for communicating between the brain and the rest of the body through sensory and motor neurons. The nervous system brings insight into understanding the interconnectedness of structure and function between the body and social behaviors. It has, at its core, basic level communication between cells. At the tissue and organ level, this involves billions and billions of cells communicating as an interconnected circuit. There are neural circuits of organized cells, from which the brain enables social behaviors related to consciousness, cognition, and emotion.[391]

Neural activity related to social behaviors, and those used for bodily functions, often communicate with each other.[107] Therefore, there is a strong interconnectedness between the nervous system and social behaviors. It is important to better understand how the nervous system influences communication and how it differs vastly between males and females.[214]

Brain energy activity can be detected through electrical activity, hemodynamics, magnetic fields, radioactivity, and X-rays.[453] Studying the central nervous system during actual behavioral displays can play an important role in better understanding communication.[391] Males have a larger brain than females on average, even when taking into account body size differences.[142, 397] This can be detected from an early age, with total brain size for males about 7.3% larger and gray matter volume larger by about 10.4% for males.[646]

Males and females have the same autosomal genomes. However, it is sex-specific gene expression that differentiates males from females. The karyotypes of XX and XY set off sex-specific gene expressions.[554] Brain differences in development between males and females start at about three weeks after conception and continue until about age thirty.[13, 142]

Ogawa, Tsukahara, Choleris, and Vasudevan (2020) highlight how the human brain becomes sexually dimorphic. Production of sex hormones heavily influences specific brain areas during developmental periods. Sex differences then emerge in tissue structures, number of neurons, and synaptic number, to mention a few differences, which create structural sexual dimorphic brains. Estrogens play a key factor with influencing social behaviors in a feminine fashion through the formation and functioning of sexually-different brain structure. If the human has developing testes, then testosterone is secreted during the embryonic period that causes masculinization, thus lessening feminization of brain structures and behaviors. These effects of testosterone last into adulthood. During puberty, the excretion increases with the testes producing testosterone and the ovaries producing estrogen, creating new cells and more masculinization of the male brain and more feminization of the female brain.

Evidence suggests structural and functional reproductive and non-reproductive brain differences between males and females. [32, 89, 439, 553, 711] Chromosomal brain differences attribute some to these male and female brain differences.[504, 553] Sex hormones also influence the arrangement of tissues in the central nervous system during development, which influences behaviors in adulthood.[439] Dr. Diana Fleischman, evolutionary psychologist, writes "knowing a brain belongs to a female allows you to predict, with 80% accuracy, her brain has more female-typical features than male-typical features." (Twitter: @sentientist 10-19-19).

BRAIN SEX DIFFERENCES CONTROVERSIES

Others argue against the notion of differences between male and female brains. Joel, Berman, Tavor, Wexler, Gaber, Stein, et al. (2015) concluded from their study that there are not enough brain structural differences to identify a male brain from a female brain. The brains of males and females have overlapping similarities. Their conclusion was based upon MRI images and brain surveys.

However, contrary evidence to their conclusion has shown sex differences in nucleus of the solitary tract, parabrachial nucleus, basil ganglia, hippocampus, cerebellum, cortical circuits, gray matter, white matter, caudate, anterior cingulate gyrus, and amygdala to mention some of the sex brain differences.[77, 142, 345, 553] Chekroud, Ward, Rosenberg, and Holmes (2016) state that Joel et al.'s (2015) criteria was too strict to designate a male brain from a female brain. According to them, Joel et al.'s criteria of requiring a dimorphic form to distinguish male from female brains, and also having a degree of internal consistency of male or female components within a single brain, should not be the only criteria to make a conclusion. Chekroud et al. (2016) sampled over 1,500 individuals and were able to predict male brains from female brains with over 90% accuracy based upon statistical analyses of brain physical characteristics distinguishing the two different types of brains.

Anderson, Harenski, Harenski, Koenigs, Decety, Calhoun, and Kiehl (2019) point out that Joel's (2015) data collecting methods and statistical analyses are less precise than more modern technologies and statistical analyses. Anderson et al. (2019) describe using source-based morphology consisting of multivariate means to quantify gray matter measured with magnetic resonance imaging; these advance the parcellations using machine-learning to categorize sex. This approach is able to take into account many different brain regions simultaneously, whereas Joel et al.'s (2015) study relied upon single characteristics to draw conclusions.

Anderson et al. (2019) provides evidence of 93% accuracy using this contemporary approach to predict sex from brain data. They also mention that brain sex differences are related to observable behavioral differences.

Glezerman (2016) also makes reasonable arguments to dismiss Joel et al.'s claims. He draws attention to their methodology. Joel et al. (2015) limited their methodology to still images of the brain. Having still images of the brain overlooks gonadal hormones influencing sex-specific brain development.[553] Glezerman highlights that the human brain is not realistically understood in isolation, but rather through its function as part of a system.

Glezerman identified functional differences in areas of the brain responsible for cognitive and physical tasks along with experiences of emotions. He takes the position that the functions of the brain differs male and female brains. Specifically, gonads function differently between males and females from variances in the areas of the hypothalamus, pituitary, and gonad axis to mention a few. The hormones are similarly secreted in these areas but males having a more constant release of the hormones while females have rhythmic release of hormones. Thus, gonad functional differences help distinguish male brains from female brains. Bodily functional differences between males and females are a result of functionally different male and female brains. This difference in hormonal release in the hypothalamus region is important because this area of the brain is responsible for linking stress and behavioral reactions. In particular, anxiety and mood are greatly affected during this process.[465] This happens because the hypothalamus connects the brain to the endocrine system.[440]

Other research also supports the notion of differences between male and female brains by highlighting brain hemispheric differences.[504] Males tend to have a brain that is much more lateralized than females.[305, 562] One particular side of the male brain is often responsible for a particular task, whereas the female brain is more likely to use both sides of the brain more for a particular function.[271] This sex difference is observed through language communication differences later on in life.[284]

Language differences can also be traced to brain structural sex differences. A locus in 3p26.1 has been identified in the female brain that is associated with higher cognitive empathy from females; it has been linked with recognizing another person's mental state with a corresponding word that it represents.[689]

SEX HORMONES AND DEVELOPMENT

Sex hormones can influence motor coordination.[439] It has long been documented that males outperform females with visuospatial tasks.[39, 441] Evidence of this has been found with tracking objects as early as four months of age.[701] Perhaps sex hormones can give an explanation for this sex difference. Sex hormones play a part in the development of the human brain, often understood as neurobiological.[504]

The human brain starts on course to become female unless exposed to androgen sex hormones.[476] Sex hormones influence structural and functional brain developments through cellular and molecular progressions, which influence gender-linked behaviors and brain functions.[439] Hormones can also influence fetal development differently depending upon the sex of the fetus.[43]

The male brain is exposed to a different hormonal situation than the female brain before birth.[504] One such way fetal hormones can influence sex development differentiation and cognitive behavioral abilities is through testosterone. Adult males have 20-25 times—not a percentage but a multiplier—more circulating testosterone than adult women.[186] Several genes have sex-specific manifestations prior to testosterone exposure, but testosterone is a major factor for many sex-specific gene expressions.[554]

The Sry gene is encoded by the Y chromosome that starts the masculinization of the male gonads for teste formation and testosterone production.[339] This gonad difference leads to sex hormone differences between males and females, which leads to tissue function sex differences. The absence of the Sry gene in females leads to the development of the ovaries. Plasma levels of steroidal hormones differ between males and females, such as estradiol, progesterone, and testosterone.[31]

A fetus is masculinized by testosterone through the canonical androgenic pathway, which serves as a backdoor pathway. The testes of the fetus are necessary for canonical androgen production. Androsterone is the primary backdoor androgen for male fetal circulation, which is sex dependent. As a result, males have more androsterone and testosterone due to synthesis by fetal testes and nongonadal tissues, before birth than do females.[486]

Males have a surge of testosterone in weeks eight through twenty-four of gestation. This surge can influence a sexually dimorphic brain structure, psychological characteristics, and human behaviors.[283, 481] The mother's testosterone levels at this time are also much higher with a male fetus than a female fetus.[726] The placenta is also responsible for masculinizing the male fetus.[486] Embryonic fluid can give insight into fetal hormonal levels. Testosterone levels can be tested through embryonic fluid and have been shown to have a major impact with sex differentiation abilities.[37, 283, 481]

SEX HORMONE EFFECTS

Sex hormone differences early in life impact gender communication differences later in life. Males have been found to score higher on mental object rotation. These sex differences were consistent with higher male fetal testosterone levels.[37] Additional research has shown that male sex hormones have a positive effect on spatial ability; this is because the male sex hormones impact the areas of the human body responsible for spatial abilities.[121, 283] This has even been evidenced by females who have higher levels of these male sex hormones performing better on spatial tasks than females who do not.[53, 267]

Male hormones are also related to male typical behaviors for both males and females. Higher levels of androgens have been linked to children playing with male-type toys and later in life for careers that usually have more males in these professions.[54, 500] Higher androgen levels have also been linked to more aggressive behaviors for both males and females.[205] Higher testosterone levels have a relationship with lower empathy for both males and females.[689]

Estrogen is another sex hormone that also influences brain development, reproductive development and function, neuroprotection, neuro function, neuro circuits, and subsequent behaviors. It operates through the central nervous system during important times of stages of development, with females having much higher levels than males.[18, 122, 481] Females can have up to 20 times—not a percentage but a multiplier—more estrogen than males.[620] These high levels of estrogen lead to a structurally dimorphic brain for females as well as behaviorally, such as social investigation, recognition, memory, and anxiety.[481]

One specific brain sex difference is that females have a larger and more active hippocampus.[202, 257, 345, 646] McEwen and Milner (2016) clearly lay out estrogen's impact on sex development with the hippocampus. Estrogen effects the extrahypothalamic brain functions that include learning and memory in the hippocampus and prefrontal cortex regions, and also excitability and seizures in the hippocampus region. Estrogen can serve to protect the brain, such as with neuroprotection in the hippocampus, nigro-striatal pathway, and cerebral cortex regions.

Cardiovascular regulation is influenced by estrogen in the paraventricular nucleus and brainstem. Fine motor skills, coordination, reaction time are all influenced by estrogen in the nigrostriatal pathway and also cerebellum areas. As estrogen levels increase, motor control of skeletal muscles decreases. This can be one explanation for more anterior cruciate ligament knee injuries in female athletes.[291] Estrogen levels are linked with pain sensitivity, migraines, and depression.[26, 681, 320]

Daily fetal heart rate rhythm can also differ depending upon the sex of the fetus. This is important because it not only adds to one more sex difference before birth, but also shows that the heart rhythms are influenced by the suprachiasmatic nuclei of the hypothalamus.[618] The hypothalamus develops differently in females from the influence of sexual hormones, such as estrogen.[481] The hypothalamus connects the emotion, limbic, and cortical brain centers with the major peripheral stress system.[222]

When stress is encountered, the hypothalamus releases cortisol.[591] One can therefore connect the dots that before birth heart rhythm rates are different between males and females; these are influenced by specific areas in the brain that are responsible for emotions and dealing with stress. Males and females after birth are likely to experience, behave, and communicate emotions differently from these pre-birth differences in these areas. It is important to understand where we begin in these areas of emotions and stress in order to determine whether social and environmental factors can be attributed as causes in these areas after birth.

FETAL SEX SURVIVAL

Males and females have different threats to their survival early and later in life.[480] Maternal functions relating to threats to their fetus differ between sexes. Mothers who are bearing a male fetus have higher levels of disgust sensitivity. Sensitivity serves as a means to protect and repel potential dangers to the fetus, such as the mother vomiting to prevent the ingestion of a harmful carcinogen. It is plausible that male fetuses need more protection from external dangers; higher levels of disgust by their mother is one form of protection because these are observed in the first two trimesters, when the fetus is most vulnerable.[726] More protection from mothers carrying male fetuses might be necessary because any problem with an X alleles is greater with a male only having one X, whereas a female with two X's is averaged out with the alleles.[31]

Maternal hormonal factors can influence fetal development.[236, 296] Fetal stress exposure, such as maternal stress and exposure to stress hormones like cortisol, can be handled differently by males and females. This results in different communication outcomes later in life. Sandman, Glynn, and Davis (2013) describe how a female fetus that is exposed to stress is likely to adapt to that stress and survive. However, the male fetus is more vulnerable to negative health impacts of stress and less likely to survive. This reduces the number of weaker males affected by stress, but increases the birth of females that can be more affected by stress. However, those males that are more vulnerable to stress are less likely to be born. In turn, this increases the number of females in society that are more vulnerable to negative health effects of stress. The female fetus that is highly susceptible to stress will then display these behaviors later in life. Such females are likely to show signs of an enlarged amygdala, fearful temperament, anxiety, and affective problems well into preadolescence, along with damaged executive functioning and neurological signs associated with these behaviors. The amygdala connects fear perception and physiological responses. One can see how an enlarged amygdala can lead to hypersensitive fear responses in behaviors.

CONCLUSION

There is overwhelming evidence of biological sex differences prior to birth. These sex differences are responsible for developmental differences that are observable later in life through gender communication, behaviors, and emotions among others. These anatomical, physiological, and sex hormonal differences have an impact on an individual long before any societal influence.

CHAPTER 5

PROCESSING INFORMATION

Our survival is dependent upon how well we perceive the environment and people around us.[268] Males and females understand the world around them differently. This includes the way they communicate with others and understand other people. Our understanding of the world and social behaviors originates from our brains.[22, 277] Our brains make predictions about what is likely to occur from the incoming stimuli processed and then behaviors are exhibited.[615]

Males tend to have larger brains both in terms of weight and size.[562, 578, 646] Sex brain differences do not end with size. Brain sex differences, both structurally and functionally, have been found to influence the processing of information differently between males and females, such as emotions, learning, memory, language, and social skills.[250, 277, 578]

SEX HORMONES

Sex hormones contribute to sex differences in brain development. The sex hormone testosterone plays a vital role in the masculinization of many nuclear structures in the male brain during critical developmental periods. One such development is the amygdala, which is responsible for emotional and stress-related processing behaviors. Sex differences have been found for both emotional and stress-processing.[347]

Sex hormones not only play a role with brain development, but also with cognitive functioning.[439] This happens from sex reproductive steroids, testosterone and estrogen, modifying neural activity and influencing the central nervous system.[266] Pletzer, Harris, and Ortner (2017) investigated sex differences concerning attention during neuropsychological assessment tasks. In the study, men were found to have a higher sustained operation attention speed compared to women. For women, accuracy for the attention tasks was higher during their early follicular, rather than their mid-luteal, cycle phase. The performance accuracy for the women in the study coincided with their progesterone levels. Mid-luteal of their cycle had higher levels of progesterone and lower accuracy performance scores. The early follicular stages of the women's cycle were associated with lower levels of progesterone and higher accuracy scores on tasks. Hence, their sustained operation attention speed fluctuated during their menstrual cycles. These findings are consistent with previous research finding the menstrual cycle to influence cognitive strategies of women when performing particular tasks.[589]

PERFORMANCE SEX DIFFERENCES

These sex differences can also influence general intelligence between males and females.[674] General intelligence is determined by a variety of different specific factors that create the overall general score. Those individual specific factors have noticeable sex differences and influence overall general intelligence scores. Superior spatial ability by males have been well documented beginning early in life, even as early as infancy.[392]

Males and females have differences in the locus coeruleus and norepinephrine areas of the brain that are responsible for sex differences with memory, spatial ability, and perception.[277] Van der Linden, Dunkel, and Madison (2017) found that males scored better on the specific tests within general intelligence for spatial orientation, which is consistent with previous research finding better spatial abilities for males.[121, 283, 589] They also found that males outperformed in continuing attention and inhibition, which is consistent with males having more compartmentalized focus from intrahemispheric brain connections.[305, 562] They found that females scored better on episodic memory tests, which is consistent with previous research of females that are more attuned with other people.[589, 689] The medial prefrontal cortex is responsible for understanding how others feel, and, when artificially stimulated, enhances understanding of others only in females but not males.[8] The effects of estrogen on the prefrontal cortex and hippocampus also effects memory.[439]

Structural brain differences help explain these intelligence sex differences. Kong, Huang, Hao, Hu, and Liu (2017) investigated early stages of spatial navigation and brain activity between males and females. They found males outperformed females with spatial activities, and had neural activity higher in the bilateral parahippocampal area of the brain when performing spatial tasks. The bilateral parahippocampal is responsible for assisting navigation behaviors. Males who had higher activity in the parahippocampal area also had a better sense of direction, whereas females did not. The authors concluded that it is a combination of both structural and chemical brain sex differences accounting for spatial activity performance variances and activation dissimilarities. This is consistent with previous research, which indicates that prenatal high levels of androgen exposure by males prior to birth enhances spatial ability over females and is often due to shaping and activating the areas of the brain responsible for spatial cognition.[392]

Goldstein, Seidman, Horton, Makris, Kennedy, et al. (2001) found males to have a larger inferior parietal lobe of around 20% even after accounting for a larger male brain. This area of the brain is responsible for mental rotation task performance. Other research has found males to have bigger parietal cortices related with visual-spatial processing, while females have more volume in the temporal and parietal areas (surroundings of the Sylvian fissure) that are associated with language processes.[250]

Females also have larger areas of the brain influencing the limbic system, which are responsible for language, relationships, memory.[578]

Additionally, estrogen negatively impacts spatial navigation by way of nigro-striatal pathway and the cerebellum.[439] It has been found that males have more activation in the spatial areas of the brain when performing spatial tasks, and females have more activation in the language areas of the brain when performing language tasks.[659]

SEX STRUCTURAL BRAIN DIFFERENCES

One area of the limbic system that differs between males and females is the hippocampus, which is larger and more active in females.[202, 257, 646] The hippocampus is responsible for memory and excitability and is larger in females even at an early age.[345, 439] By recognizing that the hippocampus is part of the limbic system, one can understand how memory and language are more connected in the female brain than the male brain. Furthermore, these structural brain differences are consistent with previous research finding females outperforming males with language tasks.[589]

Another component of the limbic system differing between males and females is the amygdala. Some of the responsibilities of the amygdala are emotion, memory, and stress-processing, and it plays a sex-specific role difference.[202, 473] Kogler, et al. (2016) investigated resting-state functional connectivity (rsFC) of the amygdala for both males and females. They found a significant difference in rsFC of the left amygdala between males and females. Women showed stronger rsFC between the left amygdala and left middle temporal gyrus, inferior frontal gyrus, post central gyrus and hippocampus, which are those regions associated with face processing, inner-speech, fear, and pain processing. The stronger rsFC in those areas for women indicates they are more sensitive to social cues such as faces. The stronger connection for women between the left amygdala and the inferior postcentral gyrus is consistent with previous research that women report greater sensitivity to pain than men.[191]

These rsFC differences suggest a superior performance for women with face processing, which can attribute to social intelligence differences between males and females. The association of rsFC of the left amygdala suggests a stronger connection with rumination, which is used for perceiving threats and negative emotions for women. They found a stronger connection between the left amygdala and left hippocampus for women. The hippocampus is related to negative emotion conditioning and memory. Having more activation in these areas for women may lead to a negativity bias perception due to remembering threats, negative emotions, and fear more than men.

The fusiform face area is the part of the brain that processes facial features.[402] Women have been found to have more activation in the fusiform face area when experiencing stress from viewing emotional faces. This indicates women had more sensitivity to social experiences involving faces and emotions, while men actually had less activation in this area.[434] Women have even been found to be more emotionally sensitive to subliminal faces.[683] Additionally, women have been found to process faces much more quickly.[239] Taken together, these findings further illustrate different emotional experiences between men and women who are exposed to the same emotional stimuli.[153]

Also of interest Kogler et al. (2016) found an interaction of the left amygdala and the sex hormone cortisol, the hormone responsible for regulating the left amygdala and emotions. Cortisol plays an important role with connecting the left amygdala with other parts of the brain. The researchers found it to have opposite effects between men and women. For women, cortisol was negatively related between rsFC of the left amygdala and striatal regions, mid-orbital frontal gyrus, anterior cingulate gyrus, middle and superior frontal gyri, supplementary motor area and the parietal-occipital sulcus. These are areas responsible for emotion regulation; as cortisol levels increase in women resting-state functional connectivity decreases between the left amygdala and emotion regulation areas, thus indicating less emotional regulation. On the other hand, men had a positive association of cortisol levels and rsFC of the left amygdala with these same structural areas responsible for emotional regulation, alluding to more emotional regulation and action execution.

As cortisol levels increase for men, their memory of a particular negative event is likely to decrease from the influence of the cortisol rise.[281]

These findings on amygdala sex differences support the notion of emotion regulation and processing sex differences with neural circuits as contributing factors.[710] Fearful experiences might be remembered more by women and lead to more depression and anxiety. On the other hand, the positive relation between cortisol levels and left amygdala rsFC with men is related to emotion regulation and rewards. This can widen the gap with men having more emotional regulation experiences and more positive memories of rewards than women. From the findings previously described, negative emotional events that trigger increases in cortisol levels in men are likely to be remembered less than in women. For men, this is consistent with previous research finding that cortisol's role with emotion regulation helps reduce the effects of negative emotions in areas of the brain such as the amygdala.[317]

Specific physical brain differences regarding emotional activation are prevalent across the cortex and can help explain these emotional experience sex differences.[202] The prefrontal and (para-) limbic brain areas are responsible for emotion regulation and can explain male and female emotional processing differences. Vagally mediated heartrate variability can serve as a biomarker for the engagement of the prefrontal and (para-) limbic brain areas during emotion processing. Resting state vagally mediated heartrate variability was found to be related to emotion regulation only in men, which indicates a sex difference in emotion regulation.[399]

Filkowski, Olsen, Duda, Wanger, and Sabatinelli (2017) found that men have more activation in the mediodorsal nucleus of the thalamus (MDN). Stronger activation in the (MDN) for men is associated with more cognitive control, attention, and emotion regulation for men compared with women. Women showed more activation in the amygdala, periaqueductal gray, and superior colliculus regions suggesting emotional stimuli having a greater impact on women especially negative emotional stimuli compared to men. In other words, parts of the brain responsible for emotion regulation were found to differ between males and females, therefore emotion regulation is likely to differ as well.

Additional research has shown that there are sex differences regarding emotional stimuli and emotion regulation. Women have been found to show greater activation of the dorsal attention network during reward and punishing tasks compared with men.[170] The dorsal attention network is comprised of dorsal lateral prefrontal cortex, frontal eye fields, middle temporal motion complex, and superior parietal lobe, which are areas responsible for external stimuli attention that include rewarding and punishing.[124, 160, 507] These findings further illustrate areas of the brain that are more active for women during positive and negative events, while also indicating more vulnerability to emotional experiences.

Another explanation for these gender communication dissimilarities is sex brain hemispheric differences. Males have more connections within a hemisphere, whereas females have greater connectivity between brain hemispheres.[305, 504, 562] The corpus callosum posterior portion (splenium/isthmus) is larger in females, which enables better intercommunication between both sides of the brain. This can help explain why social interactions play a bigger role with females, such as verbal fluency superiority.[250]

Brain structures are not the only contributor when processing, but also the composition of those structures regarding gray and white brain matter. Brain gray matter differs from white matter. Gray matter is comprised of somatodendritic tissues of neurons; white matter is constructed from myelinated connecting axons.[250] White matter helps the brain communicate to its different areas and impacts behaviors.[528] Brain gray matter is responsible for cognitive functions.[431]

Females have thicker cortex across both hemispheres in the brain.[345, 562] While the female brain might be smaller in size, the cortical thickness makes up for it with increased efficiency.[562] Females have more thickness of the cerebral cortex within inferior frontal gyrus; this equates with Brodmann areas 44 and 45. Females also have more gray matter in Brodmann areas 44 and 45, which is found to be 20% larger than for males. This is important because these areas of the brain play an important role with verbal fluency and verbal memory tasks.[367] Furthermore, the cerebellum plays an important role with emotional processing.[200]

SEX STRUCTURAL PERFORMANCE DIFFERENCES

Connectivity of both areas of the brain and white matter play an important role with creative thinking. Females having more connections to different areas of the brain helps give them better intuitive thinking than males, and plays an important role in creativity.[305] It makes sense that more different areas of the brain are needed for more creative thinking than simple isolated thoughts. Findings indicate a positive relationship only for females between white matter structures and higher levels of creativity.[649]

Connectivity differences between males and females is structurally different. Sex differences exist on intelligence tests. Pletzer (2016) used fMRI imaging to examine brain activation of males and females performing math problems. Two different types of math problems were performed; one was number magnitude processing (subtraction) and the other arithmetic fact retrieval (multiplication). The findings confirmed that males used different neuronal systems pertaining to different parts of the brain while performing these two different types of math problems; women used the same neuronal system within the same areas of the brain for both types of problems. Men had more activation in the intraparietal sulcus for number magnitude processing; their angular gyrus had more activation when performing the achromatic fact retrieval. Again, no differences were found in females performing the same tasks.

These findings indicate that women and men use different neural substrates for number processing. This is consistent with previous research that found women use verbal memory strategies to solve spatial tasks.[684] Females activate distinctive frontal areas when solving spatial tasks.[307]

ACTIVATION SEX DIFFERENCES

How we process information is often dependent upon how we see it, starting with ourselves. We often understand the world around us based upon our own body size, scale, and visual field.[672] Other visual influences are the neurons responsible for understanding another's movement actions; these are located in the cortex of the brain called mirror neurons. Mental simulation is activated from these mirror neurons.[101] Females have more gray matter where mirror neurons are found, and also more activation, which helps with understanding others.[102, 455]

Males and females have attention differences with objects; males focus more on spatial aspects, and females focus on details of the objects and language representations.[441] Kurth, Spencer, Hines, and Luders (2018) found males and females activating different areas of the brain when solving object rotation problems. The foundation for their study was well-established research in which males outperformed females with mental object rotation tasks. It was previously established that males use parietal regions while females activate frontal and inferior temporal regions; thus, different interhemispheric brain connections are used between males and females for the same object rotation task.

Extending this line of thinking, their study investigated the role of the corpus callosum with mental object rotation tasks. The corpus callosum connects both sides of the brain and is constructed of topologically organized fiber tracts. A thicker corpus callosum was associated with better mental object rotation only with women. This is because women use both sides of their brain more for object rotation tasks. Overall, their findings indicated better mental object rotation for men compared to women. This is consistent with previous research results showing particular women with more raw cortical thickness having better object rotation performance.[562]

Kurth, Spencer, Hines, and Luders (2018) interpreted their results as women depending upon an efficient interhemispheric communication for mental object rotation. Women use a higher-order cognitive process for mental object rotation that involves object identification, working memory, and language representation that involves selected areas of the corpus callosum that included the parietal, temporal, and frontal brain regions involving interhemispheric pathways. Men use a more automatic or "global" approach of matching shapes involving parietal regions that have been found to be responsible for spatial processing. This automated/global approach is related to better mental object rotation performance than the higher-order cognitive process women use for mental object rotation.

Similar sex differences have also been found with men using the global approach to outperform women that rely upon details for decision-making with the Iowa Gambling Task. There are possible evolutionarily and biological sex differences genetically inherited from men having a much larger territory to roam for resources when hunting outside the cave using a more global approach, while women paid much more attention to object identification details of their baby's needs.[671]

CONCLUSION

Males and females perceive and interact with the world differently. This stems from differences with visual perception, sex hormones, brain structures, and gray and white brain matter. Taken together, these different areas of the human body unite a better understanding of different functions and processes that lead to different communication behaviors and task performances. These different areas display consistent themes explaining gender communication differences and task performance strategies.

PART 3

OH HOW WE DIFFER, COMMUNICATIVELY TOO!

CHAPTER 6

TALKING ABOUT GENDER COMMUNICATION

BIOLOGICAL BASIS OF GENDER COMMUNICATION

Most gender communication research is exclusively studied from a cultural perspective. This perspective takes the position that males and females communicate similarly and whatever differences exist are the result of culture and society treating males and females differently.[614] This line of thinking is flawed. It has been known for over a thousand years that males and females communicate differently from an early age, but only recently has it been discovered that brain sex differences between males and females are major contributors.[22, 52, 238, 550]

Cultures and societies have changed and are continually in flux, but the same reoccurring gender communication differences are present and consistently found because biology is the root of gender communication differences.[97] Biological sex underpinnings for language gender differences is created through evolution from males and females having different needs in order to survive. One evidence of this is the FOXP2 gene that is responsible for communication.[7] It has been found that boys have less FOXP2 protein in the left hemisphere cortex than girls.[73]

Language skill developmental sex differences can be traced back as early as infancy.[7, 586] Often, neural processes are automatic and relatively inflexible.[411] Much of our brain processes used during language is from internal endogenous continuous progressions.[76] It was covered in the previous chapter that overwhelming scientific evidence of structural, functional, and sex hormonal differences have been found between male and female brains.[22, 250, 347] These differences often can be traced back to evolutionary means of survival tactical differences between males and females.[25]

Gender discourse is rooted in biology, from gene expression and sex hormones influencing brain development, and functioning along with the central nervous system; these gender communication differences tend to be relatively stable components of our personalities over time.[97, 467]

Cultures cannot entirely change gender communication tendencies that are in the human brain stemming from genes, heritability, and biological underpinnings that are responsible for cognition. Sex hormones manage how fetal neural networks develop in the human brain while inside the womb. In turn, this influences the developmental sex differences in verbal development and spatial skills especially at the onset of hormonal changes brought by puberty.[97]

Evidence of this is that girls minimally outperform boys in reading and writing in Grade 4, but these differences in performance drastically increases as children advance in age. This has been consistently found over different periods of time and in different cultures.[550] One biological contributing factor is that word processing has sex-specific practices in the brain.[256] Regarding word processing, males have more visual connections while females have more auditory connections indicating that word processing is gender differentiated.[157]

It has been clearly demonstrated that sex hormones influence physiological functioning of the human brain responsible for communication differences between males and females, giving females superior language and communication abilities.[7, 577] Behavioral sex differences stemming from hormones have been observed in infancy.[376] Testosterone levels prior to birth have been found to reduce language performance of boys at age two.[293]

At one month of age, testosterone levels have been found to negatively influence language development and performance with both males and females. This is true even after taking social factors into consideration. Males have much higher levels of testosterone even at one month of age, which is considered mini-puberty, at which testosterone levels are clearly much higher in males.[365] Language developmental sex differences have consistently found girls starting as young as one to three years of age outperforming boys with language acquisition and performance tasks, and boys having more language and speech disorders that include neurodevelopment disorders.[7] One form of evidence of this later in life is female superiority of naming objects.[268, 441] As a result, females have consistently been found to have superior social cognitive abilities.[259]

In children, girls have more interhemispheric connectivity enabling better bilateral activation for language use.[62] Females having more interconnections in their brain and superior neuronal networks, partly due to functional connectivity, increases their capabilities of social stimuli understanding. This allows for better communication.[7, 305] These biological influences on gender discourse are often expressed by females as a feminine communication style and by males as a masculine communication style.[97]

Over the last several decades, women's roles in our society have changed dramatically; women earn the majority of higher education degrees, including Master's and Doctoral degrees.[667] This has translated to a huge surge of women in professional and managerial positions and women-owned businesses.[666] However, gender communication has remained stable, thus indicating the minimal influence of culture on gender communication differences.[25] One reason for this consistency is that social behaviors including verbal communication with others originates in our brains.[22, 277]

HIPPOCAMPUS

Sex hormone levels influence the size of specific brain areas responsible for language.[7] Language use is partially determined by the cerebellum, which is more symmetrical in the female brain.[477] These structural sex differences may explain why brain activity gender differences have been found during language tasks.[184]

Much of our communication originates from memory. The hippocampus plays a major role with memory and connecting it to language. The female brain has a larger hippocampus with more activity, even at an early age.[202, 257, 345, 646] This distinction is important because the hippocampus is part of the limbic system and is responsible for language, relationships, and memory.[578]

The male brain has high amounts of testosterone in the hippocampus where memories are created. Often these memories are unconscious and have androgens surrounding the male hippocampus.[573] The exposure of the male hippocampus to high levels of testosterone creates a distinction from a female hippocampus. The male hippocampus soaked in testosterone is related to areas such as aggression, power, status, and competition.[179] These attributes are likely to influence male social interactions with a more single-topic focus as is needed during competitions.[99] With females having up to 20 times more estrogen, it influences memory by way of the hippocampus.[338, 439, 620]

Estrogen has been found to physically change the hippocampus[45] and has been linked positively with language performance.[338] Therefore, with females having higher levels of estrogen in their hippocampus, they are better equipped to use the hippocampus' functions of connecting memories, with emotions, and language. Females have been found to have a stronger emotional connection to their personal memories.[74] One can easily understand how sex hormones influence the hippocampus differently. Additional brain sex difference areas are the temporal and parietal areas (surroundings of the Sylvian fissure) having more volume in the female brain and playing a vital role with language processing.[250]

GRAY MATTER, WHITE MATTER

Gray matter in the brain is responsible for information processing.[97, 431] Overall, males have more gray matter comprised of active neurons than females.[712] One can infer that males are able to focus and process information on fewer topics more intensely than females. Therefore, males can communicate about one particular topic in-depth but have more difficulty with tying in other topics and also emotions. One exception is females having more gray matter than males in Brodmann areas 44 and 45, which is at 20% larger than males in areas responsible for verbal fluency and verbal memory tasks.[367]

White matter in the brain is responsible for connecting the networks in the brain processing areas.[97, 528] Overall, females have more white matter for neural connections between different areas of the brain than males.[712] This is especially important when considering that females have a larger hippocampus that is responsible for memory connected to emotion and sensory regions of the brain.[97, 439] This enables females to communicate about different topics, past or present, understand nuance behaviors, and tie in the emotions of others much more easily because communication between these different areas flow more easily.

As a result of the emotion, memory, and language areas being connected, females benefit greatly from talking about their problems by relating to personal experiences and using feeling words. On the other hand, the male brain has fewer connections to memory, language, and emotions leading to communication of fewer memory details, emotional experiences, and relational experiences.[97]

CORPUS CALLOSUM

Though the previously covered individual structural brain components are sex differentiated and play a role in gender communication, how they coordinate together during the communication process is also important to understand. The human brain relies upon different components simultaneously during communication. How well these different individual pieces connect to each other alters the communication process. Sex differences are present regarding connections throughout the human brain.[712]

The corpus callosum is comprised of neural fibers in the middle of the brain that physically connects both sides of the brain and also coordinates communication between both sides of the brain.[97] Females have more connections between both sides of the brain with a larger and thicker corpus callosum posterior portion (splenium/ isthmus). Males have more connections within each side of their brain.[305, 504] Females are better able to connect information and selective attention with language processing.[97, 637]

As early as childhood, sex brain functional differences have been found during language processing, with girls having more activation in different areas of the brain during language tasks, while males use fewer areas of the brain for language.[720] The thicker corpus callosum that includes the parietal, temporal, and frontal brain regions for females is often associated with the higher-order cognitive processing involving working memory and language representation activated simultaneously. This is indicative of females using both sides of their brain in a coordinated fashion.[368]

Females use bilateral processing of their brain during language verbal fluency tasks, while males use the left side of their brain.[177] Thus, males process language on the left side of their brain, but emotions are processed on the right side. This leads to males having less emotion comprehension, and also communicating less emotionally, while having a greater focus and being less distracted from contextual cues.

Compared to males, females are able to bring in more cognitive functions during language processing, which can lead to a more complicated assessment in decision-making. For example, with females, while some of category A should be implemented, categories B, C, and D are also considered. Males, on the other hand, process information more compartmentally, resulting in decision-making as category A or B or C or D.

LANGUAGE SOCIAL UNDERSTANDING

Females have a superior ability to understand social situations and also process social information.[334] There are multiple explanations for this. They have more interest in human faces as demonstrated by higher levels of arousal to faces than males.[536] This leads to a huge female advantage with emotion recognition of other people.[709] Also, females have more efficient activity when it comes to listening.[9, 223] Evolutionary evidence suggests that this came about because small group interactions were necessary for females in order to survive.[25]

Sex hormonal differences clearly account for some of the female language social understanding advantage.[577] Gender differences in language abilities likely begin before birth. The male sex hormone testosterone and the female sex hormone estrogen shape the human brain differently and influences social cognition.[481] Testosterone levels measured from umbilical cord samples were associated with language development for boys measured at two years of age, such that higher levels of testosterone were related with less language development.[293] As early as four-weeks, levels of estradiol (estrogen) is associated with articulatory skills, while at five months testosterone levels have an inverse relation with articulatory skills.[542]

Changes in these sex hormones early in life predict later language development and performance. The surge of testosterone levels for boys and estradiol levels for girls is important to understand how these changes influence later language performance. Testosterone levels at one month of age negatively impact language performance at thirty months of age even after taking into account social factors.[365]

At five months of age, testosterone levels are associated with lower language performance later at age four, while estradiol levels at five months of age are related with better language performance later at four years of age.[586] One possible explanation for these associations between sex hormones and language performance is the changing of the brain from these sex hormones. Testosterone has been found to decrease gray matter in the Wernicke's area and Broca's region of the brain, both of which are responsible for language performance.[263]

This is important because gray matter in these areas is responsible for the functioning of language processing.[97, 431] These influences of sex hormones with language performance continues through adulthood. Estrogen is higher in females and has been linked with better language performance; as women age and their estrogen levels decrease, so does their language performance.[338]

The ability of females to more easily use both sides of their brain is a key attribute with language performance and relationship building with others; this is evidenced by females empathizing and understanding nonverbal cues of others while partaking in the conversation at hand.[97, 177] Females understanding nonverbal cues is also made possible by females having larger vocal amplitudes.[592] Estrogen intermingling with other neurochemical systems in the brain helps females have a better understanding of others.[481] This better understanding is evident by higher levels of empathy and understanding of others' emotions.[250, 606]

Socializing is often more emotionally rewarding for females because they experience increased levels of oxytocin that intermingles with the dopaminergic system when socializing, which leads to them feeling more relaxed.[419, 606] Oxytocin is a nonapeptide, which can also be used as a neuromodulator in the central nervous system. Oxytocin also enables a better understanding of people and social situations, partly due to an increase in empathy and memory of social cues.[606] This can lead to females being more likely to seek out social situations and pay closer attention when engaged. Additionally, they are better able to smoothly join a group conversation that is already taking place.

Females have emotion capacities on both sides of their brain that are exchanged between both sides, allowing an easier expression of emotions through language. Males experience emotions on the right side of their brains, but process language on the left side, with fewer connections between both sides of their brain hemispheres. This creates fewer capabilities for males to understand social situations from a lack of interconnectedness of both hemispheres that decreases the ability to pay attention to nonverbal cues while involved in conversations.[97] Therefore, males listen and communicate in a more linear fashion. Evidence of these sex brain structural differences regarding emotion and language processing is present when either the right or left side of the ventromedial prefrontal cortex is damaged.[547]

BLOOD FLOW

Not only do these brain structural sex differences favor females, blood flow favors them as well. Females have more blood flow and neural activity through both sides of their brain that are designated for emotion, creating words, and connecting words to memories, sensory, and contextual cues. Blood flow is also higher for females in the cingulate gyrus within the limbic system in the midbrain that is responsible for connecting sensory input information with emotions, which allows a better ability to focus on voice, tone, gestures, and facial expressions.[97]

In other words, the main areas of the brain responsible for language have more interconnected blood flow for females, allowing for them to use both sides of the brain when communicating, while males understand emotional communication at a slower rate and are more compartmentalized, leading to more focus but bringing in fewer topics, memories, and emotions at the same time. This is consistent with previous research that has shown men to have more compartmentalized brain activation when viewing faces and processing them more slowly.[239] This makes sense because faces are involved with emotional information.

LANGUAGE DIFFERENCES EVIDENCE

These structural and functional sex differences in language areas of the brain clearly demonstrate male and female language differences stemming from biology.[386] Examples of these gender communication differences have been consistently noted for decades. Females have continually been found to have better language abilities than males.[550] Brain connectivity differences during language processing have been found between boys and girls.[86]

Early childhood gender communication differences have found girls to be more talkative and to use relationship-bonding speech, while boys are found to use more direct communication and to articulate their independence.[386] Natural consistent communicative differences have been found between males and females.[23]

Deborah Tannen (1990) was one of the first scholars to label male talk as focused on content and task, and less on building relationships as "report" talk, and females using talk to build relationships and connecting with others as "rapport" talk (p. 76). Rather than different cultural influences as she suggested, sex hormones account for sex-specific typical communication patterns and gender verbal performance differences.[338, 481, 536]

More recent than Tannen's work, Simaki, Aravantinou, Mporas, Kondyli, and Megalooikonomou (2017) also identified gender communication differences. They did an extensive review of previous research studies investigating gender language use differences. They found that females use more adjectives, which is considered admiration of the other person, communicate less directly through questions, use more indirect requests, and use more hedges and more polite strategies and phrases, while males use stronger and straightforward language. These examples for females are centered on the importance of the relationship with whom they are communicating with for the intentions of politeness, compliments, and less direct to not offend the other person. The male strategies are more focused on the information of the conversation, and less about the relationship of the individuals communicating. A more individualistic communication style by males is physically displayed through fewer mimicked and synchronized behaviors and less cooperation in relationships.[413, 668] Females have been found to have higher levels of mimicked and synchronized behaviors when communicating.[224, 682]

These gender language distinctions that Simaki, Aravantinou, Mporas, Kondyli, and Megalooikonomou (2017) found are consistent with Tannen's categories of rapport relationship building communication for females, and report topic directness communication by males, thus illustrating consistent gender communication differences through several decades.

Recent findings by Leaper (2019) are consistent with the gender communication themes of male and female language differences described by Tannen (1990) and also Simaki, Aravantinou, Mporas, Kondyli, and Megalooikonomou (2017). Leaper (2019) found in video-recorded conversations that females used more affiliative strategies for requests including subtle communication for recommendations, justifications for requests, acknowledging the other person's perspective, and asking the other person for ideas or support. On the other hand, males communicated in a more self-emphasizing manner consisting of direct suggestions. Self-disclosure gender differences were also found. Females used more self-disclosing statements and exhibited more active listening to others' self-disclosure through elaborations and subtle comments. Males used more disaffection in their responses and comments that were irrelevant and adverse. Supportive listening and closeness were highest for female dyads and lowest for male dyads. These findings further support the trends found throughout decades of research that female communication is more focused on other people and their relationship with them; this is compared with males, whose communication is more task-oriented.

Relationships play such an important part in the lives of females that they often have their menstrual cycle synchronized with females they live with. Even more specifically, females living together are more likely to have menstrual headaches than a female living alone. These findings indicate that relationships play a major role with females biologically and are better able to empathize with others because they are having the same biological experiences.[201]

Case and Oetama-Paul (2015) have a more modern label for these gender communication differences described by Tannen and also Simaki, Aravantinou, Mporas, Kondyli, Megalooikonomou (2017) and Leaper (2019). However, Case and Oetama-Paul (2015) provide strong support for the consistent gender communication differences throughout many decades by attributing biological sex as a major contributing factor. They use affiliative to describe female language because the female brain has more network connections to different areas of the brain and is characterized by relationship goals and language use. The female brain has much higher levels of oxytocin, bonding chemical, that rises during relaxing conversations and falls when feeling unnoticed. Oxytocin with females is related with communication that is relational, empathic, person-oriented talk, collaboratiive, indirect, and more sensitive to sensory stimuli; these translate into behaviors such as more head nods, eye contact, smiling, and asking more open questions when communicating.

Female language usage often results in fewer direct words such as 'can' and 'could' so that the other person is not offended and the relationship is maintained. Other such female language includes words like 'let's' rather than a direct order; another example is saying 'I'm sorry' as a means to convey understanding rather than an actual apology. Females also use their superior language abilities to handle conflict less directly than males, such as by gossiping and excluding others.

Male language is labeled by the above authors as the assertive style characterized by a dominance hierarchy of one-upmanship language, while avoiding weakness and vulnerability such as through self-disclosure. This style is heavily influenced by much higher levels of testosterone for males, which is associated with competitiveness and aggression. It conveys control, autonomy, directness, status, things, and theorems that translate into such behaviors as listening for facts, asking more closed questions, less eye contact, more interruption, offers of advice for problems they hear, and listening for blatantly obvious vocal tone changes for emotion cues.

Science was not as advanced at the time of Tannen's work as it is today when measuring and quantifying biology's role for gender communication differences. Therefore, Tannen attributed these differences entirely as social learning through different cultural experiences as a male or female. However, more recent research using more advanced scientific research designs and statistical methodology has found biological sex differences consistent with Case and Oetama-Paul's (2015) description of females using a more empathetic communication approach and males as more focused on a particular topic approach.[647]

Other research has also found women to use a communication style that Case and Oetama-Paul (2015) describe as an empathetic communication approach.[385] Having a more pro-social orientation, such as empathy, is related with more mimicked and synchronized behaviors during conversations.[413] Even nonverbal communication research confirms these findings, with females displaying more mimicked and synchronized behaviors, indicating a greater concern for relational communication and relationship building.[224, 682] The greater mimicked and synchronized behaviors by females allows for shared cognitive circuits to better understand others.[301] In turn, better social cognition of others occurs.[451]

Advances in scientific research has found males using a more assertive and competitive speech style, and females using a more empathetic and affiliative speech style that stems from brain structural and biochemical differences; these are found across a variety of different cultures and research designs with millions of participants.[97] An additional piece of evidence supporting biology's influence in gender communication is that males self-disclose more to females that are in their follicular stage of their menstrual cycle.[290] This likely occurs because this is a fertile time in a woman's menstrual cycle; estrogen levels are higher and reproduction potential is high. Males biologically know that self-disclosure plays an important role with female partners.

The male language use of an assertive and competitive communication style is not a result of culture or parenting boys consistently with this style, as Tannen might suggest, but rather is the result of thousands of years of evolution needing aggression in order to survive to get resources and mates that influences testosterone levels.[25] Adult males have 20-25 times more circulating testosterone than adult females.[186] Testosterone has been consistently associated with aggression, power, status, and competition.[179] For instance, testosterone levels change differently from competition between males and females.[1]

A male language pattern is a combination of fewer connections to different parts of the brain for more compartmentalization communication; this goes along with much higher levels of testosterone associated with competition, which requires concentration on one particular task or issue at a time. Competition is a social experience, it is associated with testosterone and is also linked with male communication patterns.[99] To suggest that male communication styles are entirely socially learned is irresponsible and reckless.

The gender communication and sex differences between males and females regarding language style is consistent with sex differences with oxytocin and testosterone levels. Oxytocin and testosterone have opposing effects in socialization. Human social cognition and bonding is positively associated with oxytocin, while testosterone is linked with more self-oriented, asocial, and antisocial cognitions and behaviors.[129, 606] The differing effects of oxytocin and testosterone clearly resemble the different communication patterns between males and females previously described.

Females are superior with verbal skills.[283, 589, 338] Previous research has consistently found females outperforming males on language tasks. It is quite plausible that the superior language performance of females is related to the ventral frontal cortex region of the brain, which is responsible for social cognition, interpersonal judgement, and decision-making.[97] In order to communicate effectively, a person needs to understand other people,

SPATIAL COMMUNICATION

Females are not superior to males on all tasks. It is well-documented that males and females differ in spatial performance tasks; males have superior performance, likely due to evolutionary survival necessities.[25, 352] Part of these sex differences come from males focusing on spatial aspects regarding objects, while females focus on details of each object along with language associations with each object.[441] It has been shown that males and females use different cognitive strategies when performing spatial tasks as early as age five.[492] Males also have a better memory for visual and spatial events.[684]

Sex brain activity differences have been documented when performing spatial tasks.[352] Males have been consistently found to outperform females with spatial abilities, usually with moderate differences, in research studies.[469] The male advantage comes from having a 20% larger inferior parietal lobe, which is key with mental object rotation abilities.[241] Males also have more blood flow in the right-hemisphere, which is responsible for spatial abilities. The spatial superiority for males and inferior language skills often results with males physically expressing emotions. The male cerebral cortex connects emotion with action.[97]

Spatial language communication gender differences occur as a result of the spatial sex differences just described. It is much easier for a male to buy a woman flowers to express love than to say it or write it on a card. Additionally, males have early exposure to androgens in the areas of the brain responsible for spatial performance that enhances their spatial ability.[392]

On the other hand, estrogen detrimentally effects female spatial performance by way of the nigro-striatal pathway and the cerebellum.[439] Regarding the spatial tasks of communicating or understanding directions, it has been found that males are much better with cardinal directions (North, South, East, West), while females do as well or sometimes better with landmark directions (i.e. turn left at the third pond and then turn right after the fourth parking lot).[441]

One can easily understand how these spatial gender communication differences are essential to recognize in such tasks as finding a location to meet, visual aids in presentations, and parking a vehicle, just to mention a few examples.[723]

CONCLUSION

Centuries of evolutionary survival needs have created biological sex differences that are observed in gender communication language differences. These biological sex differences are consistently found alongside gender communication differences. As time goes on, societies and cultures change, but biological sex differences responsible for gender communication are far slower to change.

CHAPTER 7

SHE FIGURED HE UNDERSTOOD; LITERALLY HE DID NOT

Males and females have different brain functions when processing emotions, language, and other cognitive information. Males tend to rely much more on the right side of the brain for cognitive functions involving emotions, while females have the advantage of using both sides of their brain more effectively for emotion and language.[177] This is evident from the different sides used in the ventromedial prefrontal cortex distinguished by sex.[547] Males have more visual connections for processing language while females have more auditory connections.[157]

SEX BRAIN CONNECTIONS

The corpus callosum—connections to both sides of the brain—is different between males and females.[712] Males have more intra-hemispheric brain connections, while females have more inter-hemispheric brain connections.[305] In addition, the smaller callosal splenia for males assists the left side of the brain for language information and is processed and understood in a linear fashion. Furthermore, males having fewer connections to both sides of the brain reduces their ability to understand nonverbal cues in a conversation. Males also have more separation and compartmentalization with regard to emotion and language compared with females.[97] Previous research has also found males to process social information in a more compartmentalized fashion.[239] This separation for males makes it more difficult to express the emotions they are feeling as proficiently as females through language, as well as to process emotions while involved in a conversation. This lack of understanding nonverbal cues results in males understanding language more literally.

Females, on the other hand, communicate much more indirectly with a heightened nonverbal awareness. This can be displayed through subtle indirect behaviors that are intended to be noticed and understood. Some linguistic examples of female indirectness are using 'can' or 'could' rather than specifically telling someone to do something, using 'sort of' rather than outright dismissing someone's comments, and using 'let's' for more inclusive language.[97] This gives females the advantage of selective attention during language processing.[637]

EMPATHY

The aforementioned communication biological sex differences lead to differences in understanding between males and females—in particular, empathy. Empathy is defined as a combination of biological and situational influences that enables a person to perceive and understand another person's emotions through automatic processes, while realizing that they are separate from their own.[131] Females tend to show more interest in empathy than males. Females evaluate faces more quickly and positively than males, and also process them differently.[239, 536]

When viewing faces, females have more powerful processes that lead them to be more sensitive to faces.[334] When viewing emotional faces, females experience more activation in the fusiform face area, which is the part of the brain that processes facial features.[402, 434] This enables females to better distinguish between different subtle facial expressions.[358]

Not only are visual cues of emotions analyzed at a deeper level, females are better equipped to distinguish emotions from tone of voice.[592] A large part of this superior listening is due to females having a more efficient brain network and more connections to both sides of their brain.[223] Sex hormones for females also contribute to female superiority with understanding communication. Females have higher levels of oxytocin during social situations.[419]

Often, oxytocin interacts with estrogen to improve social understanding of others.[481] This is important because oxytocin promotes heightened social awareness of others by working with the dopaminergic system.[606] Additionally, fluctuations in the sex hormone estrogen in women as a result of their menstrual cycle changes the hippocampus.[45, 400] Estrogen is linked with better language performance, social inquisition, recognition, memory, and pain sensitivity.[26, 338, 481]

The female sex hormone progesterone increases functional connectivity in the hippocampus.[28] This is important to note because females have a larger and more active hippocampus.[202, 257, 345] The hippocampus is responsible for connecting language, memories, and relationships with others.[578] Therefore, the hippocampus, which is responsible for language and relationships, is larger and highly influenced by sex hormones found at much higher rates in women. One can easily infer that these attributes are advantageous for females with language production, processing, understanding, and memory.

One can clearly link the biological sex differences previously described as creating a sex difference with empathy. Females being better equipped to understand nonverbal communication while simultaneously engaging in a conversation is a huge advantage over males, who predominantly use language and less nonverbal processing during conversations. It is through nonverbal communication behaviors that emotions are understood.

Females are better able to connect to the emotional state of others during conversations. This creates a huge advantage for females to understand communication through nuance behaviors and emotions, while males are more likely to understand the literal conversation with limited emotional processing of others to assist their understanding.

EVOLUTIONARY EXPLANATIONS

The biological sex differences in conversational comprehension are likely to have some evolutionary underpinnings. It was necessary for females to have small group social interactions in order for them to survive, such as protection, food, and mate selection.[25] One can easily draw the inference that those females with better biological equipment to socialize were more likely to find a mate, reproduce, and survive along with their offspring. Thus, their biological traits for superior socializing skills were passed onto future female generations and those who did not have these biological attributes likely did not survive or have offspring who survived.

It has been well documented that males outperform females with spatial and object rotation tasks.[25, 352, 441] This has proven to be evident from an early age.[492] Males also have a better memory for spatial and visual experiences.[684] The male strength in these areas indicates physical movement and physical objects for understanding the world around them, including the social world.

For instance, males physically act out and display specific emotions they want to express, either in place of verbally communicating them, or to accompany the emotional words. The cerebral cortex for males helps to explain these phenomenon because emotion and action are closely connected in the male brain.[97] These spatial and object rotation abilities of the male brain give an important clue as to how males understand communication, both when sending a message and receiving one. Males understand communication best when it is literal, specific, and used with concrete language and examples. These characteristics of language closely align with spatial and object skills that also rely upon concrete representation, rather than abstraction or vagueness.

Males and females communicate and understand the world quite differently. Males tend to understand the big picture, bottom lines, and surrounding contexts, while females tend to remember the details. This is evident with spatial understanding, such that males understand generally where they or objects are located in an area, whereas females cognitively perceive the details of the objects and language associations for each object.[441] This is also evident with stimuli, such as males seeing the whole picture, and females seeing the details constructing the individual parts of the big picture, including using more critical descriptions of color tones.[277, 614]

It is easy to understand how gender communication differs. With males having a superiority with spatial skills and object rotation, along with big picture understanding of a stimuli or location, they are more likely to understand the general conclusions from conversations; they focus less on the specific details, especially if they perceive these details as less relevant. Therefore, they are less likely to understand subtle communication, hints, and use of humor for specific points.

Males are also more likely to understand literal language, concrete terms that they can visualize, bottom line takeaways, and representation of ideas such as similes and metaphors. When communicating with a male, females should understand that subtle hints, comments, and gestures are less effective than direct explicit communication accompanied with a visual display.

On the other hand, women are more likely to read into subtle comments and behaviors for additional meaning and emotional cues regardless of whether they were intended or provide additional information. They are likely to communicate less directly because they assume others understand these nuances as well. Males must put all of the different pieces and subtleties together when communicating with a female. This is because there are more options to communicate with a female beyond straight explicit and fact-driven communication.

CONCLUSION

There are biological sex differences that can be clearly linked to gender communication and understanding differences. The female brain's ability to better understand nonverbal communication creates a huge advantage in understanding others. Her ability to use both sides of her brain during communication enables a much better understanding of subtleties in communication. The communication of males is much more explicit both in sending messages and understanding messages from others.

CHAPTER 8

HE ANSWERS ONLY QUESTIONS ASKED; SHE ANSWERS UNASKED QUESTIONS

The way males and females communicate during conversations can differ greatly. Evidence of this exists as early as infancy.[586] This can be especially true when asking and answering questions. Prior to birth testosterone of boys have been found to be detrimental to language abilities for them at age two.[293] At one month of age, testosterone differences between males and females hinders future language development abilities for males.[365] Brain structure and connectivity differences provide great insight into conversation differences.[712]

Brain activity also differs between males and females when using language to communicate.[184] The male brain tends to function in a much more compartmentalized fashion by having one side function for a particular conversational topic. The female brain is much more likely to use both sides of the brain during a conversation topic.[177, 239, 271] Therefore, males are more probable to communicate information that they deem necessary and relevant to the discussed topic, while females are better equipped to expand more dynamically with the overarching topic.

BODY SYSTEM SEX DIFFERENCES

Body systems function differently for males and females; this is a result of different brain functions.[712] Females have more interconnections between different areas of their brain, allowing for different areas to communicate more effectively with one another.[305] Differences in the limbic system between males and females contribute to language differences. The limbic system advantage for females contributes to superior performance with memory, language, and emotion, all of which play a larger role in her communication.[578]

The larger hippocampus in females provides additional insight into gender conversational differences.[257, 345] Females show more bilateral activation in the hippocampus with emotional perception.[202] The hippocampus is responsible for memory and is located in the same limbic system that is responsible for language.[97] The female hippocampus assists with remembering emotional details more so than with males, with males being more likely to recall the general themes of the emotional episode. These differences are partly due to the interconnectedness of the hippocampus and the locus coeruleus (LC). The (LC) directs attention to particular stimuli.[277] The female larger hippocampus, which is responsible for language, emotion, and memory, would interact with the (LC) to focus more on these areas during conversations. Sex differences have been observed regarding the role of the (LC) for male attention to the gist of information, while females are directed by their attention to details.[277]

It is essential to acknowledge the impact of sex hormone differences when understanding the hippocampus. Sex hormones play a vital role with regulating the hippocampus for cognition and mood regulation.[424] Males have much higher amounts of testosterone surrounding the hippocampus.[573] This is related to aggression, power, status, and competition.[179]

Conversely, females have much higher levels of estrogen surrounding the hippocampus.[439] This is linked to physically changing the hippocampus.[45] Estrogen is associated with language performance.[338] Estrogen and testosterone influence the neural control of social behaviors contributing to a sex-dimorphic brain, such as with tissue structures. These tissue structures create neural circuits that are partially responsible for sex-specific social behaviors.[481]

The effects of different sex hormones on a vital area of the brain responsible for memory, emotion, social recognition, and language influences gender communication. Language performance, social learning, and social recognition have been positively associated with estrogen partly due to enhancing social cognition by interacting with other neuro chemical systems in the brain.[338, 481]

One can then conclude that estrogen helps females more with different functions of the hippocampus, such as language expression about previous memories and elaborating about emotional experiences. For males, the associations for testosterone are aggression, power, status, and spatial ability.[179, 684] These categories have fewer emotional ranges and are more focused on a particular task that is necessary with competition.[99]

It has been found that sex hormones are related to these gender communication differences. Higher levels of testosterone are related to a better performance for the gist of understanding in communication, while lower levels of testosterone decrease the big picture performance.[524] As early as one month of age, testosterone begins to negatively impact expressive vocabulary, contributing to language superior performance in females over males later in life.[365] As a result, males are less likely to activate their hippocampus with a variety of emotions in a short period of time when recalling past memories, and will likely stay on one topic at a time. Therefore, more elaboration of past memories injected into conversations expanded upon with emotional expressions would be expected more from females.

CONVERSATIONAL GENDER DIFFERENCES

The aforementioned language-functional differences can be observed during conversations.[284] When a male is asked a question, he often answers without a lot of detail and without referring to previous related events. That happens because males understand the world around them—as well as communication interactions—more holistically; males focus on the central essential information from the individual pieces fitting together for a conclusion.

Evidence of this has been found with numbers. Males are more likely to perceive multi-digit numbers holistically as one number, while females are more likely to processes them as individual numbers placed together.[277] These gender differences have also been evidenced by males processing large shapes constructed from smaller individual shapes more quickly than females, who process the smaller shapes more quickly.[589] Males are also more likely to remember experiences involving visual and spatial occurrences.[684]

Lack of details and emotions does not mean that the male is not interested or does not care about details. It is much more difficult for a male to tie together separate pieces of information spontaneously because one side of his brain or the other is functioning during a conversation.

On the other hand, the female brain can more easily use both sides of her brain for the same conversational topic.[97] This can allow her to bring in other topics related to the discussion, as well as previous related events in rich detail. She is better equipped to recognize the details and peripheral information. Females are better able to remember emotional autobiographical memories.

Some of these differences in gender communication can be traced back to males and females encoding memories differently. Females are more likely to differentiate similar but different events, while males are more likely to perceive these separate events as the same.[277] This alludes to males remembering the overall central theme of experiences, and females focusing more on the details. The details distinguish similar events.

CONCLUSION

Males and females communicate and understand communication differently. These differences do not reflect a lack of interest by males or a lack of focus by females. Rather, it is a difference in how males and females understand and communicate in conversations from biological underpinnings.

CHAPTER 9

HE FORGETS OUR LAST CONVERSATION, HOW PREVIOUS CONVERSATIONS RELATE TO THE CURRENT ONE, WEEKEND PLANS, HOW SHE FEELS ABOUT...

Males and females remember conversations differently.[367] These are not minor differences, but can range from the general topics, details, other people involved, and emotional experiences to name a few. Several physiological sex differences help with understanding these gender differences regarding memories and conversations.

SEX PHYSIOLOGY AND RECALL

Males and females employ different cognitive strategies during recall.[310] It is much easier for females to connect different areas of their brain for conversation recall due to more interhemispheric brain connections.[305] Females have a better memory for faces relating to events that happened.[640]

The part of the brain responsible for a large proportion of these differences is the hippocampus. It connects memories, language, and emotional experiences together with females having stronger connections, more activity, and is much larger even at an early age compared with males.[202, 257,

[345, 439, 646] This may contribute to females having a much more heightened social awareness. Oxytocin also rises to higher levels for females during social interactions.[419]

Oxytocin interacts with estrogen for improved social awareness.[481] This increase of oxytocin for females creates stronger emotional experiences for females, especially for negative ones.[606] Therefore, females are more likely to remember negative experiences, and in more detail.

A possible explanation for males recalling less information from conversations can be physiology. Females have a much better coordinated system for listening.[9, 223] Females also have more connections between listening and emotions that tie together for memories.[547]

CONVERSATION TOPIC RECALL

Ever wonder why a male can better remember last week's major sporting event than a conversation you just had with him? Male spatial versus language abilities can account for some of this difference. As was covered in a previous chapter, males have a superior ability when it comes to spatial ability and object rotation.[25, 352, 441] A male is much more likely to remember conversations that involve visual imagery than abstract thoughts.[684] Males have more visual connections for word processing.[157]

This can be explained by fMRI results showing greater activity for males when recalling visual imagery than verbal cues compared with females.[310] Some examples of visual imagery in conversations are pictures, examples, analogies, action movements, and physical involvement by the male during the conversation. When having a conversation with a male, it can be beneficial to use more explicit nonverbal gestures.

Recall of conversations can also be impacted by the number of changes and subtopics within a given conversation. Females have a superior ability for memory recall of language due to larger gray matter for BA 44 and BA 45 areas of the brain.[367] Not only is this larger area of the brain for language important for female recall, but females have a much better ability to efficiently use both sides of their brain during conversations; the corpus callosum between males and females are distinctly different.[177, 712]

This is supported by the existence of sex differences when activating the ventromedial prefrontal cortex. These sex differences contribute to cognitive functioning differences.[547] Verbal fluency is one such cognitive function that is enhanced for females from efficient use of both sides of her brain.[640] Staying on topic helps concentration and recall for males, rather than bouncing different topics around during the same conversation. Additionally, having different smaller conversations at different times is better for male recall than one large conversation all at once.

A female is more likely to remember conversations that connect to an emotional component.[26, 338, 481] Females pay more attention to details in objects, such as faces and more details of color tones.[441, 614] As a result, females are better able to understand micro facial expressions displaying emotions.[358] Increased emotional processing associated with female recall improves memory recall.[310] This will enable the female to better empathize and connect with the conversation. This will also utilize more areas of her brain.[592] The more different areas of the female brain that are activated, the better the chances are for more detail recall in the conversation.

The higher levels of oxytocin in females during social interactions is important to understand with conversational recall.[419] Social awareness is promoted by oxytocin through the dopaminergic system.[606] Therefore, conversations that females find more interesting, stimulating, unexpected, and exciting have a greater chance of being remembered than conversations that do not capture her attention and affect her body chemical system.

IMPROVING CONVERSATIONAL RECALL

One way to increase conversational recall for both males and females is through applying expectancy-violations theory. The powerful role of expectations during social interactions has been supported by research for years.[10, 248, 383] One of the great benefits is the adaptability to different contexts and people.[169]

Burgoon's (1978) experiment helped to shed the initial light on the powerful impact of communication expectations during social interactions. This experiment focused primarily on proxemics expectations.

Participants who were unaware of the experimental design walked into a room and were asked to have a conversation with a researcher who was secretly part of the experiment and was sitting in a chair. Each participant was then asked to move their chair to whatever distance they felt comfortable to communicate with the other person.

Three separate conditions then followed. The researcher either kept their chair at the distance determined by the participant, or they moved their chair closer to the participant or farther away. The researcher keeping their chair at the distance set by the participant served as the normative or expected distance. Moving the chair closer or farther away from the participant served as a violation of the participant's communication expectations, in particular for proximity.

These communication expectations that were violated can be perceived as either negative or positive. If the participant viewed the unexpected change in distance favorably, then that was a positive violation of expectations. On the other hand, if the participant did not like the unexpected change in proximity, then that served as a negative violation of their communication expectations. The normative distance was thought to be determined by the relationship between communicators, situation of the encounter, power each person had in relation to the other, and perceived valence.

Burgoon's (1978) article was a central piece that started bringing attention to communication expectations, which was initially studied with proximity. However, communication expectations can play a vital role in communication outcomes beyond proximity, such as with conversations. Evaluations are made by people interacting in conversations when their communication expectations are violated.[378] These communication expectation assessments are important to understand because communication outcomes occur as a result.[169, 315, 721]

One such communication outcome affected by violations of communication expectations is emotional experiences.[10, 169, 248] The important takeaway from Burgoon's (1978) experiment is that violations of communication expectations play a more vital role with communication outcomes than expected behaviors. They are also remembered more.[496] It takes more mental effort to process information that we are not expecting because we have to exert greater attention, effort, and energy to understand what is unexpected, compared with quickly and easily processing information that is expected and makes sense.[378]

Communication expectations are created from previous communication interactions.[169, 315, 721] Males and females are likely to retain more information from conversations that involve unexpected information or behaviors, compared with normally expected conversational topics. Therefore, males and females both increase how much they remember when it contains unexpected components.

Furthermore, another person's communication expectations are based on previous communication interactions. When it becomes necessary to have an important conversation, one should consider violating those communication expectations in an effort to increase the recall of the conversation. This can be done by using more powerful words, vivid details, more powerful gestures and facial expressions, vocal tones, and giving information that is unexpected. These are all ways to achieve higher levels of conversational recall.

CONCLUSION

How we make sense of the world and people around us is often the result of conversation. It is necessary to understand conversational recall gender differences. These differences can be explained through biological sex differences. Males and females are likely to remember conversations differently depending upon the topic. Expectancy-violations theory can help both males and females with conversational recall.

PART 4

FEELS SO GOOD.

CHAPTER 10

HOW DO YOU FEEL?

Emotions play an important part in everyone's life. Believing the role of emotions to be the same between males and females is reckless.[178] Sex hormones and genes on sex chromosomes are responsible for structural and functional emotional differences between males and females.[40] Males and females have structural brain differences before birth that lead to emotional differences in adulthood as well.[680]

SEX HORMONES AND EMOTIONS

Males and females experience emotions differently due to sex hormones. Sex hormones influence the entire brain, such as cognitive functions and mood that is distinguishable between males and females.[430] Emotions are processed differently as a result of sex hormones changing brain synapses.[303] Estrogen and a larger hippocampus that is more active makes females more sensitive to social situations.[202, 257, 345, 424] Estrogen can even change the hippocampus physically.[45]

Additionally, prolonged stress can physically change the brain and its behavioral and emotional functions in differing ways between males and females.[443] This makes females more susceptible to negative social interactions and can partially explain why they are twice as likely as males to be diagnosed with depression.[348]

DEPRESSION GENDER DIFFERENCES

The brain also has sex differences regarding areas responsible for emotions.[250] Kong, Chen, Womer, Jiang, Luo, et al. (2013) found that major depressive disorder differs between males and females in the cortico-limbic-strial neural system, which is responsible for regulating emotions. Females with major depressive disorder have less gray matter in the limbic regions; these areas are related with emotional processing.

Conversely, males with major depressive disorder have less gray matter in the striatal regions, motor and reward areas receiving dopaminergic inputs. These differences lead to females having more anxiety issues and men having more substance control problems. Dopamine dysfunction in these areas also contributes to these differences.[175, 364] Substance control problems are also related with fetal androgen exposure, which is one more contributing factor.[92]

Pain is often a part of depression. Females are more sensitive to pain due to sex hormones, such as estrogen, and also cognitive functioning.[333, 447, 656] For females, the menstrual cycle and also menopause play a vital role with estrogen levels creating emotional oscillations and influencing muscle control; for males, emotions can fluctuate from seasons and time of the day.[97, 291, 333] Therefore, the changes of emotions differ between males and females.

MALES AND EMOTIONS

Filkowski, Olsen, Duda, Wanger, and Sabatinelli (2017) highlighted some brain structural and activation sex differences when viewing emotional stimuli. Males were found to have more activation in the mediodorsal nucleus of the thalamus (MDN), which is responsible for coordinating visual attention such as when viewing emotional stimuli. Males were also found to have more activation in the left superior frontal gyrus (SFG), which is partly responsible for emotion regulation.

Having more activation in the MDN, which is partially responsible for visual attention control, and the SFG, which helps control emotions, gives some credence for men having more cognitive control with their emotions. This has been supported by other researchers as well.[435, 731]

FEMALES AND EMOTIONS

Females are more influenced by the limbic system, which is responsible for emotions, than men.[578] Filkowski et al. (2017) illustrate that females have shown more activation in the bilateral amygdala and hippocampus. Females also show more resting state functional connectivity activity after experiencing posttraumatic stress disorder.[272] Again, with the hippocampus being responsible for memories and emotions, these findings indicate emotional experiences to last longer with females; the extracellular signal-regulated kinase 2 phosphorylation in the hippocampus has also been found as a contributor to female emotional instability.[435] With the amygdala responsible for processing cognition and emotion, it is no surprise that females also display a greater range of fluctuations regarding brain activations to emotional stimuli.[423] Females also often exhibit more heart rate variability when resting than males.[703]

Further influences of female emotional instability are the effects of menopause reducing estrogen levels and decreasing functional abilities associated with the hippocampus, such as emotional memories.[333] Estrogen level changes in males appear to not have these same effects on emotional stability.[430] One can conclude that estrogen levels are related to emotional functioning in females, such as higher levels of estrogen related with emotional memories, while a decrease in emotional memories occurs as estrogen levels decrease.

Filkowski et al. (2017) highlighting higher levels of activation for females in the bilateral amygdala increases attention for females with emotional stimuli. Other research is consistent with this notion, indicating that sex differences found prior to birth contribute to females being more emotionally sensitive as adults.[680]

BRAIN SEX DIFFERENCES

Males and females differ biologically when processing negative emotions because males use an evaluative approach and females use an affective approach.[415] Amygdala sex differences account some for females more impacted by negative emotional experiences.[183, 423] The amygdala helps process emotional stimuli.[423] The locus coeruleus (LC) is also different between males and females in both structure and function. The (LC) plays an intricate role with adverting attention toward particular stimuli, such as signaling for females that detail information is important to attend to while for males the general information is important. The (LC) can therefore influence sex differences regarding emotional memories by working with the amygdala.[277, 572]

Additionally, females have more activation in subcortical brain areas in response to emotional cues relating to harm avoidance.[19] Filkowski et al. (2017) point out that females having more activation in the dorsal midbrain is important because it encompasses the periaqueductal gray (PAG). The human (PAG) activates in response to various emotional stimuli. Females were also found to have more activation in the locus coeruleus (LC), which is responsible for emotional processing.

Females have more emotion capabilities on both sides of their brain, while also having language and emotions integrated; males process emotions on the right side of their brain and language on the left side with fewer connection capabilities between their sides. Emotions flow less easily to the left verbal side of the brain for males. As a result, males communicate about emotions in a linear fashion. The more interconnected female brain plays an important role with emotional processing.[305, 423]

The connections of the female brain allowing for an easier pathway to transfer emotional information to different sides of her brain is influenced by estrogen.[183] Females experience greater emotional sensations and activate different areas of their brain than males—for instance, when watching different emotional music videos.[249] With greater integration throughout the brain, having more activation in the anterior cingulate cortex and right hippocampus when viewing negative faces, it is not surprising that women are about twice as likely to be negatively impacted by depression than men.[363, 683] Additionally, women are much better at recognizing emotions, indicating that they avert more attention to the emotions of others.[2]

NEGATIVE EMOTIONAL SEX DIFFERENCES

This higher activation for females in emotional areas can lead to more emotional problems.[217] Particularly true is negative emotion susceptibility for females.[635] Females have been found to have much higher brain activation when viewing subliminal negative faces.[416] Females also report more distress with negative emotional stimuli. Their menstrual cycle midluteal phase—low estrogen levels—greatly hinders females from suppressing negative emotional stimuli.[417] Likely, this indicates the important role of estrogen with females for combating negative emotions.

Females have more activity than males in the anterior cingulate cortex, an area of the brain responsible for attention and emotion, and the right hippocampus, when viewing subliminal sad faces.[683] Females also have a visual physiological response to viewing angry faces with their pupils either expanding or contracting indicating stress and a risk for major depressive disorder.[362] Considering this evidence, it should come as no surprise that females are better at recognizing emotions of others because of the role of the hippocampus with emotions.[709] Additionally, the higher resting heart rate variability indicates that females have less emotional control; this leads to more anxiety and depression than males.[703] Anxiety in females contributes to less emotional self-regulation than it does with males.[217]

SEROTONIN SEX DIFFERENCES

Sex differences with brain functioning from sex hormones have been well established, such as higher levels of depression in females.[104] Depression falls under the category of a neurobiobehavioral disorder.[702] Males and females are susceptible to depression for different reasons socially, with females more from interpersonal relationships, and males from career goals.[336]

Understanding depression as a biological function, serotonin is a neuromodulatory transmitter that helps regulate, excite or inhibit emotional states, such as happiness, vitality, and euphoria.[34, 357] It has been commonly accepted for more than forty years that the serotonergic system is sexually dimorphic, impacting the neurobiological pathways that are involved with functioning in areas such as mood and mood disorders, depression treatments using serotonin, and as a neurotransmitter; all of these indicate genetic risks.[512]

Perry, Goldstein-Piekarski, and Williams (2017) lay out the biological structural components of the serotonergic system that influence neurobiological pathway differences between males and females. These structural differences create functional sex differences that partially explain females having higher levels of depression. For instance, individual gene differences having a role with serotonergic metabolism plays a role with depression. It has been found that females have a much stronger heritability of depression than males, further indicating genetic sex differences.[337]

The serotonin transporter 5-HTT controls synaptic serotonin levels; cell surface expressions of 5-HTT sites are aligned with serotonin levels.[660] Perry, Goldstein-Piekarski, and Williams (2017) address sex and gene linkages regarding the serotonin transporter-linked polymorphic region (5-HTTLPR); this is in the serotonin transporter gene (SLC6A4) that codes for the protein moving serotonin from the synaptic cleft to the presynaptic neuron. These structures create sex differences regarding serotonin metabolism. More vulnerability to depression can occur from stress due to its functioning.

Females have been found to possess lower serotonin receptor binding, which provides evidence for depression sex differences.[204] Only females with depression have less serotonin transporter availability, compared with healthy individuals of the same sex.[632] Females that have transformed 5-HTTLPR serotonin receptor binding can have lower levels of serotonin, but this functioning difference is not found with men.[405] These lower binding levels are associated with higher levels of neuroticism, which is related with negative emotional states.[660] Lower levels of serotonin are related with processing emotions more negatively.[204]

The 5-HTTLPR serotonin receptor binding functioning can lead to females having more risk of depression, anxiety, and internalized behaviors related to depression. However, for males this can lead to aggression, conduct disorder, and externalized behaviors.[254] Therefore, the functions of serotonin for males and females differs in its role with depression.

Perry, Goldstein-Piekarski, and Williams (2017) point out the X-linkage's detrimental effect with serotonin's ability as a neurotransmitter. Specifically, they address the sex chromosome X-inactivation. Depression has been connected with several X-linked genes. MAOA is an X-linked gene responsible for regulating neurotransmissions by degrading serotonin. MAOA-H increases the risk for depression and anxiety, particularly for females. With the X chromosome having a functional impact on serotonin, it makes sense that it is involved with depression for females, who have two X chromosomes when males only have one. For instance, depressed females have lower methylation at the MAOA locus.[446]

Sex hormones must be considered when understanding the serotonergic system; this is because they have an interactive effect that impacts its functioning differently between males and females.[46, 356] Perry, Goldstein-Piekarski, and Williams (2017) highlight the interaction between sex hormones and gene products effecting the rates of serotonin biosynthesis. For instance, depression for females mostly occurs during major hormonal changes in their lives. On the other hand, testosterone is an antidepressant for both males and females.[442]

Increasing testosterone levels is associated with increasing serotonin reuptake transporter binding, which can be an effective treatment for depression and anxiety by increasing serotonin levels.[356] Another example of sex hormone effects with the serotonin system is with the TPH enzyme, which controls the amount of serotonin synthesis, predicting depression levels in females, but not with males.[609]

Socializing can effectively treat depression in females. Females often find socializing to be a stress relief and positive emotional experience; this is felt from the resulting raised levels of oxytocin interacting with the dopaminergic system.[419, 606] Expressing positive emotions can also help to relieve stress from positive experiences and facial feedback.[219, 624]

STRESS GENDER DIFFERENCES

There are biological explanations for sex differences as they relate to stress.[178] Sex hormones influence functional cerebral asymmetries, which result in brain functional sex differences responsible for emotions and behaviors.[271] The hypothalamus is responsible for regulating emotional reactions to stress. There are a few genetic sex differences regarding the hypothalamus. Seven genes encoded on the Y chromosome have been identified as having male-specific expressions, and only a few on the X chromosome were found only for suppressing activation.[561] While the actual physical composition of the hypothalamus might not differ much between males and females, the activation and regulation from sex hormones does differ, with females having a more sensitive hypothalamus that circulates more stress hormones following a traumatic event.[490]

Changes in ovarian hormones play a role in premenstrual dysphoric disorder, postpartum depression, and postmenopausal depression, which indicates depression correlations with hormonal changes in females. The highest levels of depression occur during puberty, following pregnancy, and perimenopause.[15] Creatine is necessary for brain energy balance functioning and fluctuates much more in women as a result of their menstrual cycle.[285]

Females are more affected by stress and female sex hormones, such as circulating ovarian hormones, which play an intricate role with depression. For instance, depression is more common for females when peripheral estrogen levels increase during puberty than it is before this sex-specific hormonal onset.[287, 308] Dramatic decreases in estrogen for females can also lead to depression, such as around age fifty with the onset of menopause.[593]

Decreased female estrogen levels increase the risk for prostaglandins, which is related to neurogenic inflammation.[135] Not coincidently, women over age fifty initiate divorce at a much higher rate than men over fifty.[565] These findings point to estrogen playing a vital role in combating female depression.[15] It is essential for females with depression to find the right hormonal balance.

For men, higher levels of testosterone is beneficial with better cerebral serotonergic functioning, leading to less depression.[510] Testosterone can be used as a possible antidepressant.[206] An added advantage for males is that testosterone does not cyclically fluctuate like estrogen does for women.[15] Behaviors are often associated with different hormone levels.[283]

Around age fifty, sex hormonal influences begin to reverse with women's estrogen levels decreasing and men's testosterone levels decreasing; this results in less feminizing of women and more feminizing of men.[97] However, we often try to understand others' emotions from our own perspective. This can be detrimental when trying to understand someone who is not our biological sex.

The inability to understand another's emotional state is linked to physiological health and stress management detriments.[44] Sex hormones can influence mood through the hippocampus.[424, 439] An fMRI study involving female participants found that increasing their testosterone levels activated more of their amygdala and hypothalamus when they viewed angry faces.[275] This action response to threats highlights the role of testosterone. Most likely, these results allude to a male biological underpinning for action against negative social threats. Along these lines, sex differences have found higher aggression levels related more to males than females.[283] This is consistent with findings that testosterone is linked with more individual orientation along with antisocial cognitions and behaviors.[129, 606]

On the other hand, the increased levels of oxytocin females experience when socializing with others is linked to increasing their memory of social cues.[226, 606] If social cues are remembered more by females, then the emotions related to the social cues create a stronger and longer lasting social memory. Hormonal replacement therapy can be an effective solution for female depression.[243]

CONCLUSION

The robust influence of sex hormones with emotions covered in this chapter gives insight into understanding behaviors, communication, and psychological health. Sex hormones influence emotions, and emotions influence how we perceive others as well as ourselves, including how we feel, behave, and also communicate. Observing one's own or another person's communication and behaviors can give some insight into their body chemical distribution.

For example, if a woman who is experiencing and exhibiting signs of depression around her late forties and early fifties, she might be reacting to lowering levels of estrogen. On the other hand, a male who becomes less active in competitive hobbies, experiences decreased spatial abilities such as driving a car or putting a golf ball might be experiencing lower levels of testosterone. These changes in behaviors that are considered abnormal should raise awareness; one should see a health professional to measure body chemical levels, particularly sex hormone levels.

CHAPTER 11

CHILL, DON'T STRESS

Humans have basic emotional needs that have been passed down genetically. We have a need for social relationships for both psychological and physical health.[212] One such need is to find a mate. This need helps to satisfy one's need for social bonding along with passing on one's genetics.[19]

AFFECTIONATE COMMUNICATION AND STRESS

The romantic relationships that we have can greatly impact our stress, both positively and negatively.[207] Affectionate exchanges with another person, such as through touch, can lead to stress reduction and better well-being.[313] Kaldewaij, Koch, Zhang, Hashemi, klumpers, and Roelofs (2018) found affectionate communication to be directly associated with lower cortisol levels related to the stress response. Others have also found positive physical outcomes from receiving affection, such as oxytocin increases to reduce stress, blood lipid levels, lower blood pressure levels, and blood glucose levels, which are known for diabetes risk.[208, 209, 210,]

STRESS GENDER BRAIN DIFFERENCES

Stress for women and men differ, and evidence of these differences has been found throughout all stages of life.[40] Sex hormones and genes on sex chromosomes effect the structural and functional responses to stress differently between males and females.[40] Different areas of the brain are activated during stress for males and females. During stress, males have more activation in the caudate, midbrain, ACC, and thalamus, which are areas responsible for instrumental action and motor function. On the other hand, females in stress were found to have higher heart rates and more activation in the occipital lobe, right temporal gyrus, and insula, which are areas responsible for visual processing, verbal expression, and emotional experience.[602] Females have more resting state activity, such as in the prefrontal cortex.[286] The prefrontal cortex is responsible for organizing social behaviors according to the stimuli and context encountered.[349]

Actual sex differences in brain activity has been found with stress in the medial prefrontal cortex.[438] Females have a stronger emotional connection with their personal memories, often consisting of more negative memories of childhood and romantic relationship memories.[74]

Young, Bodurka, and Drevets (2017) investigated males and females diagnosed with major depression, and found that females with major depression had more brain activity during negative autobiographical memory recall than males with major depression or individuals not diagnosed with depression. For females diagnosed with depression, these negative memories were activated much more in the middle prefrontal cortex (mPFC), insula, and thalamus indicating that negative biographical memories are much more personally processed and more difficult to divert attention away from them. This leads females to be more susceptible to depression from stressful experiences. Males with major depression had brain activations of negative autobiographical memories that were similar to other males undiagnosed of depression.

These findings are consistent with other research that found females to have higher activation in the dorsomedial prefrontal cortex during stress (dmPFC); this indicates for females high levels of internalizing and thinking about stressful events that can easily become overwhelming. Males had less activation in these areas, leading to less thinking about the stress and internalizing the stress.[602]

Additionally, Young, Bodurka, and Drevets (2017) found that during positive autobiographical memory recall the reverse. Females were found to have reductions in the hippocampal/parahippocampal region. Females also had reduced activation in the middle prefrontal cortex (mPFC). Taken together, this suggests females find positive autobiographical memories less relevant, rewarding, and stimulating than males. Depressed females find these positive memories less relevant, rewarding, and stimulating than females not diagnosed with depression. Depressed males recall positive autobiographical memories similar to males not diagnosed with depression.

STRESS AND GENDER SOCIAL AWARENESS

People who empathize more experience higher levels of stress from that of others.[156] Females are more sensitive to stress as a result of heightened social awareness and processing.[114] Part of this is due to having more areas of the brain impacted more easily.[305] Females have more activation in the locus coeruleus to environmental stressors, which plays a vital role with emotional processing.[202]

Females experiencing stress have stronger emotions and feelings connected with sensory and semantic processing, and more automatic nervous system activation.[602] Females show heightened responsiveness to social interaction involving rewards and punishments from others, as indicated in more brain activity in the dorsal attention network, which brings more vulnerability to negative effects from stress.[170] This is evident by earlier detection of emotions, added activity in the amygdala, and greater limbic activity when processing emotional information, better emotional memory, and more integrated brain for emotion and cognition processes.[16]

Females also have a higher chance of getting a menstrual migraine when living with another female. This can occur from both females having synchronized menstrual cycles.[201] These findings indicate that females experience stress related to social functions, while males experience stress associated with action and movement. While females find communicating as an effective means to lower stress, males can lower their stress levels through activities.

STRESS AND GENDER REACTION DIFFERENCES

Males and females have different neural circuits involved with emotion representation and incorporation.[710] Males have an evaluative approach to negative emotions, while females use an affective approach.[415] There are physical changes to the brain after prolonged stress that regulate behaviors and emotions that differ between males and females.[443]

Males with major depressive disorder have reduced gray matter in striatal regions, which are the reward systems. Females have reduced gray matter in the limbic regions, which are emotion and memories areas. Thus resulting in males having less impulse control and females having more anxiety disorders.[351] Perhaps males having less impulse control partially accounts for the fact that 75% of people arrested are male and 80% of people arrested for violent crimes in the United States are male.[190]

Females have a more sensitive limbic system, which controls emotions. Furthermore, females tend to have more activation in the hippocampus, which is responsible for emotions and memories.[202] Females have more resting state functional connectivity activity in the hippocampus after developing post-traumatic stress disorder.[272]

Estrogen interplays with the hippocampus for females. When estrogen levels are at their highest during the ovulatory phase, the hippocampus physically enlarges.[45] The enlarged hippocampus and added estrogen contribute to females being more vulnerable to stress from social situations.[257, 345, 424]

The hypothalamus is another area of the brain that has sex activity differences during stress. The hypothalamus is responsible for physiological reactions to a stressful event. While it differs only slightly in physical presentation between males and females, sex hormones play a large role with females having a more sensitive hypothalamus that releases more stress hormones following a stressful experiences.[490, 561] Actual stress activation responses is heightened in females.

Orexins activate responses to stress such as neurobiological systems by promoting the acute stress response-stimulating orexin neurons. Females have a much higher orexin system expression to stress that can exaggerate neuroendocrine and behavioral responses.[251] This means females are more affected by negative emotional experiences than males, which can lead to more stress.

Females have more pain sensitivity, due in part to brain structures and functions.[447] Amygdala—emotional processing part of the brain—differences between males and females accounts for some of the higher vulnerability to negative emotional experiences to stress by females.[183] Females have a stronger resting-state functional connectivity between the left amygdala and the left middle temporal gyrus, inferior frontal gyrus, postcentral gyrus, and hippocampus, areas of the brain associated with face processing along with fear and pain processing.[347]

Because females have more activity in the areas of the brain that process fear and pain, this results in greater stress from those events. Females also have observably more brain activity when viewing subliminal negative faces.[416] Again, more brain activity for females when viewing negative faces subconsciously indicates female sensitivity to stressors, such as negative emotional experiences.

Observations of female sensitivity to negative social situations can be visually observed outside of a research experiment. When viewing negative faces, one can actually observe changes in female pupil size indicating an automatic physiological reaction.[362] Female sensitivity to emotional stimuli can go the other way as well in social situations. Light, Grewen, and Amico (2005) found women lowered their blood pressure and blood glucose levels when they were involved in more affectionate communication. Burleson, Trevathan, and Todd (2007) also found stress levels to lower the following day for middle aged women who had more affectionate communication. Females are not only more prone to stress from social situations but also with different brain activity and higher levels of stress when sleep-deprived.[242]

As most people who have been in a long-term romantic relationship can attest, relationships can also create higher levels of stress and negative physiological responses. Positivity or negativity involved in conflict plays a major factor with physiological outcomes to stress.[519] Laurent, Powers, and Granger (2013) found relationship conflict impacted the physiology of women more than men. Timmons, Arbel, and Margolin (2017) found that women were able to recover physiologically from conflict stress much quicker if they had positive social support from their husbands.

To better understand these gender differences regarding stress, one should look at the role that the serotonergic system plays with stress.[512] Serotonin neurotransmission differs between males and females and also plays a role with handling stress as a mood regulator. Differences in sex-specific pathophysiological pathways regarding serotonin can partially explain higher levels of depression in women compared with men.[553]

Victor, Drevets, Misaki, Bodurka, and Savitz (2017) found similar neural activity of women not diagnosed with depression with that of both sexes diagnosed with depression. For women, the hippocampus and anterior cingulate cortex have been found to have more activity when viewing subliminal unhappy images than viewing subliminal happy or neutral images. The use of subliminal images indicates a biological constructional influence to these activities, rather than socialization or conscious effort. This activity is consistent of people diagnosed with depression.

SEX HORMONES AND STRESS

Sex hormones influence reactions to stress differently between males and females because they change the brain synapse.[303] Females have higher dopamine system sensitivity in acute and repeated stress and have hyperarousal reactions to stress.[42, 560] Females have more sensitivity to pain due in part to body chemicals.[447] Females are more reactive to the stress reaction chemical cortisol, responsible for directing energy to attend to stressful events. Stress can impair vital areas of the brain such as the amygdala, hippocampus, and anterior cingulate cortex.[473] This can damage amygdala involvement with the hippocampus, memory and emotion regulation, leading females to be more sensitive to mood disturbances and focus on negative information following a stressful experience; this is partially due to sex hormonal changes on the HPA axis, and brain circuits responsible for stress responses.[16]

For females, but not males, cortisol levels have also been found to have a negative association with resting-state functional connectivity with the amygdala, vital with processing stress, and the anterior cingulate gyrus that is responsible for emotional processing, learning, and actually feeling psychological emotions, such as pain.[347, 429] Thus, females experiencing stress have increased cortisol levels, which disrupts emotional processing and learning. When the reactions to cortisol do not function properly and levels remain high, negative physiological effects on the body resembling stress are likely to occur.[457]

Reasons for the described differences of stress-processing between males and females can be traced back to birth; evidence suggests females are more sensitive to emotional experiences.[680] Females are diagnosed with depression around twice as often as men.[283, 683] They are also at a twofold risk of developing post-traumatic stress disorder after an extremely stressful experience.[272]

Males have higher levels of testosterone, which does not fluctuate nearly as much as estrogen for females in the brain areas impacting stress levels. Estrogen fluctuations with females can bring about negative outcomes to stress, such as migraine headaches.[135, 422] Sex hormones can impact the hippocampus, which can in turn affect stress through mood changes.[424, 439]

The female menstrual cycle plays an intricate role with her sensitivity to stress.[114] Females are more prone to feel stress from negative emotional stimuli, which is most vulnerable during their menstrual cycle midluteal phase.[417] Female menstrual cycles influence stress levels through sex hormones such as estrogen, such as high levels during puberty, following pregnancy, and perimenopause.[15]

These extreme levels of sex hormones can cause stress from the associated psychological stress of depression, resulted from imbalanced levels of estrogen.[308] Lower levels of estrogen in females can also lead to more stress through declines in neural and cognitive integrity along with dysregulation of emotional processing such as premenstrually, late perimenopause, and following menopause.[16, 276] These low estrogen levels related to stress increases the chances for females to develop menstrual migraines and depression.[135]

The early use of hormone therapy to help women reach optimal estrogen levels is better for addressing physiological and psychological problems compared with waiting, such as later stages of menopause.[268] The likely optimal level of estrogen for females is an inverted U-shaped-level, in which estrogen levels are not too high or too low.[422] Finding a balance with estrogen levels for females can play an important role with stress reduction.[15] A woman's menstrual cycle can also fluctuate her creatine levels necessary for proper brain energy and functioning.[285] One can conclude from these findings that stress plays a larger emotional role for females.

Affectionate communication prior to a stressful experiences can lead to lower levels of stress.[502] An underlining connection between affectionate communication and stress reduction is oxytocin.[210] Affectionate communication such as intimacy can lead to positive outcomes to the endocrine system, immune system, cardiovascular system, and neuro activation and chemistry.[295, 519]

Another effective means to deal with stress is to delay cortisol increases in reaction to a stressor for emotion regulation. This can be done through cognitive reappraisal and distraction by reducing the potency of negative emotional experiences.[317] This can be done by perceiving a negative emotional experience in a different light, such as its irrelevancy to larger life issues.

CONCLUSION

Stress plays a different role for males and females. These include the physiological reactions, different causes, sex hormone differences, and different ways to reduce stress. One cannot effectively treat stress in a unisex manner. The biological underpinnings are far too different to treat stress the same for males and females. This chapter provided ample evidence of brain and sex hormone stress differences between males and females.

PART 5

DO YOU UNDERSTAND?

CHAPTER 12

WOMEN'S 6TH SENSE

FEMALE BRAIN 6TH SENSE
There is a difference in reading and understanding social cues between males and females across cultures and historical periods; this is likely due to biological predetermined differences in social behaviors.[504] Females overall have been found to have better social cognitive abilities.[259] Different areas of her brain are better able to communicate with each other from having more interhemispheric connections.[305]

Females have better neuronal networks from functional connectivity that allows for better social processing.[7] Females can engage in conversations, while simultaneously interpreting social cues due to more areas of her brain working in coordination. Females at an early age pay more attention to faces, which helps develop their social understanding of others later in life.[441] Females have an innately superior ability to perceive details of objects, such as people's faces and micro-emotional changes in faces.[268, 358] Females had an evolutionary need to understand their offspring's facial cues in order for their genetics to be pass down from generation to generation.[2, 100, 482, 536] This indicates a heightened social awareness for females.

Females have more resting state activity in the prefrontal cortex, which is responsible for organizing social behaviors regarding stimulus and context.[286, 349] They are able to use more areas of their brain and quicker when processing emotions because estrogen helps to protect the cerebellum.[439] The cerebellum helps with emotional processing.[200] When viewing human faces, females have more biological responses indicating more sensitivity.[334] They process faces quicker.[239] They have more activation when viewing emotional faces in the fusiform face area of the brain that processes facial features.[402, 434]

Females even have more activity in emotional areas of the brain when viewing subliminal faces.[416] Females also perceive faces more than males in objects, and this is termed pareidolia, which has more activation in the female brain areas associated with emotion, such as the right STS, BA22; posterior cingulate cortex, BA22; orbitofrontal cortex, BA10.[537] The orbitofrontal areas have also been found to be larger in females.[22] Females remember more details of social interactions, especially involving emotional cues, such as in the face.[277] Not only faces, but other nonverbal cues are better understood by females.[538] For example, females have a superior ability to understand emotion in voice nuances.[592] Females also have better social perception as a result of larger areas in the brain that are part of the limbic system.[578] In addition, females have a larger insula that is responsible for processing sensory and emotional experiences.[578, 602]

EMPATHY

Psychological sex differences exist between males and females. It has long been found in research that females are better social empathizers.[283] Evidence of this has been found early in childhood with sharing behaviors.[52] Part of this is their ability to focus more during conversations and become less distracted by irrelevant information.[637] Females score higher with trait empathy that relates their response to another person's anguish.[113]

Females have more empathy than males; this is indicated by higher stimulation from automatic processing in their brain when viewing other people's faces, along with a better understanding of nonverbal body cues.[536, 538] Females score better with cognitive empathy, which is the ability to understand another's mental state and predict their likely behavior. Warrier,

Grasby, Uzefovsky, Toro, Smith, et al. (2018) conducted a study in which males and females looked at a photo of a pair of eyes, then ascribed a word to that person's mental state. Females outperformed males, and the authors identified a locus in 3p26.1 within the female brain as a partial explanation to female outperformance. This finding supports the notion that females are superior in nonverbal communication, which, in this case, meant understanding another person's nonverbal emotional expression. Females have consistently been found to have higher levels of empathy throughout their lives that is evident through their communication behaviors as well as choices in careers and hobbies.[647]

Superior female empathy can be observed through physical behaviors, as well as brain activity. Male and female lover pairs have been observed having similar cooperative behaviors when performing a task, while at the same time having similar areas of the brain activated. It was much quicker and easier for females to adapt their behaviors to their partner's than it was for males to adapt to their female partner's behaviors suggesting that it takes more cognitive effort for males to empathize with others.[491]

Additionally, physiological mimicry and synchrony for couples has been found to be higher when the male partner has higher levels of empathy.[125] This indicates that it is the male with less empathy holding back mimicry and synchronous performance. This is what previous research has found with females having higher levels of mimicry and synchrony during conversations, indicating more concern for relationship building.[224] A pro-social communication style, which is consistent with female communication, is associated with displaying more mimicked and synchronized behaviors.[413] Females often have synchronized menstrual cycles with other females in the home, and are more likely to experience a menstrual headache if other females in the home have one.[201] This enables them to better empathize with their female house mates.

Synchrony and mimicked behaviors between people in a relationship are important because it is linked to more positive behaviors, better understanding of others, stronger relationship bonds, and more positive emotions.[451] Synchrony and mimicked behaviors enable a better understanding of the other person as cognitive circuits are shared between the individuals, often reducing the differences between the individuals and focusing on the pair as one.[301]

Testosterone is associated with preferences for more individuality, and thus, fewer social interactive behaviors with others.[129, 606] Testosterone levels are associated with less abilities to empathize.[472] Testosterone has been linked consistently with male-type behaviors, such as aggression.[283] Less social communication by males is associated with less synchrony and mimicked behavioral displays.[413] Most people do not want to constantly socialize with an aggressive person.

INSULA

Another source for female empathy comes from the insula. Females are found to have more gray matter in the insula.[406] Notably, gray matter is constructed of somatodendritic tissues of neurons, which help the processing and functioning of that area of the brain.[250] Females also often have more activation in the insula than males.[302] One can then easily conclude that the insula plays a larger role in the female brain compared to the male brain.

The human insula is mysteriously located deep within the lateral sulcus of the brain, and is not seen from the surface; it is responsible for sensory and emotional processing along with making decisions. The insula has a direct connection with the automatic nervous system; emotional processing directly affects automatic physiological processes.[663] This can be explained by the insula directly relating to sensory-motor coordination.[511] The insula serves as an intuitive feeling.[652, 688] This intuition comes from the superior ability of self-awareness to process a deep level of meaning concerning others' behaviors, such as empathy from social emotional thinking.[70, 539] The insula is stimulated by such emotions as happy, sad, disgust, frightened, and sexual.[715]

The insula's role with empathy, derived from sensory perceptual information, is automatic processing and is broken into four areas by Kurth, Zilles, Fox, Laird, and Eickhoff (2010). The four areas are sensorimotor region, central-olfactogustatory region, socioemotional region, and cognitive region. The insula not only serves to feel emotionally what others feel, but also physically as well.

As was previously covered in an earlier chapter, females are more sensitive to pain.[333, 656] Coincidently, the insula is activated when painful stimuli is felt.[71] The insula may serve as a thermosensory function because it has been found that cold temperatures are processed and understood and felt through the insula.[597] As was previously covered, females often have more activation in the insula to stimuli, perhaps the insula solves the mystery that females more often feel colder than males at the office, home, etc. due to more activation in their insula and the thermosensory function.[302, 597]

Taste sensations also activate the insula.[714] Sound plays an interesting role as well. The insula is activated from different sounds to decipher emotional meaning, which plays an important role between sound and empathy.[580] Taken together, these heightened sensory awareness activations enhance the ability to detect new stimuli.[663] This can create a female sense that something is amiss when walking into a room; females may also notice that someone is not acting as they usually do. It can also be as simple as understanding others on a deep individual level.

OXYTOCIN

Oxytocin also plays an important role with female empathy superiority.[230] Oxytocin improves perception of social and emotional stimuli.[508] One way it does this is through intermingling with estrogen in the brain.[481] Females experience higher levels of oxytocin when communicating with others, which increases their memory of that social interaction and makes for a more enjoyable social experience.[606] Therefore, if females have a more accurate memory for social interactions, then they also understand social interactions more than males.

BIO EVOLUTION

Female superior empathy abilities might come from bio evolution. Our primitive female ancestors stayed back at the cave raising the offspring, while the male was outside hunting. Those female mothers back at the cave who understood what the baby was communicating and feeling were more likely to have their genetics survive and passed down. Those who did not understand the emotional states of their offspring might not have known when their offspring were feeling ill or hungry, and their offspring were less likely to survive and carry on the mother's genetics.

Another important factor with the enhanced empathy of females identified by Warrier et al. (2018) is the association with language. We often understand the mental state of others through communication. In their study, it was essential to have the language ability to match a particular word with the mental state of the other person. Hence, empathy ability and language skills are often similar. Females are likely to empathize better as a result of better nonverbal communication, along with the ability to gain information through their superior verbal communication skills.

SENSES

It has been covered in this chapter that females have a superior ability to understand beyond what is seen during social situations. A major contributing factor is the female's superior ability to analyze their surrounding environment. Females have superior abilities in each of the five senses.

Smell and Taste

Females have more sensitivity and preferences to taste and smell.[630] Females tend to have more brain activation to food stimuli.[105] This is evident by males and females having different cravings for foods.[261, 264, 426] Neural brain activation and sex hormonal differences help to explain these gender differences with smell and taste. The female menstrual cycle has been found to fluctuate cravings and calorie intake.[261]

The insula has been found to play an active role for food, regarding smell and taste.[261, 650] As was previously covered, the insula more strongly influences females than males because it is comprised of more gray matter in females.[406, 578] Additionally, females have more activation in the insula when viewing food.[302, 341, 389] These factors likely contribute to female heightened sense awareness, such as with taste and smell. Women's keen sense of smell helps lower their cortisol levels when they smell their partner's scent and increases their stress cortisol level when inhaling that of a stranger in stressful situations.[289]

Much of what we think we taste derives from smell.[629] Females are better than males with smell, as is evident by their outperformance in recognizing and naming a smell, ability to determine whether two smells are different, and being able to detect smells at much lower concentrations.[361] Females have superior tasting abilities, enabling them to become more aware of different nuances between tastes.[227] For example, it has been found that women rate red wine as having a more intense taste, but men rated it more favorably.[631]

Touch

Females have a better sense of touch.[3] They can sense touch more easily and are more delicate to pain through touch.[322] They also have stronger resting-state functional connectivity (rsFC) between the different areas of the brain responsible for pain sensation and processing, thus providing evidence of higher susceptibility to pain.[191, 347] Estrogen for females likely plays an important role in touch.[333, 656] Estrogen is also highly influential in female muscle control.[291]

Hearing

Males and females differ greatly with subcortical auditory processing.[360] Females have more auditory connections for word processing.[157] Females are able to hear a larger range of sounds, which allows them to better understand emotions from tones of voices.[592] This hearing advantage is exacerbated by having more efficient pathways in the brain to transfer information to both sides of the brain.[223]

This efficiency can be observed through neuronal activity of the cochlea to the brain stem having a more efficient and shorter route for females to process and distinguish different sounds.[613] Females have more blood flow in the cingulate gyrus, which is responsible for aligning incoming sensory information with emotion, such as sounds from another person's voice.[97]

The sex hormone estrogen also is related to superior hearing abilities in females. As estrogen levels fluctuate with women during hormonal changes, so does their hearing ability; higher levels of estrogen are associated with more sensitive hearing, and lower levels of estrogen have less hearing capabilities.[613] This can be beneficial from an evolutionary perspective in that estrogen and hearing ability are better for women when they are of reproductive age, compared to when menopause begins and both estrogen and hearing abilities decrease after their children have been raised.

Sight
Mirror Neurons

There are sex differences in the visual perception and its neural basis that lead to males and females visually seeing the world and others differently.[675] Simplistically, body size influences the relativism of visual perception by understanding objects and people in relation to our own body size, scale, and visual field.[672] This creates seeing the world around us in a relative fashion.

Females also have been consistently found to have more sensitive vision.[268] Females have more parvocellular-projecting gangion cells (P-GCs) in their retina, having a primary role of taking in central visual information, and are responsible for perception of form, fine details, and color.[17, 393, 698] In addition to superior central vision, females have been found to have better peripheral color vision.[464]

(P-GCs) play a vital role in fine details and color; an artificial intelligence technology system has been created to detect fabric defects by using machines that imitate the functions of human (P-GCs) in the human retina.[393] Females also use more details to describe color tones.[614]

Females use more exploratory visual scanning of other's faces, enabling them to understand more about the other person from taking in more nonverbal information.[126] This enables them to have a better ability to perceive subtle emotional facial changes.[640] Specific neurons responsible for understanding others are mirror neurons. These mirror neurons help create a sense of simulation of movement actions, as well as preparing to display those same observed behaviors.[101] The same neural circuits responsible for action and subjective experience of emotions are activated in one person simply by observing the behaviors and emotions in others.[102] Women have more activation than males with mirror neurons.[455]

Those neurons responsible for understanding and preparing to mimic another person's action movements are mirror neurons that consist of gray matter neural cells, often activated when communicating with others.[101, 641] The areas of the body and brain that mirror neurons are activated consist of sensory, emotion, and motor areas.[229, 395, 640]

Females have more gray matter in the areas where mirror neurons are found, often display more empathetic behaviors, and have a more powerful activation with mirror neurons when communicating with others. This gives an advantage over males with emotional recognition, imitation, emotion contagion, and interpersonal sensitivity, leading to a greater empathy ability.[102, 455] Therefore, females have superior mirror neuron abilities to better psychologically and emotionally imitate others, which is at the essence of understanding others.

Color

It is understood that females have a better sense for colors, such as more attention to color and a bigger color vocabulary.[268] The X chromosome, of which females have two, accounts for much of the color sensitivity from genes located on it.[471] Genes for L-cones and M-cones are located on the X chromosome, which help with determining the spectral sensitivity of hues. As a result of the X chromosome, color blindness is only found with males and accounts for about 10% of males. Additionally, testosterone plays a role with connectivity between the thalamic neurons with the cortex that is needed for neuronal inputs for color appearance perception that creates sex differences with color hue differentiation. Therefore, females have been found to have a better hue perception of colors and description details.[5, 614, 630]

Some females are actually better equipped to see colors because they have an additional color receptor or cone in their retinas, enabling them to better distinguish different color shades.[630] This is evident with females performing better at matching shades in dentistry than males.[506] Also, color preferences have been found across different cultures in that males prefer darker colors and females prefer lighter colors.[628] These biological sex differences with perceiving color might give some truth that the best style a man can choose to wear is chosen by a woman.

CONCLUSION

It should come as no surprise that females are superior at understanding others. The biological underpinnings help to bring the evidence and explanations together. This comes from social awareness and superior sensory perception. This superior sixth sense by females has been fine-tuned for thousands of years and has played a vital role with the perpetuation of the human species for thousands of years.

CHAPTER 13

THE MAN TRANCE

Males and females rest and relax differently, both in how and to what extent. It is important to recognize these differences because miscommunication can occur over relaxing.

RESTING MALES

Males tend to have a lower brain activity level and fewer heartrate changes than females when resting.[202, 703] Additionally, the sex hormone of testosterone enables males to have more emotional control due to lessening depressive effects and also creating more emotional stability.[15, 206, 510] This lower brain activity and balanced emotions enable males to shut off more of the outside world than females are capable of doing.

When a male is in this state, it is time to recharge and relax without outside distractions. One can easily understand how a male in this psychological and physical state can be misinterpreted by a female as ignoring her and unconcerned about her needs. Any attempt for a meaningful conversation with him during this time will have little success. Without this shut down state for males, stress is not properly attuned to.

RESTING FEMALES

Females tend to have more brain activation in emotional areas, bilateral amygdala and hippocampus, making it more difficult to control emotions and intentionally go to a resting mental state quickly.[202, 423] Females have a more powerful resting-state functional connectivity of the amygdala, gyrus regions, and hippocampus connecting memories, actions, and language all together when trying to rest.[347, 703]

Furthermore, female resting state is negatively impacted by cortisol (stress hormone) levels in that more of their brain is activated from the stress, and less likely to achieve a restful state.[347] All of these higher brain activities for females in emotional areas makes it more difficult to control emotions, such as shutting them all down at once to rest.[435] Females often have more changes in their heart rate when resting, likely do to more activity in different regions of the brain occurring simultaneously that leads to more anxiety and less of an overall resting state.[703]

The evidence from this section indicates that many more conditions need to be aligned for females to get to a state of rest. Any distractions that can activate one of these areas jeopardizes her rest.

SEX HORMONES AND REST

Sex hormones also play a pivotal role with inhibiting the female's ability to shut down emotional activations in order to rest. Estrogen plays an important part with emotional regulation. Too much or too little estrogen for females can create destress.[287, 308, 593] As was previously covered, females increase their oxytocin levels when interacting with others.[419, 606] One can easily understand how communicating with others can help her relax.

RESTING ACTIVITY GENDER DIFFERENCES

Males and females have differing ideas about relaxing. For males it often consists of activities that take little to no psychological or physical efforts. Some of these activities include watching television without any specific show in mind, fishing, napping, playing video games, enjoying a favorite beverage without much conversation with those around, and surfing the

Internet. For females, resting activities are more engaging and can include conversations without a specific purpose, shopping, eating out, and exercising with a friend.

As was previously covered in this book, males are much more compartmentalized, focusing on one task at a time.[99] If the task is rest, then it is rest time, and other areas are essentially shut off. Females have many more connections to different areas of their brain that are often activated at the same time.[97] This is especially true with emotions flowing more easily from one side of the brain to the other for females.[423]

It is more difficult for females to control emotions that are flowing across both sides of their brain than it is for males that have emotions concentrated in one particular area. Therefore, female rest may come in the form of talking with a friend about an emotionally positive or relaxing memory; relational connection with the friend through conversation can be restful as well.

CONCLUSION

Males are much better equipped to flip the off switch in their brain and body. It may appear to the uninformed that a man is in a trance or is in a semi-conscious state. Either might be the case but it is nonetheless rest for him.

PART 6

NAVIGATING GENDER COMMUNICATION.

CHAPTER 14

EVOLUTION AND PROBLEM SOLVING

FROM THE BEGINNING

Much of our communication and behaviors today can be traced far back to our primitive survival beginnings.[25] These interactions have been biologically in place for thousands of years. Our primitive ancestors needed survival skills, such as accurately understanding their surrounding environment, which also involves the people within it.[268]

The fundamental structures of our brains help with making predictions about the stimuli information we take in, which leads to behaviors that are anticipatory for those predictions.[615] It is not entirely society and culture that creates these predictions and gender communication differences, but rather these differences are reflective of the survival needs of our ancestors. Our survival needs came first and these gender communication differences are observed and recognized at some of the earliest stages of life; this occured well before social learning from people around us, schools, television, movies, music etc.

It is essential to recognize and understand these innate gender communication differences; not doing so can be detrimental to biological sex health treatment differences, psychological health treatment differences, and understanding others in both personal and professional relationships.

Our earliest ancestors had different gender roles. This was necessary for survival. Those who did not recognize this complimentary dependence between males and females greatly diminished their chances of adding their genetics to the evolutionary pool. They were less likely to attract a mate, reproduce, and acquire the resources necessary for their offspring to survive and carry on their genetics.

EPIGENETICS

Not only are the necessary traits for survival passed down to modern civilization, but also the behaviors of these ancient ancestors. The genetics we inherit create a relatively stable structure from which our behavioral experiences can only alter to a limited extent. One such way behavioral experiences can change our genetic output is epigenetics. Through the process of epigenetics, one's behaviors and experiences can alter their genetics future generations inherit.[372] The behaviors might not change DNA that is passed down to offspring but rather how that DNA functions, such as changes occurring in the sperm or egg prior to conception.[438]

Prenatal factors related to the mother can alter information that is transferred from the mother to the child during pregnancy.[94] For example, it has been found that before conception paternal and maternal obesity can impact the child.[161] The behaviors that you partake in today can modify the genetics you pass down to your offspring to some extent. Even during pregnancy, the mother can pass along valuable information to the developing brain of the fetus that is necessary for survival in a changing environment.[78]

The traits that were necessary for survival and that created distinct gender roles between males and females were passed down to future generations along with the behaviors exhibiting these traits, thus reinforcing these genetic features even further. However, there are limitations to how much behaviors change our genetics. For example, no matter how much all of us practice running, almost none of us will ever have the ability to win an Olympic 100-meter medal, but we can all learn to run faster given our preordained biological abilities.

MALE BIOLOGICAL TRAITS

The early gender roles for ancestors thousands of years ago were complimentary to each other and were necessary for surviving and contributing to the genetic pool. Males and females resided in a cave for shelter and protection. On average, males have larger body masses and more muscle proportion to fat along with more muscle strength and power.[138] Their larger body, along with strength, helped them gather resources, such as clubbing something over the head to drag back to the cave for their partner and offspring to eat.

The male brain has more intrahemispheric connections that allow for a better bond between perception and coordinated action that is important with spatial abilities.[305] Furthermore, males have 20-25 times more testosterone flowing in their bodies than females.[186] High testosterone levels in males play a necessary evolutionary role for attracting mates, reproducing, and hunting to provide resources for their offspring.[25] Testosterone is associated with more individualistic behaviors that can be attributed to antisocial cognitions.[129, 606] These communication attributes serve the male well for hunting by himself.

The effects of high levels of testosterone in males can be observed during competitive events today.[1] Competition is a social event in which concentration on one specific task is required and resembles that of male compartmentalization communication patterns.[99] Testosterone changes is not limited to sporting competitions.

Testosterone levels of a male can fluctuate depending upon the attractiveness of the males around him that are competing for female mates.[68] Coincidently, female fantasies often involve being desired in a similar fashion as desired goals found in competitive sports.[67] Testosterone is linked to strength and aggression along with visual motion abilities.[179, 268] It is also associated with more masculine types of interest, starting at birth.[500] The much higher levels of testosterone in males is likely a major contributing factor to 80% of people arrested for violent crimes are male.[190]

Early sex hormone exposure during development creates sex differences in tissues within the brain, influencing the way they are organized as well as activated in a sex-specific manner by creating a sexually differentiated brain. Sex hormone exposure also controls gene transcription, which influences gene expression.

The influence of sex hormones on brain tissue impacts visual perception of objects and movement. Estrogen levels have been found to impact spatial abilities of women. Women in the late follicular menstrual phase with high estrogen levels perform poorer in spatial performance, compared to men and women not in that phase that have lower estrogen levels.[120] Males on the other hand, have a more natural tendency for perceiving movement.[268]

Nazareth, Huang, Voyer, and Newcombe (2019) describe the consistent findings from numerous research studies of males outperforming females on spatial tasks, usually with moderate performance differences. Evidence of males' superior ability to track objects has been found as early as four months of age.[701] Females are distracted more from irrelevant information, and also perform slower after a mistake when performing spatial tasks.[185, 637]

Sex hormones such as androgen, a male-typical sex hormone, has been linked with spatial ability with both males and females because it influences areas of the human body responsible for spatial abilities development. Hence, higher levels of androgens are associated with better spatial abilities.[640] Females born with congenital adrenal hyperplasia are exposed to higher levels of androgens prior to birth that impact their spatial abilities development; they outperform females without this condition involving spatial tasks.[267]

Evidence of androgen exposure and spatial abilities begins at an early age.[259] Some of these tasks include reaction time to movement, visual acuity, line alignment, motion direction, and line relations.[608] The spatial abilities of males are linked to early exposure to androgens during development and muscle coordination.[96, 392] Males also have a better memory for events involving spatial performance tasks.[684] This is evident with males having less pupil dilation when performing a spatial task, indicating less cognitive effort is needed.[91] Nazareth, Huang, Voyer, and Newcombe (2019) reviewed many spatial studies and found that males outperform females much more after age thirteen, which is consistent with a larger sex hormone difference between males and females.

Androgen sex hormones also influence the development of the cortical streams that coordinate with aimed attention.[268] McGivern, Mosso, Freudenberg, and Handa (2019) describe how visual attention sex differences attribute to spatial ability differences. The primary visual cortex is the main way that we visually perceive the world and is comprised of these cortical streams, such as the dorsal stream. The dorsal stream helps detect motion for the visual cortex that enables the ability to determine space relations of objects. Males are more likely to focus their attention to space between objects that better enables them for tasks such as aiming objects they throw, more precision following moving objects, and rotating objects mentally. Furthermore, males are much better with tasks involving cardinal directions (North, South, East, West). These spatial gender differences are necessary to recognize in order to communicate with others more effectively and to better understand communication. For example, spatial communication is pertinent when traveling to new places, understanding a diagram, or trying to park a car.[723]

Additionally, some of this superior spatial ability is likely due to the male retina. Males have more magnocellular-projecting gangion cells (M-GCs) in their retina primarily taking in peripheral visual stimuli information and are responsible for visual motion.[17, 698] This visual advantage helped the primitive male chase prey and then find his way back to the cave to bring the prey to his partner and offspring. Spatial and motion abilities today are necessary for certain careers and athletic feats.

The biological athletic strength advantage of males leads to a particular gender role. As a result, the male would be responsible for leaving the cave and bringing back resources for their female mate and offspring. These resources often consisted of protein that entailed hunting and killing other animals. One can easily see how these male biological traits have evolved.

As primitive males left the cave, it took high levels of testosterone to run around for hours hunting down prey, and superior motion abilities to strike the prey. Those males who had higher levels of testosterone and superior spatial ability were able to find their way back to the cave with the food, while those males who lacked sufficient testosterone or spatial abilities likely got lost and did not make it back to the cave, or returned with no food, resulting in their offspring not surviving to pass down their genetics. As has been previously noted in this book, males are inferior to females regarding language abilities. It does not take much language ability to hunt down prey, kill it, and find your way back to the cave.

FEMALE BIOLOGICAL TRAITS

The gender role of our early female ancestors is also present in the biological makeup of modern females. Females from thousands of years ago had a high responsibility of sociability for survival. Often, the female would stay back at the cave tending to and nursing the offspring. The first language of any human offspring is nonverbal communication.[83] It became essential for mothers to understand nonverbally what the baby was communicating, such as if they were ill, hungry, sad, tired, wanted to play etc.

Those mothers who had superior language abilities, nonverbal communication, and empathy increased their offspring's survival chances. Those mothers who lacked skills in those areas were less able to understand whether their baby was in danger such as being ill or hungry, thus decreasing their chances of having their genetics passed on by their offspring surviving.

Modern day females have superior nonverbal communication skills used for empathizing with others. They are biologically equipped with more interconnections to both sides of their brain to participate in the conversation, while also simultaneously observing the other person's nonverbal behaviors and micro facial expressions.[97, 177, 358]

McGivern, Mosso, Freudenberg, and Handa (2019) address female attention to object details. Females perceive the visual world through the visual cortex by relying more on the ventral stream that allows for more attention to object features, such as color and form. Additionally, the ventral stream spreads into the inferior temporal cortex that allows for better semantic representation of objects. In turn, females have better recognition of objects both explicitly and implicitly, verbal fluency for naming objects, and both episodic and autobiographical memory. Regarding navigation ability, females perform equal or better than males when landmarks are used. Again, it is the attention to details of the object of landmarks that draws females' attention. For example, females use more details when describing color tones.[614] From this female superiority for attention and memory of object details, females have a better memory for faces from events that occurred.[640] Females have a natural tendency to perceive people's faces with greater detail and subtle emotional changes.[268, 358] Females also have better auditory connections for word processing.[157] These traits enable females to have superior social cognitive abilities.[259]

Female retinas also help with this ability. Females have more parvocellular-projecting gangion cells (P-GCs), enabling them to see more color and detail.[17, 393, 698] This ability for females to see more color has been found in peripheral vision as well.[464] Women focus more on details when making decisions.[671] One can see how these abilities can be beneficial when a newborn baby's first channel of communication is nonverbal communication, thus it becomes essential for the mother to understand facial expressions, nonverbal gestures, and skin color changes indicating health problems.

Not only does sight contribute to females having a superior nonverbal ability, but superior hearing does as well.[9, 223] In spoken communication, everything but the specific words themselves are considered nonverbal communication, such as pauses, rate, pitch, and volume.[83] Having a better hearing system for females helps to distinguish these different nuances from their baby to determine his or her needs. Again, these superior nonverbal communication skills found with modern women were passed down from generation to generation by those who had those abilities to contribute to the genetic pool for future generations, and those who lacked such abilities likely did not contribute their genetics.

Females are superior in nonverbal communication, but they also have superior language abilities; this is partially due to having up to 20 times more estrogen.[338, 620] Estrogen plays a large role in areas such as social understanding, recognition, memory, and pain sensitivity.[26, 338, 481] Estrogen interacts with oxytocin in the brain for better social understanding.[481] Estrogen is also associated with more sensitive hearing, which can serve females well during social situations.[613]

Additionally, females having much lower levels of testosterone helps their vocabulary and language development from as early as their first month of life. Early levels of testosterone have been found to negatively impact expressive vocabulary and language development in infancy that continues later in life, even after taking into account social factors such as sex, age, and paternal education.[365]

Other research has even found that testosterone levels prior to birth reduce language performance for boys at two years of age.[293] Hence, testosterone hinders language development for both males and females starting at an early age, and males have 20-25 times more testosterone.[186] Females also have better selective attention during language performance.[637] Having superior language abilities was vital for mothers thousands of years ago to communicate with their offspring for survival.

Covered in a previous chapter that females have a sixth sense, which enables them to understand others' communication more accurately due to the way their brain is structured.[305] A larger insula that consists of more gray matter is one such feature.[406, 578] The female insula is also typically more active as well.[302] The insula is responsible for physiological sensory processing.[663]

The sensory perception activation of the insula enables females to empathize with others for a clearer understanding of other people during communication by feeling both emotionally and actually physically similar sensations.[369] For example, it plays a role in deciphering different sounds to determine another's emotions.[580] It gives females an added intuitive feeling understanding.[652, 688] This intuitive female feeling was necessary thousands of years ago to not only understand the needs of their offspring but also to better understand friend from foe.

Females also have a heightened sense of smell, which also plays a bigger role in their lives.[627, 658] This is necessary to understand the baby's needs, along with possible threats from the environment, such as an incoming rain storm or threat from fire. Taste is also activated in the insula.[714] The female insula has more activation when viewing food.[302, 341, 389] This was necessary thousands of years ago for the mother to taste healthy food and distinguish it from dangerous food before feeding her offspring. Additionally, having cold temperatures processed through the insula helped these mothers have a better sense of the temperature of food along with whether their baby might have a fever.[597] The female superior senses abilities was key with her and her offspring survival.

CONCLUSION

What we observe today pertaining to gender communication differences has been instilled in each of us from thousands of years of genetic imprinting. The gender communication behaviors and roles we take on in modern society are reflective of our ancestors' needs for complimentary survival between mothers and fathers. It is irrational to attribute these gender communication differences as magically appearing only from modern society, such as movies, television programs, pictures in magazines etc. Rather, often is the case that art imitates life.

PART 7

RELATIONSHIPS AND INTIMACY.

CHAPTER 15

SEXUAL INTIMACY, THE DOUBLE STANDARD?

A double standard is defined as "any code or set of principles containing different provisions for one group of people than for another, especially an unwritten code of sexual behavior permitting men more freedom than women."[155] According to this definition, there are different social judgments and codes of sexual behavior between males and females. While the standards may differ between societal acceptance of sexual behaviors between males and females, there are biological underpinnings that help understand the origins.

GENDER AND OFFSPRING UNCERTAINTY

Both males and females have a basic need to know that the offspring they are raising are genetically their own. Females always know with 100% certainty their offspring. The baby was inside the mother for nine months and they physically see the baby born with half of their genetics. The same cannot be said for males. Males cannot always be 100% sure that their female partner is giving birth to their offspring. There is enough of a window of opportunity for a woman to become pregnant through multiple sexual encounters to make it nearly impossible to specifically know the exact sexual encounter in which conception occurred.

Lum, Sundaram, Louis, and Louis (2016) created an advanced sophisticated model revealing that, during a normal menstrual cycle for a woman, there are at least twelve days that pregnancy can occur after sexual intercourse. This particular model was created from advancements in science and has increased precision for pregnancy predictability. Having almost absolute certainty about who the mother of the offspring is may contribute to societal pressure to reduce the number of possible fathers by creating the societal female sexual standard.

Possibly, this has exacerbated beyond the realistic biological timeframe of possible pregnancy through generations. In other words, instead of only having concern about female sexual encounters when conception was possible, perhaps males are wired to think well beyond that timeframe to months or even years concerning previous partners for that female. This is not a rationale assurance for certainty of their offspring, but rather some sort of evolutionary over-adjustment.

INFIDELITY PROBLEMS

Infidelity is more common than one might think. Balon (2015) points out that humans have historically been polygynous, and recent studies have documented that 97% of mammals are not monogamous. Regarding primates, only gibbons appear to be monogamous, while gorillas are polygynous and chimpanzees go without paring.

Saunders, White, Dawson, and Mawson (2018) conducted a study in which they DNA-tested birds who lived in the same nest. They found that in 27% of the cases, a male bird living in the nest was raising an offspring, likely unknowingly, with DNA differing from his. For humans, non-marital births were 40% of all births in 2015.[265] It is legally established that a married man is the father when their wife gives birth. However, hospitals now require either a voluntary paternity acknowledgement or from a court order. This is necessary because a child is allowed access to their father's health history, life insurance benefits, social security benefits, and inheritance.[548]

The process to voluntarily acknowledge paternity at the hospital was established in 1993 by Congress.[540] Later, federal legislation added that paternity recognition was required for a man to put his name on the birth certificate of the child that acknowledges the rights and responsibilities of paternity.[541]

Sometimes determining fatherhood can become difficult. One example involves twins within the same mother having two eggs fertilized by two different fathers.[444] Another difficult circumstance is determining the father of a child when two brothers have sex with the same woman.[159] It is important to be able to establish the biological father because his involvement in the child's life can positively impact the child's psychological and physical health and development.[604]

Never trust a pretty face? It has been found in one study that those rated as more attractive are more likely to have shorter marriages and are more likely to divorce. One possible reason given by the authors is that attractive people have more alternatives if they are unsatisfied in a relationship.[425] Then perhaps the better choice is someone less attractive with a wider face.

Not so fast. Arnocky, Carre, Bird, Moreau, Vaillancourt, Ortiz, and Marley (2018) found that both men and women that have a higher width-to-height face ratio have a higher sex drive. Additionally, men who had this higher ratio had more desires of infidelity. It is thought that higher levels of androgens such as testosterone can help create these facial features during development. As we know, testosterone is associated with sex drive.[127]

Polo, Muñoz-Reyes, Pita, Shackelford, and Fink (2019) found similar results with men with higher facial width-to-height ratio and skeletal muscle mass having more relationship partners and unrestrictive attitudes about sexual behaviors. These authors also attributed their results to testosterone.

GENDER MATING DIFFERENCES

Another possible biological explanation for the gender sexual double standard is testosterone. Testosterone is found at 20-25 times more in males but has been linked to sexual desire with both males and females.[80, 127, 186] Males who do not have a partner usually have higher levels of testosterone than males with a partner, such as males actively searching for mating experiences have the highest levels of testosterone.[253]

A physical indication of testosterone levels can be signs of acne for both men and women.[80, 304] Testosterone also plays a role with males having bigger positive responses to sexual images.[388] This likely coincides with the need to ensure that some of their DNA is successfully passed on by having more sexual partners, and being less concerned with a relationship or less successful mating attempts.

For females, women with wider hips are found to be more sexually promiscuous. This is thought to occur because wider hips reduce childbirth injuries or mortality.[617] Also, females that have shorter speech vocal tract length have more sexual partners. For males, physical size and a low-pitched voice were associated with having more sexual partners.[669]

SEXUAL DESIRE & FUNCTIONING
Attention
In order for sexual arousal to occur, one's sexual attention must happen first. The senses play an important role, with touch being among the most important.[344] There are some differences for gaining sexual attention. Most males are more captivated by visual cues, focusing more sexual attention as it pertains to females, while female sexual interest can occur from viewing males or females.[140, 141, 526]

Humans are able to discern between one-trillion different odors.[87] Body odors play a key role with initial stages of mate selection.[408] Human sweat can communicate sexual socioemotional meanings.[730] One way body odors influence mate selection is where a woman is in her menstrual cycle plays a role with gaining the sexual attention of males. For instance, a person's emotional state can be communicated to others through body odors, such as sexual arousal.[146, 147, 707] This helps with the olfactory system's major role in mate selection.[109]

Chemosignals are particular body odors that influence sexual attention for both males and females by activating areas of the brain responsible for sexual arousal.[707] Chemosignals play an important role for males understanding when a female is more fertile, thus increasing potential reproduction success.[290, 470] Males are able to distinguish scents between a female's high and low fertility state; they find the high fertility state more attractive.[234]

Odors play a more powerful role for females.[658] Chemosignals consisting of subliminal odorants, such as the steroid compound androstadienone, provide females information about the quality of potential mates regarding their genetic fit.[498] Females desire a male with different genetics to decrease the chances of genes that are detrimental to the health of the offspring.[707] However, oral contraception reduces the ability to evaluate the chemosignals of males.[551]

Sexual desires play an important role with gaining sexual attention in relationships. One particular facet is the difference between desired sexual closeness and actual sexual closeness. The closer they align, the better sexual satisfaction is in the relationship and orgasms.[221] In order for partners to meet one another's sexual needs, sexual attention and desire is necessary. It has been found that prioritizing sexual needs can increase sexual attention and desire.[459]

Arousal

Sexual arousal as a response to sexual attention from stimuli originates in the brain and differs between males and females; this is partly due to sexually dimorphic brains.[344, 481] Most males are only sexually aroused by sexual stimuli of females, while females can become sexually aroused by sexual stimuli of both males and females.[299] Males have a stronger sexual drive and rewarding feelings from sexual cues, which includes visual sexual stimuli.[353, 526, 639] For instance, males become sexually motivated after smelling the distinct chemosignals of females that were sexually aroused.[707] Males exposed to the scents of a female in a fertile state of her menstrual cycle are more aware of her heightened sexual arousal and mimic her with increased sexual motivation.[439]

Sexual arousal has been found to be influenced by testosterone for both males and females, but males have 20-25 times more testosterone.[80, 127, 186] However, the role of testosterone with female sexual arousal is a much more complex issue. Some research has found endogenous testosterone not playing a role with human female sexual arousal with naturally cycling females.[570] Other researchers have failed to find ways to use testosterone for improving female sexual desire through pharmaceutical research.[59]

For all non-human female mammals, only estradiol has been found to improve female sexual arousal.[93] For female humans, estrogen has been consistently found to drive sexual motivation and arousal.[481] This calls into question testosterone-only therapy treatment for human females. Suprapysiological levels of testosterone implementation has been shown to improve low levels of estrogen therapies to help with female sexual arousal.[93]

Testosterone that is exogenous can interact with estrogen receptors by converting testosterone to estradiol or through the influence of binding proteins that increases accessible levels of estradiol.[655, 686] Therefore, the conversion of testosterone to estradiol is what helps female sexual arousal.[525, 655] Precise levels of estrogen can clearly be linked to the specific fertility phase of a female's menstrual cycle.[75] Therefore, estrogen-only therapies might be the better approach for improving female sexual arousal.

When females have difficulty becoming motivated from sexual stimuli, this can lead to them feeling anguished. The cause can extend beyond simple testosterone or estrogen levels, such as neurological malfunctioning. Sexual functioning consists of hormonal and neurochemical actions within the brain and among the central nervous system and the sexually sensitive areas of the body.[481] More specifically, sexual functioning consists of cognition in the form of attention, emotions, motivation to express sexual behaviors, and automatic and neuroendocrine functioning.[526]

These interconnections take in sensory information; when perceived as rewarding, this information prepares the body to take action; but when the information is perceived unfavorably, behaviors are then inhibited. Female lack of sexual desire may stem from inhibitory overactive excessive functioning of the prefrontal cortex that includes neuromodulators consisting of serotonin, opioids, and endocannabinoids.[344] Serotonin helps constrain satisfaction, opioids regulate sexual rewards associated with behaviors, and endocannabinoids helps the functioning of relaxation.[516] Each of these areas might be overworking to limit and reduce sexual feelings and subsequent behaviors.

Another possible reason for female lack of sexual desire is underperforming of the excitation functioning of the limbic system, which includes neuromodulators such as norepinephrine, oxytocin, dopamine, and melanocortins.[344] Norepinephrine and oxytocin help regulate sexual arousal with the limbic system, while melanocortins and dopamine assist with attention and physiological desire functioning.[516] These areas might not be functioning strong enough.

It makes sense that oxytocin functioning plays an important role with female sexual motivation due to relationship bonding playing a large role with female sexual arousal.[526] Thus, there might be imbalanced levels in one or more of these neuromodulators that are responsible for healthy sexual motivation functioning.

Health professionals should use effective communication to address the problems of female patients with sexual problems. Lara, Scalco, Troncon, and Lopes (2017) outline one effective communication approach. The health professional should teach the physiology of female sexual responses consisting of desire, excitement, and orgasm. The next step they suggest is educating about the sexual health for healthy sexual experiences. Finally they suggest addressing sexual pleasure as an important factor for physical and emotional health. Health professionals should also be aware that oxytocin increases for both males and females during sexual arousal indicating the importance of relationship bonding during sexual arousal.[581]

Orgasm

The euphoric sexual arousal sometimes climaxes with an orgasm. As with the other previous sexual arousal areas addressed, there are some orgasm differences between males and females.[353] Males progress toward an orgasm much more quickly than females.[501] Arcos-Romero and Sierra (2020) describe the contributing factors for males to have a pleasurable orgasm as age, sexual sensation desire, sexual gratification, and focus on partner sexual pleasure. They highlight the importance of age with females, along with response to sexual cues, sexual motivation, sexual gratification, and focus on meeting partner's sexual desires.

There are some different prerequisites for male and female orgasms. It is not whether a prerequisite is present that makes male and female orgasm probability differences, but rather the degree to which prerequisite(s) are present.[344] The quality of the relationship that the female has with the male plays a much larger role than it does for the male.[526]

Males achieve orgasms much more frequently than females.[353] One can conclude from the available evidence that the female orgasm is much more complex prior, during, and after. To begin with, psychological factors play a much larger role leading up to an orgasm for females. Females are more likely to become sexually aroused when they identify with characters in an erotic film, compared with watching an erotic film in which they do not see similarities to themselves.[240] The relationship with her sexual partner is also important to have trust and a psychological connection, both of which impact relationship satisfaction.[167] Often, it is also important to the female that the male sexually desires her.[67]

Oxytocin, a relationship-bonding hormone, also plays a crucial role with the intensity of orgasms.[344] Oxytocin increases for both males and females during orgasm.[581] Sexual desire is highly psychological for females, thus the relationship significance to a female orgasm. It is closely linked with her emotions and brain activity.[24] She also needs to feel the right emotions in order for an orgasm to even be possible, because emotional suppression and negative emotions such as depression and anxiety are related to sexual motivation and arousal.[167]

One effective approach for women to achieve better sexual desire and orgasms is sexual mindfulness. She should focus in a non-judgmental way on the present moment of the physical sexual senses and embrace the sexual arousal. She can practice this when not involved in sexual activities through visualization training of psychologically experiencing her goals prior to the actual experience.[678]

Kontula and Miettinen (2016) specifically address the orgasm factors covered above. They found that physical sexual activities such as sexual experience, masturbation, and more sexual partners did not improve the likelihood of female orgasms. Surprisingly, they found that those women who masturbated frequently had less satisfying sexual lives partly due to more difficulties with achieving orgasm. Rather, they found prioritizing achieving an orgasm, sexual desire, sexual self-esteem, and communicating openly with their sexual partner as important factors that increase the likelihood of experiencing an orgasm.

One physical factor that they did find to increase the chance of a female orgasm is sexual intercourse that lasts around fifteen minutes; less time reduces the chances and longer intercourse time minimally improves its chances. Additional physical factors were the female's level of activity. If she was more active, such as taking the on top position and/or using multiple positions, this increased the chances of having multiple orgasms. They also found that if the woman received oral sex prior to intercourse that also increased chances of her reaching orgasm during intercourse.

More physical involvement of the female needed for achieving an orgasm is placing more importance on it and becoming more actively involved in the relationship. These findings are consistent with previous research that also finds emotional regulation to play an important role with sexual motivation and arousal, which in turn greatly impacts relationships for both males and females. One effective strategy is emotional reappraisal, which is reframing the way one perceives an emotional event.[167]

A woman's menstrual cycle can play a huge role with her sexual desire that is needed to entertain the possibility of an orgasm. This occurs from her menstrual cycle affecting her cognition, motivation, and behaviors.[72] A woman's sexual desire peak is near ovulation, when her fertility opportunity window increases along with levels of estrogen. As estrogen levels increase, her sexual desire increases and her food intake cravings decrease.[571] Thus, biological evolution kicks in, shifting the focus from food to sex in order to increase the probability of reproduction.

A woman's menstrual cycle not only affects her sexual arousal and motivation, but has also been found to influence the males around her. Males look at females differently depending upon the stage of her menstrual cycle. Males scan women's faces in a more consistent pattern that greatly enhances facial recognition when the woman is at her highest fertility level.

This pattern includes scanning facial features in close proximity to each other and longer time viewing the lower portions of her face.[470] This is an important timeframe for men because it greatly enhances their chances of successful reproduction; in effect, the male wants to ensure there is no reproductive mistaken identity.

Hoffmann (2019) found that men who smelled the sweat of women in the follicular period of her menstrual cycle—which is associated with higher levels of estrogen—had higher sexual arousal even when the female was not sexually aroused. Also, those men who smelled the sweat from a female who was sexually aroused had more genital arousal than when they smelled the sweat of a non-aroused woman, indicating sexual arousal contagion. It was also found that males self-disclosed more information when smelling the sweat of a female in the follicular phase of her menstrual cycle.

Sexual activities are a form of exercise, so it should come as no surprise that women can experience orgasms from exercise. These include abdominal exercises, climbing, and weight lifting. Motions in the abdominal and pelvic areas can illicit clitoral pressure to initiate an orgasm.[274] Orgasms can be caused from other factors as well including fantasies, imagery, during sleep, stimulation of brain and spinal cord, childbirth, drugs, and epileptic seizures.[350]

Not only are causes for orgasms different between males and females, normalcy of pre-orgasm varies as well, with males returning to normal levels much quicker, while females can even have multiple orgasms afterwards.[344, 501]

BIOLOGICAL SEXUAL DIFFERENCES

There are differences with the location of the female sex organ, vagina, for females between different types of mammals. Some mammals have the vagina in close proximity to the rectum, as is the case with birds. However, in primates, there is more separation between the vagina and rectum, such as found with human females, who also have a much longer distance between the vagina and rectum.[503] This human female vagina location has evolved to this location to enable more sexual intercourse from the front, creating emotional bonding during intercourse.

With the human female vagina being more frontal, intercourse can occur with the male and female both facing each other, exchanging emotional cues from facial expressions, such as eye contact, sound of breath, etc. This face time allows for more relationship bonding to occur, rather than having intercourse only for reproductive purposes. Human sexual intercourse has evolved to a more emotionally intimate moment.

The male sex organ, penis, is unlikely to change in size after his developmental growth period has stopped during his life.[531] However, the female sex organ, vagina, can change for a variety of reasons during her life experiences.[665] What is relatively consistent is that both women and men prefer a vagina that is perceived to be tight during intimacy.[461]

CONCLUSION

There is a double standard in society regarding acceptable sexual behaviors for men and women. These standards can be traced back to biological reasons. The woman is always certain the offspring are hers but the male cannot be as sure. Infidelity cannot be ignored in mammals, which goes for humans as well. Males and females also differ regarding sexual attention, arousal, and orgasm. There are numerous psychological and physiological differences. Often these differences are not whether one sex has them or not but the difference lies in the degree to which each sex has them.

CHAPTER 16

SHOULD WE DATE, PROCREATE?

EVOLUTIONARY MATE SELECTING

The perpetuation of the human species is rather complex and intriguing to understand. The major influencing roles of our biological tendencies when choosing a mate have been in place for thousands of years, even while cultures and societies have changed.[25] Therefore, it is necessary to address our biological history in order to understand how the human species got to where it is today. To not understand or to try to change these biological instinctual factors will lead into directions of which we do not know the long-terms effects.

When we meet someone for the first time, we often have mutual eye contact to establish a recognition, followed by scanning the face and then the rest of the body. When looking for a possible mate, these areas are assessed for potential partner status.[149] Different strengths, weaknesses, and sexual reproductive features and functions also come into play when we view another person's face, eyes, and body and consider them as a possible mate.[25]

It was previously covered how females are more invested when choosing a mate to reproduce with. They have the offspring within them for about nine months. Therefore, they invest nine months of their life into one offspring that is theirs. A male might have less certainty about whether the offspring is his because there is a twelve-day conception window each month.[412] However, the male is able to mate with other females to increase the chances of passing his genetics onto a healthy offspring.

The differences in gender investment when choosing a mate creates different factors for males and females. Thousands of years ago, the female stayed back at the cave raising the offspring, while the male went out and hunted to bring back resources for their mate and offspring. This has led to an evolutionary genetic trail of females seeking a mate who has the potential to be a provider of resources.

Males, on average, have larger body mass, strength, and higher muscle to fat ratios, which were helpful when resources needed to be physically gathered.[346] Additionally, males have 20-25 times more testosterone that provides strength and endurance to hunt.[25, 179, 186] Those males who have these attributes are more likely to find a mate and have their genetics contribute to future males having higher levels of testosterone and strength. Though these desired attributes are still deep within us thousands of years later, their specifics have adapted as cultures have changed throughout history.

MALE ATTRACTIVENESS

Male expecations have changed from dragging back a dead animal to eat, to now having the financial resources to provide what would be considered today's wild game to eat (groceries). Instead of dragging resources back to the cave by hand, providing more modern resources attract female mates such as a fancy transportation mobile such as an expensive car, car service, first class commercial, and private jet to mention a few examples.[213] A high paying position or title that he has working for an organization is also valued for resource providing potential because females are one thousand times more sensitive to salary for attractiveness of a male than it is for attractiveness of a female.[687]

Physical abilities are also important; ask any high-profile professional athlete about his female fans.[1] Mautz, Wong, Peters, and Jennions (2013) investigated some male physical attributes deemed attractive by modern females. Females seeking a mate look for factors include a larger penis size, greater shoulder-to-hip ratios, and height. However, these variables interact as well. They found that penis size increases male attractiveness to an extent, but not if it is to extremes. The researchers found larger penis size to be more attractive for taller men much more than it did with shorter men. Thus, greater height and penis size resulted in more attractiveness, likely as a result of sexual selection evolution. These attributes tend to contribute to the notion of physical strength as attractive.

Foo, Simmons, Peters, and Rhodes (2018) found that females find male strength attractive, but that male strength decreases ejaculatory quality when mating.[213] A lower-pitched voice in males is also viewed as more attractive and associated with having more sexual partners, while a higher-pitched voice in females is linked with more attraction.[669] If a female finds him humorous then his attractiveness increases even more.[176] Power and resources being highly valued in a male for thousands of years has not changed; just their forms have changed.

FEMALE ATTRACTIVENESS

Qualities desired in a female mate include being healthy enough to not only take care of their offspring inside their body for nine months, but also to live long enough to help care for the child after birth. This helps to explain the emphasis on female physical attractiveness.[687] Biological evidence for emphasis on female attractiveness is that males are more visually sexually stimulated than females.[231, 388] Males have more activation in the orbito-frontal cortex when viewing an attractive female face than females do when viewing an attractive male face, which is the area of the brain responsible for sensation when observing a stimuli.[118] Males are biologically programmed to direct their attention to female physical attractiveness when searching for a mate.

During the 1950's Marilyn Monroe was considered highly attractive.[588] This was likely due to food not being as abundant as it is today. Therefore, a female with a larger body size was perceived as having the ability to have access to more food resources when it was less available. Subconsciously, this likely registered in society as the ability to nourish a baby within the womb and then nurse it after birth increasing the chance of producing a healthy offspring.

Today a much thinner body size is considered attractive.[648] This can be challenging because women have a higher body fat percentage.[677] However, the body proportions of different areas of the female body have not changed much for attractiveness. A common measure of body shape attractiveness for females is the waist-to-hip ratio. Today's waist-to-hip ratio attractiveness is .7, which probably has not changed much from the attractiveness of decades ago, but the overall body size for attractiveness has decreased.[149]

Today's society has much more food available, especially low-quality foods with high amounts of carbohydrates and calories. Therefore, it takes more resources to have a smaller female figure, such as buying high-quality food and a gym membership. The smaller figure looks healthy today and is associated with higher quality of food to nourish a baby in the womb, and exercise implies that the mother will have the physical abilities to help nurture the baby into adulthood.

Occupations have also changed from the 1950's from more industrial and physical labor to modern technology occupations that require few physical demands, such as typing for most of the workday. The central theme has stayed consistent with female attractiveness as an indicator of youth and health to reproduce and help raise the offspring. The theme has changed from having enough food to having better quality food.

It has been found recently that women with wider hips have a more active sex life.[617] The wider hips make it easier for a woman to give birth, and increases the chances of successful reproduction for males. Perhaps females with wider hips attract more males due to the increased chances of providing a healthy birth. However, more sexually active the female, the more assurance the father needs that the offspring is his. One small indication of offspring certainty is that both males and females prefer a tighter vagina.[461] Furthermore, tighter overall body is probably perceived as healthier and more likely to have this feature.

APPLYING EVOLUTIONARY ATTRACTION

In both males and females, scarcity is highly valued and sought. What is less available is wanted more, especially for females seeking mates. Females tend to be more selective in choosing mates than males, but that choosiness wanes when female competition for the same mate increases.[489] Females have a better sense of attention to sexual features regarding other females.[140] Some of these features they can sense in other females include the desires that males seek, such as youthfulness and healthiness in females.

However, it has transformed over time from having enough food to having quality of food and regular physical activity. Females searching for resources and protection in males has changed from physical strength to financial wellbeing to purchase high quality food, healthcare, transportation, and clothing.

Face preferences resemble evolutionary sex differences. Gender differences in opposite facial attraction preferences exist. Males are found to prefer new faces, while females find familiar faces more attractive.[401] These findings likely indicate a male desiring to increase his chances of healthy reproduction by having more sexual encounters with different partners. On the other hand, a more involved mating investment for females is valued for having the same mate in which familiarity and commitment are of upmost concern.

Consistent with familiarity, females prefer faces that resemble their brother's facial features.[585] Similarity also plays a role with attraction. Males and females find potential mates more attractive when their faces resemble each other.[566, 567] Perhaps males prefer a new face that resembles their own, and females prefer familiarity due to their extensive reproduction investment.

Understanding what each gender prefers in a mate is helpful, but knowing what indicates interest is an added benefit. Wade and Feldman (2016) found differences between men and women in terms of which behaviors are most effective when flirting with the other gender. Much of the effective behaviors refer back to the evolutionary desires previously covered. Women displaying flirtatious behaviors suggest sexual access to a particular man, which was found most effective. These behaviors included intimacy, touching, and dancing with him. On the other hand, males sharing their resources with a woman were rated as most effective. These included asking her out for a date, being attentive to what she said, complimenting and spending time with her, etc. These are important to understand, because men often overvalue the usefulness of large actions and undervalue the usefulness of smaller actions. This is likely because men are not as subtle as women.

BODY HAIR

Body hair is associated with sexual maturity.[704] Therefore, thousands of years ago, humans who had body hair were likely perceived as more sexually mature and having a higher probability of successfully reproducing, compared with those who did not have body hair. This is how we humans have ended up with body hair today, passed genetically by those who were more sexually active and thus attracting more mates.

The question becomes how much is enough for humans. As can be observed during any casual visit to a zoo, humans tend to have noticeably less body hair than other primates. This is likely due in part to human males and females preferring mates with less body hair as a way to reduce the likelihood of their mate having a parasite, such as men's preference for female shaved genitalia.[535] From an evolutionary perspective, men probably prefer women with less body hair because that is associated with more youthfulness. Women prefer men who are clean-shaven, except having some hair around the areolae, pectoral region, and sternum. However, if facial hair is preferred, then hair that connects the lower jaw to the mustache and covers the cheeks with facial hair is more attractive than patchy facial hair. The second rating of male body hair attractiveness is to be clean-shaven overall, and the last is more body hair over more areas. Additionally, more body hair in men is acceptable because it is associated with the sought-after sex hormone of testosterone.[158]

There are some similarities and differences for males and females when choosing whether or not to groom their pubic hair. Around half of women remove all of their pubic hair, and this number is higher for younger women and is due to appearance, preference by their sexual partner, and cleanliness.[418, 638] Women groom their pubic hair more often and more completely than men. Women are more likely to groom for a hairless appearance, which men prefer in their sexual partner. Factors influencing women's choice of pubic hair grooming techniques are a stronger feeling of cleanliness, comfort, attraction, peer-influence, and cost effectiveness. Shaving tends to be a common pubic hair grooming choice by both men and women, with itching as the most reported side effect.[88]

However, itching isn't the only side effect. There is a relationship between pubic hair grooming and sexually transmitted infections and disease. Grooming increases the risk of epidermal microtears that can lead to more exposure during sexual activity. Another less likely contributing factor to infections is sharing grooming tools, such as razors. However, there is an upside to pubic hair grooming, which is the decreased chance of getting pubic lice.[487]

A small study conducted by Schild-Suhren, Soliman, and Malik (2017) found that women shaving all of their genital pubic hair with a razor can be a contributing risk factor for genital inflammation, vulvar dysplasia, and malignancies. An association was also found for women with shaved pubic hair and recurrent inflammation, along with vulvar dysplasia and cancer. The manipulation of the skin by a razor may contribute to more health risks. More information about safe pubic hair grooming should be disseminated with the general public, especially those entering puberty.[150]

UNCONSCIOUS ATTRACTION

Prospective mates not only evaluate what is seen, but what is smelled as well. Humans are able to distinguish differences for over one-trillion odors.[87] Each body odor is created from a distinct genetic marker.[370] Human body odors activate neural activity in areas of the brain, which is different from processing odors of inanimate objects, and assists with processing social information to form unconscious perceptions of others. The human visual system likely acts complimentary with the olfactory system that is responsible for smell and is always ready for stimulation.

While the human visual system may look for similar traits, the olfactory system plays a larger role for females in a variety of ways, such as sniffing out dissimilar gene-coded traits in a potential mate for genetic variability and a better quality immune system.[361, 505, 658] The steroid compound androstadienone is a subliminal odor that males give off, which helps females determine potential fit.[498] The more pleasant a woman finds a male's body odor, the more sexually aroused she becomes.[623]

Interestingly, the insula plays a part in smelling a potential mate.[505] As was previously covered in an earlier chapter, females have more gray matter in the insula, and often more activation.[302, 406] The insula has a direct path with the automatic nervous system, in which emotional processing impacts physiological responses.[663] Emotions play a much larger role with female sexual arousal than it does with males.[526] Perhaps the insula's role in women's sixth sense smells out a potential mate. Females use the natural body odors of potential male partners as a form of communication much more than males do for potential female mates. Females seek mates with dissimilar genetic traits in order to reduce the effects of problematic genes.[409, 706] These body odors can come in the form of axillary bacteria odorous molecules surfacing on the skin, and also from sweat. Maybe there is something to the female's sense of smell and love. Females in love are less able to identify body odors in their male friends.[414] This is an instinctual mechanism that focuses the female on her mate so she does not become distracted by other males.

Furthermore, females who are at lower risk in their reproduction monthly cycle and are exposed to the male sex hormone androstadienone stare at female faces longer.[498] Females also have more activation in the fusiform face area of the brain responsible for face characteristic processing when looking at a female face than at a male face.[166, 402] Females scan the faces of other females that are in their high fertility stage of their menstrual cycle with scanning patterns that increase face recognition.[470] These findings indicate that females hone in on the competition for a potential mate because there is no longer a need to look at male faces when a mate has already been selected.

The role of scent communication is different for males. Males find female scent more attractive when the female is closer to ovulation; high-fertility scents are rated more attractive than low-fertility scents.[234] This is consistent with male evolutionary mating behaviors.

Pupil dilation also plays an important role. Human pupils dilate when viewing something of interest.[329] Changes in pupil dilation have been found as early as infancy, indicating pupil size changes in response to social stimulus.[189] Males look longer at attractive females and the reverse is true with females looking longer and having pupil dilation when viewing attractive males.[556] It must be understood that females usually have larger pupils under normal conditions compared with men.[724]

Pupil dilation and sexual attraction is stronger for both males and females when viewing sexually explicit stimuli.[692] Pupil dilation allows for more light to come in, which allows more sensory information. However, other indicators of sexual attraction have been identified. For males, genitalia excitement is a stronger indicator of sexual attraction to a female than pupil dilation.[111, 555] The reverse has been found for women, with pupil dilation being a stronger indicator of sexual arousal.[110, 111]

CONCLUSION

From the evidence covered in this chapter, there are some common themes. Searching for a mate is a progression of general evolutionary attributes one looks for in a mate; these are then narrowed down to individual preference. First, basic biological features are evaluated with males looking for youth, fertility, and assurance that their offspring can be identified as theirs. Females evaluate males for the ability to gain resources, which has transformed to financial wellbeing, strength,and protection.

Secondly, both males and females look for similar physical attributes as their own. They look for similar facial characteristics and body size. Familiarity seems to be a stronger attribute valued by females.

Thirdly, females find a mate through body odor chemosignals that have a different genetic makeup, making genetic defects less likely in offspring.[361] To assist this, females have more neurons and glial cells in their olfactory bulb.[483] So, perhaps maybe think twice about what perfume or cologne is consistent with your genetic chemosignal makeup. Some other chemosignal considerations are extended; for example, online dating before meeting and arranged marriages. In both of these examples, chemosignals are removed and once meeting in person, the potential partners may soon smell that their genetics are incompatible.

CHAPTER 17

RELATIONSHIP NEEDS

RELATIONSHIP PHYSIOLOGY
Affection is needed to maintain relationships.[279] It has been extensively noted that affection has physical health benefits. Females have larger structures in the limbic system, such as the right insular cortex and anterior cingulate gyrus areas responsible for attention and emotional processing and expressing, which play a larger role in relationships than for males.[578] Females also have higher levels of oxytocin when communicating with others, which reduces stress.[419, 606] Relationships often have conflict that leads to stress. However, Jurek and Neumann (2017) found that even a minor increase in oxytocin levels before a conflict can lead to more positive communication during the conflict.

SEXUAL DESIRE AND HORMONES
Sexual exchanges play an important role with romantic relationship development and maintenance.[61] Males have more neural rewarding sensations to sexual stimuli than females.[639] Males have 20-25 times more circulating testosterone, which is linked to sexual desire for males.[80, 127, 186] Hence, if males have more neural rewarding sensations to sexual stimuli and more of the sex hormone related to sex drive it just makes

sense that sexual intimacy plays a larger role in the lives of males than in females.

However, there are cases in which males have low sexual desire. Extremely intense exercise for males has been linked to sexual dysfunctions.[262] Also for men, low testosterone levels can play a major factor with lower sexual desires and drive.[134]

Petherick (2017) writes that the sexual desires of women are far more complicated to understand. For instance, there is still an open debate with only minimal evidence from blood flow research supporting the female Gräfenberg spot (G- Spot) existence. Oral contraceptives, which are used to prevent pregnancy, still have unknown effects on the sex drive. One possible cause is that the contraceptive dilutes testosterone, which needs to be converted to estrogen for female sexual desires.[525, 655, 686]

For a few women, the detrimental effects of antidepressants on sexual desire can be exacerbated from the oral contraceptive. Scheele, Plota, Stoffel-Wagner, Maier, and Hurlemann, (2016) found contraceptive use for women inhibited oxytocin brain reward emotions when viewing their partner's face. Thus, there are still many unknowns about the role of contraception with women's sexual desires.

The vast majority of divorces for people over age fifty are initiated by women.[565] There are probably several reasons for this, but one worthy of note is menopause. Women begin to experience dropping levels of estrogen starting at around age forty.[480] Estrogen plays a large role with brain functioning and behaviors.[182]

Estradiol has been found to improve sexual desire for all female mammals. Additionally, much higher testosterone levels than are naturally found with females has been found to improve hormone therapies with low levels of estrogen for human females.[93] However, lower levels of testosterone are unlikely to improve female sexual arousal.[570] It is the conversion of high amounts of testosterone converting to estradiol that can improve female sexual arousal.[525]

However, this is not as easy a fix as was previously covered for men with low testosterone levels. Talking and other cognitive therapy can also be beneficial for female libido improvement.[468, 515] Previous research has found that females experience increased levels of oxytocin that interact with the dopamine system when talking.[419, 606] In 2015, flibanserin was approved to treat women for hypoactive sexual disorder in premenopausal women, which affects at least 10% of women. It helps treat serotonin levels and was initially developed to treat depression.[468] Thus, women's sexual desires are complicated, and several possible treatments for low desire are possible.

SEXUAL READINESS

Sexual arousal is an integrated response that includes cognitive, emotional, physiological, and behavioral processes.[603] Females and males have different conditions prior to sexual desires. Males are sexually aroused more quickly and by a greater variety of stimuli.[484] Males are also aroused to a greater extent from sexual visual images.[388]

As was previously covered in this book, males are much more compartmentalized with neural connections and processes.[97] There is a clear link between male sexual arousal towards females they find attractive; it is much more complicated for females, who are sexually aroused by males and females.[621] This may explain why males viewing sexual stimuli make poor decisions even regarding non-sexual decisions.[375] Likely, males can only focus on one stimuli at once.

Females have a much more integrated body system, such as finding males with body odors indicating a different genetic code as more attractive.[361] Furthermore, their sexual readiness involves more overall areas needed to be relaxed for her to feel comfortable enough before becoming sexually aroused.[97] If one of these areas is under stress or negative mood feelings, then sexual arousal can become inhibited.

Stress impacts females much more strongly, both physiologically and psychologically.[42] Brain activity sex differences have been observed from stress.[438] Having more sensitivity to social experiences makes her more vulnerable to negative effects of stress by having more activation in the dorsal attention network.[170] Female emotional experiences have additional activity in the amygdala leading to heightened limbic activity when processing emotional information.[16]

Females are more vulnerable to the stress chemical cortisol, which spills over to the detriment of the amygdala, hippocampus, and anterior cingulate cortex.[473] This can weaken emotional regulation, causing her to focus on negative emotional experiences.[16] Negative physiological reactions associated with stress are likely to occur.[457] These physiological and psychological negative reactions to stress for females each contribute to inhibiting sexual arousal and desire.

Females have a much stronger emotional link to their personal memories.[74] Females have a more sensitive limbic system that controls emotions, such as more activation in the hippocampus for emotion and memory.[202] One can easily see how overall reduced stress and more relaxation must take place for females to feel calm enough for sexual desire. There are several ways this can be achieved to physically and psychologically remove herself from life's distractions.

OXYTOCIN, THE BONDING CHEMICAL

Feng, Hackett, DeMarco, Chen, Stair, et al. (2014) found that women have a stronger caudate/putamen response to reciprocated cooperation than men. The women found cooperative reciprocity more rewarding. However after experimentally increasing oxytocin levels, men found reciprocated cooperation positively rewarding, but the reward value actually decreased for women. The authors' possible explanation for this sex difference is that women are at higher levels of oxytocin to begin with, and non-natural increases in these levels surpasses their maximum level during reciprocated cooperation. Therefore it is less rewarding than with men.

Thus, the influence of additional non-natural oxytocin for women is not socially rewarding during cooperative reciprocity, but it is for men. Other research has found the oxytocin receptor gene to influence allelic variation and self-disclosure in romantic relationships.[152] If females have higher baseline levels of oxytocin then it only makes sense that they will self-disclose more than males in relationships, which is consistent with previous research.[97, 384]

SYNCHRONY AND MIMICRY

Indications about the health of a relationship are synchrony and mimicry. The amount of communication behaviors between matching partners indicates mimicry, and the rhythm of those behaviors is synchrony.[57, 224] Mimicry and synchrony during human communication is found in behaviors, hormones, automatic system, and the brain.[193] As behaviors and rhythms match between partners, they take on each other's emotional states.[534] In turn, they can empathize with each other, leading to more accurate understanding of each partner.[143]

Synchronized rhythms and mimicked partner behaviors related with similar brain activations are referred to as biobehavioral synchrony and is essential for relationship bonding.[192] What a person thinks their partner is feeling will then become what their partner actually feels.[600] As a result, martial satisfaction is dependent upon synchronized rhythms and matched behaviors that connect their emotional states.[437] Lovers have much higher levels of physical behaviors, rhythms, and brain activation synchrony.[193, 491]

Synchronous behaviors also mean more cooperation between the ones communicating.[668] A strong visual indication of this is nonverbal communication behaviors. Each partner matching the same nonverbal communication behaviors such as posture, facial expressions, gestures, with rhythms of speaking volume, eye contact duration, and speaking length are indicators of a healthy relationship. On a basic level it makes sense, matching the behaviors and rhythms of someone you like rather than someone you dislike.

When physical behaviors match, such as having the same behaviors or doing the same task together, similar areas of the brain activate for both partners.[57] When similar brain areas are activated between partners from synchronized and mimicked behaviors, this can lead to prosocial behaviors exchanged between the partners, more positive emotions felt, a stronger relationship bond, and a better understanding of each partner.[224, 297, 451] In other words, shared behaviors lead to shared brain experiences, which lead to positive exchanges of communication. Perhaps not coincidently, couples living together in long-term relationships show some similarities with brain network organization.[612]

LOVE PHYSIOLOGY

What makes two people fall in love? What makes two people stay in love? Is it confidence, charm, good looks, intelligence, wealth, or career position? Jeff Bezos was divorced after becoming the wealthiest person ever to live; Brad Pitt and Angelina Jolie were highly attractive with powerful careers, and that did not keep them together; Elon Musk seems charming and quite confident in himself, but three marriages have not worked out for him, so it must be something else besides these listed characteristics.

Human physiology gives consistent insight into why people fall in love and stay together. Love at the basic level is an attachment. Perhaps women feeling desired by their partner is reassurance of a committed relationship.[67] Oxytocin is often referred to as the love hormone. Oxytocin levels increase during bonding.[664] It promotes relationship bonding by reducing fear and anxiety, while promoting trust and sexual pleasure.[340] Oxytocin is a neuropeptide that increases perceptions of relationship quality by increasing activation of the reward areas of the brain by route of mesolimbic dopamine pathways after receiving touch from a partner.[359]

Dopamine is a chemical in the body that acts as both a hormone and neurotransmitter, and plays a role in motivation and reward sensations. The brain changes as a result of changes in the levels of oxytocin and dopamine in the human body when they become more closely interacted together during attachments.[193, 664] This occurs from social cues by the attached person becoming more rewarding through the newly changed neural networks.[255, 407]

Feldman (2017) addresses the process of love and attachment levels. The striatum plays an important part with the reward system of the human body; it interprets emotional and motivational information from sensory inputs during human attachments. After receiving incoming pleasant sensory information, the striatum gets dopamine inputs from different areas of the brain. The dopamine tightly coordinates with oxytocin to more precisely associate the reward feeling of dopamine. Together dopamine and oxytocin contribute to neural plasticity that is necessary for selective focus and long-term memories of the relationship partner, thus making clearer the target of the dopamine.

A better understanding is then made about the partner from trends of behaviors exhibited to their relationship partner, the reward feeling, and particular behaviors leading up to it. Biobehavioral synchrony begins to develop from these reoccurring relationship behaviors enhanced by oxytocin, along with reward feelings from dopamine. As a result, the striatum acting with the reward feeling of dopamine and bonding mechanisms of oxytocin influence which motor behaviors to exhibit in order to achieve particular goals.

In other words, the striatum makes sense of the good emotions from dopamine through coordinated efforts with oxytocin; these are experienced during love to increase the likelihood of receiving more euphoric feelings from love experiences. Striatal action has been observed in almost all research imaging studies involving human attachments. Simply put, it clarifies what needs to be done again to get this great feeling from one's partner. These processes contribute to the degree of love and the value of attachment.

Euphoric emotions play an important part in loving attachment. Love addiction can take place throughout different stages from initial relationship beginnings through the course of the relationship including termination.[84] Love addiction occurs from addictive motivators to neurochemical reactions; this is similar to other forms of addiction. Both can provide exceptionally great amounts of feelings of reward.[173]

Love and substance addiction share some of the same neurochemicals responsible for euphoric emotional experiences: oxytocin and dopamine.[193, 340] These addictions have major overlaps regarding brain function and neural chemicals, along with needs that can be temporarily met but become an obsession when unmet for an extended period of time.[65, 173] Other overlaps are "mood swings, craving, obsession, compulsion, distortion of reality, emotional dependence, personality changes, risk-taking, and loss of self-control" (p. 51).[203]

Earp, Wudarczyk, Foddy, and Savulescu (2017) lay out three criteria that can indicate a person is addicted to love, assuming that similar brain processes are occurring that are commonly found with addiction. The three criteria are: disruption of normal life, inability to partake in healthy relationships, and being a disruption to oneself and others.

If love can be addictive, then can there be a medical cure for it? Earp and Savulescu (2018) take the position that researchers should investigate pharmaceuticals that enhance or deter relationships. These pharmaceuticals can help with the complex relationships of sex drive, attachment system, and better experiences of romantic love. There are already drugs available by prescription that affect thoughts and emotions, which in turn influence relationships. For example, the contraceptive pill for women can change mate preferences.[20] Oxytocin injections can improve perceptions of a partner's touch and the quality of the relationship.[359] The common food additive β-caryophyllene can weaken dopaminergic activity to lessen reward and motivation to help cure love sickness.[390]

Earp, Wudarczyk, Sandberg, and Savulescu (2013) make the argument that some forms of love should be intervened because it can become harmful or even deadly. They contend that the human brain system for love is comprised of desire, allure, and attachment. Therefore, love is heavily dependent upon biochemical pathways impacted by hormones and neurotransmitters associated with rewards that medication used to reduce or eliminate those reward sensations can cure love addiction. All drug addictions are partially contingent upon release of dopamine rewards. Some available medical implementations can take the form of anti-love, such as antidepressants, which have side effects such as androgen-blocking reduction of libido, medication for obsessive compulsive disorder that targets serotonin levels to reduce repetitive thoughts about an individual, medication that reduces levels of oxytocin and dopamine, and desensitizing an individual via over-exposure.

RELATIONSHIP MAINTENANCE

As was previously covered in this book, females are verbally superior.[367] They are also better equipped for communicating emotionally.[439, 547] Perhaps this helps explain why males are known in society to be inferior with greeting card communication.[699] Additionally, actual gifts themselves differ between men and women.

Males have a superior ability regarding motion and spatial abilities, likely due to early androgen exposure in these areas of the brain.[17, 97, 392] These abilities usually are consistent with gift preferences. Observed males have different preferences than females starting at infancy regarding items, such as preferring toy trucks and cars due to their higher levels of testosterone.[311] Men usually want a gift they can use and do something with, such as build, fix, hit (golf), throw (football), hunt, drive (boat), etc.

It takes more mental effort to process something new or out of the ordinary.[378] Males have more neural activity and are more aroused by a variety of visual stimuli.[484, 639] Therefore, a way to maintain a healthy relationship is for a woman to wear a variety of different intimate outfits, such as designs, fabrics, and colors on different occasions. This will have more visual and sexual stimulation to the man than wearing similar outfits night after night.

It is much more complicated to understand gift preferences for women. To begin with, the relationship with the man giving the gift along with the type of gift influences how the woman perceives the gift. Nakagawa, Takahashi, Okada, Matsushima, and Matsuda (2015) found that the activation of the women's anterior cingulate cortex (ACC) differs dependent upon the man giving the gift and the gift itself. The (ACC) is associated with determining the reward response to the gift based on the activation level, evaluating the gift's social meaning. For example, they found that if the woman had no interest in the man, then no activity increase was found in this area when receiving a gift from him, but the (ACC) did increase activity levels when receiving the same gift from a man she had interest in. Additionally, the (ACC) was found to be connected to the supplementary motor area/ dosal ACC (SMA/dACC), which is within the dorsal mediofrontal cortex; this indicates that action monitoring, emotion, and cognitive processing in decision-making are all linked together.

Hughes and Aung (2017) investigated gift preferences for women, from their partners, in different stages of life. Younger women who viewed themselves as having desirably attraction attributes preferred their long-term mates to give romantic gifts, emotional support, and have wealth potential. Older women preferred receiving gifts that are domestically helpful and of financial assistance. Whereas those women not in a committed relationship and those without children preferred romantic gifts, wealth potential, and emotional support much more than married women, women in relationships, or women with children.

A takeaway from these studies is that both the giver and receiver need to be considered in the process. Aknin and Human (2015) found that a gift optimally creates closeness between the giver and receiver when the gift reflects something unique about the person receiving the gift and as importantly the person giving the gift.

Another approach to maintaining a relationship is keeping it exciting. Sharing in an exciting activity can be exhilarating for relationships. Cummins (2017) covers how excitation transfer theory can lead to greater attraction. When a person has an experience with an exciting stimuli, that excited emotion can be sustained and attributed to another stimuli. For instance, two people in a relationship who go to an amusement park and ride tall rollercoasters will feel the excitement and adrenaline from the rollercoasters. However, those emotions might not only be attributed to the rollercoaster, but also to their partner. When this happens, an individual thinks that the excitement is from the enjoyment and attraction of being with their partner and not necessarily from the scary heights of the rollercoaster. Partaking in more exciting activities can lead to both partners viewing the relationship as more exciting and the other person more attractive.

CONCLUSION

It is important for partners to know each other regarding gifts. Women tend to have a more complex system regarding affection in relationships. Her body system is more integrated and one aspect can greatly influence the rest of her system. It is important for males and females to both understand the processes of affection for the other person. For instance, men need to understand the importance of communication for a woman to reduce stress and promote relationship bonding. This can come in the form of self-disclosure, listening, and touch such as holding hands.

Love plays an important role in relationship affection; knowing the physiological underpinnings of love can help strengthen and maintain a relationship. Partners can have differences in a healthy relationship, depending on what those differences are; it is fine to have different hobbies and interests, and probably healthy to have some separate interests; however, it's essential to have similar core values with each other, such as beliefs and morals.[718] Those core values are what people hold strong that make them who they are and major differences in these areas between partners can lead to unresolved conflicts and incompatibility.

CHAPTER 18

SHE DEMANDS, HE WITHDRAWS

DEMAND AND WITHDRAW

Misunderstandings are common with relationship communication. However, recognizing common romantic communication patterns can lead to better understanding and less conflict.

A common toxic pattern is demand and withdraw, which is detrimental to both individuals and the relationship overall. It is characterized by interpersonal emotional communication patterns. As one partner demands more from the other partner usually in the form of emotional sharing, the other partner tends to shut down and withdraw from the relationship even more each time.[47] This escalates the tension, and more demand is sought leading to even more withdrawal until a boiling point hits.

Most romantic relationships in this pattern find the woman in the demand role and the man in the role of withdrawing. As the demand and withdrawal model indicates, each partner influences the other; the emotional state of one person is often transferred to the other person, so it can be detrimental to the relationship when negative emotions are transferred.[335] Negative emotions can even transfer through body odors from one person to another through chemosignals.[147] This vicious demand and withdrawal cycle must be addressed, because the tension felt by both will come out in one way or another, such as taking anger out at other people, themselves, or even pets.

The demand withdrawal relationship dynamic tends to occur for a few reasons. It takes more mental effort for men to process information relevant to a relationship.[716] Additionally, men have inferior language development and expressive vocabulary due to higher levels of testosterone starting at an early age.[365] Testosterone levels prior to birth have been found to negatively impact language abilities for boys at age two.[293] Women have more invested in a relationship, because if a woman becomes pregnant, she spends nine months carrying the offspring. Therefore, demand and withdrawal usually begins with the woman perceiving her feelings or needs are not adequately attended to by the man. When she communicates these issues with him, often times he is caught off guard thinking that everything was going all right. That can be part of the problem.

From an evolutionary perspective, the man may think that things are going well as long as he is providing resources and is physically spending time with her. As was previously covered in this book, males tend to use action and spatial activities as preferred ways to communicate the male's feelings and emotions to a woman. For example, coming home from work and taking the woman out to dinner and then to a movie is in his mind contributing above average to the relationship.

However, as was previously covered in this book, females have more emotional and relationships needs. If he does not communicate much at dinner or does so about non-emotional topics that are unrelated to the relationship, then her needs are not receiving adequate attention. When she demands more from the relationship, he perceives his relationship actions as unappreciated. He is likely to resent her communication demands and view them as unwarranted and shut down even more from the relationship. Then, the vicious cycle is likely to increase with her demanding more and him retreating even more. A man doing things with her and for her are his forms of emotional communication; meanwhile, she needs her emotional and relationship needs recognized and addressed.

CONFLICT MANAGEMENT STYLES

How the demand and withdrawal interaction is handled depends upon the conflict management style that each partner chooses to enact. Done effectively, conflict management can help strengthen the relationship. Conflict can be defined as communication interactions between two people who have incompatible goals.[321] Blake and Mouton developed five conflict management styles recognized by communication researchers (1964). Competition consists of one person getting all of the resources while the other person gets little or none. Accommodation consists of one person giving up a large portion of their desires in order for the other person to meet their own goals. Avoidance ignores the issue. Collaborative style consists of both individuals working together to meet the goals of both people. The compromising style consists of both individuals giving up some of their goals.

Which conflict style one chooses is dependent upon situational factors such as concern for one's own goals compared with concern for one's partner's goals. On the other hand, personality type tends to have a more consistent conflict management style each time there is a conflict. Females often view conflict more destructively, approach conflict more carefully, and show more concern for the relationship. Males tend to use more status conflict approaches and actions to resolve it, rather than talking it out.[599]

Gere and Impett (2018) found that reducing the importance emphasized on one's goals in a relationship was important for long-term relationship commitment. However, it can come at a cost to the woman's satisfaction.

Sex hormones also play a vital role in relational conflict. Cortisol is a stress hormone that increases with stress.[427] Oxytocin is a bonding sex hormone that helps to reduce stress.[210] Testosterone is a sex hormone related with aggression.[129, 606] Schneiderman, Kanat-Maymon, Zagoory-Sharon, and Feldman (2014) found that a person who had a partner with higher levels of oxytocin showed greater empathy. Higher levels of relationship aggression with both partners had higher levels of testosterone. High levels of cortisol for both partners were related with decrease empathy and more likely of a breakup. Therefore, it is essential to reduce stress and increase the bonding sex hormone oxytocin when having conflict communication. Having shared mimicked and synchronized behaviors can help the relationship by leading to more prosocial behaviors.[297, 491] Synchronized and mimicked behaviors can also help with understanding from the individuals sharing cognitive circuits and blurring the individual differences and focusing on the pair as one.[301]

Each partner needs to understand when the other person is ready to communicate about conflict-related issues. As was previously covered in this book, men have a much more compartmentalized brain.[97] Men are more focused on one issue at a time. Therefore, when conflict arises he needs time to reflect by himself and then come back and discuss it. It is not effective to demand that he talks about an issue right when it occurs, express his emotions about it, and try to solve it. Each of these tends to be separate brain functions performed separately by him.

She needs to understand when to bring up the issue without trying to solve it or go into depth about it right away. Rather, she should find a time for both to discuss it in detail after he is informed. Bombarding him right when he walks into the room about an unexpected issue is not effective.

On the other hand, women have a much more integrated brain.[97, 305] These connections can easily account for females having a stronger connection between their personal memories and emotions.[74] An issue that she has can easily spill into other areas beyond the initial problem, such as emotions, stress, and relating to past experiences resembling the one at hand.[345]

While the man might be able to set the problem aside and attend to other aspects of life, it might not be as easy for her. Her sleep might be interrupted and definitely she will not be in the mood for romance until the problem is addressed enough to reduce stress and negative emotions for her.[42] He should communicate to her that he understands it is an important issue to address, listen to her, and then set aside a future time they both agree to discuss it further.

He should not try to only give solutions the first time he hears it but wait to offer them for the second discussion that is more in-depth. Both partners need to reframe from using personal pronouns and the other person's name when communicating about the negative aspects of the conflict and should communicate about the specific behaviors related to negativity involving the conflict.

HELPFUL SOLUTIONS

There are some communication adjustments that can be done to improve relationships, especially regarding the demand and withdrawal negative spiral. Relationships are complicated as is the demand and withdraw cycle. Sometimes problems in relationships arise merely because each partner views the relationship differently. The demand and withdrawal cycle must be addressed and not avoided. It can be done effectively as previously described by having each partner ready to communicate about the issues and using one of the effective communication styles previously covered.

To not effectively address demand and withdrawal issues can have dire consequences, such as higher levels of anxiety for women and substance abuse for men.[175, 364] Rodriguez, Fillo, Hadden, Øverup, Baker, and DiBello (2019) found those in a relationship who avoid closeness or are with a partner that avoids closeness perceive their partners to be less satisfied and committed. Additionally, those who are higher in avoidance or anxiety have a more pessimistic view of their own relationships.

Referring back to two common themes within this chapter are timing and biology. Hoffmann (2019) found that men are more likely to self-disclose to a woman when she is in her follicular phase of her menstrual cycle, which is consistent with higher levels of estrogen. The man is likely to be more sexually aroused from her body odors at that time and in turn self-disclose more to her. Hence, a woman who wants to have an intimate and emotional conversation with her male partner is likely to have the most success when she is in the follicular menstrual stage.

Ross, Karney, Nguyen, and Bradbury (2019) write that it is optimal to resist withdrawing and acknowledge the requests. However, sometimes the man is unable to meet the demands due to their socioeconomic lack of resources. In those cases, it is actually better for the man to have a level of withdrawal from the demands.

Burgess Moser, Johnson, Dalgleish, Lafontaine, Wiebe, and Tasca (2016) studied emotionally focused couple therapy (EFT) for couples engaging in demand and withdraw cycles. This type of therapy is specifically aimed toward breaking these negative communication cycles. It focuses on the emotional and attachment needs of each partner. They found that (EFT) helped to reduce relationship avoidance, anxiety, and blame, while increasing in relationship security and satisfaction.

CONCLUSION

Relationship conflicts can make it difficult for each partner to understand the other's needs; vicious negative communication cycles can develop. Males need to understand female emotional and relational needs, while females need to understand the value placed on physical actions as emotional expressions by men, who have more limited language abilities. Relational conflict can be beneficial, depending upon how it is managed and communicated.

CHAPTER 19

DIFFICULT RELATIONSHIP CONVERSATIONS

Relationship conversations centered around problems can be difficult. If they are not addressed, then the problem is likely to persist. If the problem is improperly addressed, the vicious cycle demand and withdraw described in a previous chapter may become a pattern. The negative emotions of each person are then transferred to the other person.[335] Therefore, the goal should be to adequately reduce or eliminate problems through effective communication.

UNCERTAINTY REDUCTIONS THEORY

A common but often overlooked root of relationship problems is uncertainty. Uncertainty reductions theory was first introduced by Berger and Calabrese (1975). In uncertain environments, people seek out information to reduce their uncertainty and anxiety and better predict the situation. Having certainty in a relationship is associated with positive communication behaviors and relational satisfaction.[495] When a partner has uncertainty in a relationship, negative behaviors are likely to be exhibited as a response. These include jealousy, avoidance, spying, infidelity, destructive conflict, and allowing control.[137] Criticism is also taken personally when there is uncertainty in a relationship, leading to men avoiding certain topics.[626]

Relationship uncertainty is often associated with avoidance.[117] This was the case with the demand and withdrawal cycle covered in a previous chapter; it often involves the woman feeling uncertain about whether she was valued in the relationship. This is due to lack of communication from the man, and the man feeling uncertain as to why the woman is not satisfied from the resources and attention he has given. But his gestures often lacked the overt emotional verbal expressions that women enjoy hearing.[47]

One possible modern day solution is to make the relationship official through social media. Lane, Piercy, and Carr (2016) found that posting relationship status on Facebook was associated with positive relational outcomes such as more satisfaction, commitment, investment, and partners having less interest in other potential partners. Perhaps posting relationship status helps to reduce relational uncertainty, and leads to these positive outcomes.

As was covered in a previous chapter, men tend to communicate much more literally, and women more subtly.[177, 547, 712] This can lead to feelings of uncertainty for both, along with negative relationship outcomes. The woman may drop hints about expressing emotions that the man likely will not pick up beyond the literal meanings of the hints, which are often small and unimportant on the surface. On the other hand, the man may literally view spending time with a woman as an investment in the relationship, such as going out to eat, seeing a movie, or going to a museum, during which little outright emotional expression is expected from his perspective. The mere fact of doing things together is an emotional expression on his part.

One way to reduce uncertainty is sharing tasks.[117] Sharing tasks can communicate to the woman that she and the relationship are valued because the man is contributing to tasks he would otherwise rather not do. These can include domestic chores around the house, which would communicate investment in the relationship because both people live in the house. The man would view the woman doing tasks as literal investments in the relationship.

Another possible means to reduce relational uncertainty is touch. Jakubiak and Feeney (2019) found that couples that touched before and during a conflict reduced stress, which can improve relational security and cognitive interdependence. Perhaps a simple touch such as hand-holding communicates more relational clarity and reduces uncertainty. Additionally, research found that relational partner coordinated behaviors activate the same areas of the brain and are associated with more prosocial behaviors.[297, 491]

GENDER TIMING FOR CRITICISM

The approach to difficult conversations also differs between males and females. Males tend to build relationships and are more comfortable communicating about sensitive topics while involved in an activity with another person; this is likely due to their comfort of superior spatial abilities and task-oriented behaviors.[99, 392] This can include eating lunch, playing golf, fishing, sitting during a long drawn out baseball game, house repair projects etc.

Males prefer time to reflect on problems by themselves before discussing them with other people. Therefore, a woman should understand that scheduling a shared activity together can give him time to reflect, thus creating better conditions to bring up the issues to discuss. She should give him prior notice that she would like to talk with him about a particular issue when they are sharing the planned activity.

Females prefer for issues to be brought up quickly. From having a more interconnected female brain, problems can more easily seep into other areas of her life.[305] If not addressed, the issues can fester and grow and grow and spread to other areas of the female's life well beyond the initial topic.[183, 435] Additionally, as was covered with the demand and withdrawal cycle, she needs to feel validated by communicating about problems without distractions.[47] In particular, women have expectations for individual attention on formal dates and when spending intimate time alone.[450] It should not take place during a sporting event on t.v., activities with the children, in front of other people, or without sufficient time to discuss it.

The takeaway from this section is that when women desire to bring up a particular problem with their male partner, she should give him prior notice. On the other hand, a man needing to bring up a particular issue with his female partner should not delay, and should do so without any environmental distractions.

HOW TO CRITICIZE

Both partners are interdependent to some extent.[280] How relationship conflict is communicated is important to understand, because it can lead to disease and mortality from synchronized heart rate variability of the couple. This increases the likelihood of inflammation-related diseases.[705] The use of personal pronouns can give insight into the relationship status and inner-feelings of a person.[63]

Both males and females should discuss problems by focusing more on the issues or behaviors and less on the individual person. Additionally, personal pronouns should be limited to reduce perceiving the talk as a personal attack. These include reducing the usage of 'you' or 'I' or even individual names when criticism is communicated. The use of personal pronouns during conflict gives a clue into the demand/withdrawal vicious cycle. The use of more individual language during conflict such as 'I' is one indication of the presence of demand/ withdrawal; the individual demanding does not feel validated and needs to express their individual perspective rather than of the relationship.[552]

On the contrary, couple-inclusive language, often referred to 'we talk', has positive indications of the relationship such as interdependence, investment, and resilience.[235] Some positive psychological and physical outcomes at both the individual personal level and the relationship level have been found with relationship inclusive talk.[331, 552] Some of the physical benefits of using connecting words such as 'we' rather than separating words such as 'I' or 'me' are lower cardiovascular arousal and more positive emotional experiences.[598]

Seider et al. (2009) found separating words and less marital satisfaction was strongest for older wives. As women experience menopause, their estrogen levels decrease, along with the importance they place on their marriage relationship.[565, 593] Therefore, both males and females should engage in connecting words as a couple, such as 'we' and 'our,' rather than singling out one person to blame for conflicts. Using similar language is also associated with other positive aspects of a relationship, such as initiation and stability.[306]

RELATIONSHIP PERCEPTION

People in relationships view their partners differently than others view them. They often view them much more positively than others do, which makes sense as to why they are in the relationship. Part of this can be explained through the fundamental attribution error. We tend to perceive what happens to us positively and from our personal control; we attribute negative experiences to external factors such as other people and the context. The reverse also holds true. People relate positive aspects of another person to external factors, such as the context, while negative events happening to other people are often attributed personally to the other person. Perhaps there is a biological reaction. Maybe it makes us feel better about ourselves to view our relationships more positively than what reality may suggest. People who automatically perceive their relationship positively often have fewer thoughts of suicide.[445] This helps explain why it can be difficult to convince someone else that they are in an unhealthy relationship.

Unhealthy relationships are less stable with more extreme ups and downs than healthy relationships. Those ups can be filled with excitement and passion that keep the partners in a toxic relationship.[309] Frampton and Fox (2018) address how social media can also distort perception of a relationship and lead to negative effects, such as indirect information seeking about their relationship partner. Relationship jealousy, relationship threats, and retroactive jealousy are commonplace on social media. This can occur from social comparison, digital remnants, and again the ever important relational uncertainty. Relationship partners can become jealous of their partner's past relationships even though their partner no longer communicates with these individuals.

It also matters who in the relationship delivers the criticism. Criticism is taken much better and less harmful when it is delivered by someone with whom the recipient is familiar.³¹⁸ Therefore, it is best for the person in the relationship to talk with their partner. If a partner is unable to talk to their partner, then often a family member is better rather than a casual friend. A best friend can be similar to a family member.

EMPATHY

Empathy plays an important role in relationships. Empathy is the ability to understand the emotional state of another person through automatic processes, while also realizing these are distinct from one's own emotional state.¹³¹ Communicating empathy is important during a difficult conversation. One way to do this is by mimicking the nonverbal behaviors of the speaker, especially when the speaker is displaying relationship-connecting nonverbal behaviors.⁶⁶ Mimicking behaviors activate the same areas of the brain, which can literally help with understanding the emotions of others.²⁹⁷

Empathy is not always better in relationships. Righetti, Gere, Hofmann, Visserman, and Van Lange (2016) found that divergent interests in a relationship can lead to less satisfaction due to discomfort. Empathy can exacerbate the negative effects of divergent relationship interests through negative emotional experiences and added stress. Therefore, it is better to communicate to one's partner that they do not want to partake in an activity rather than go along with it just to avoid a conflict.

DECEPTION

A difficult conversation can stem from a person thinking that another person is untruthful. Spontaneous communication behaviors of relationship partners often give insight into how partners truly feel about each other, thus emphasizing the importance of understanding nonverbal communication.¹⁸⁸ There are some indicators of deception to consider, some from which are gender-specific while others are not. To begin, one should get an understanding of how the other person normally communicates.⁶⁶² This can be done by asking some mundane questions. If one does not know the person well, then some basic questions can help establish how the person normally communicates when telling the truth, such as where they are from, what hobbies they have, type of job etc. Then, see if there are any anomalies later in the conversation of importance.

Another indicator for both males and females is to see if their nonverbal communication behaviors are consistent. One should consider whether their emotion expressions and gestures are consistent with the emotion of the topics discussed. For most right-handed people, looking up and to their left when communicating is recalling facts of the story, up and to the right indicates they are fabricating.[530] Genuine facial expressions usually begin on the left side of the face, and posed facial expressions begin on the right side.[575] Therefore, looking to the left should be accompanied with factual information, and looking to the right associated with imaginative information.

There are some gender deception differences. It is easier to detect deception from female communicators.[4] The female communication style gives more evidence to evaluate.[97, 179, 367] However, females are better at detecting deception, partially due to their higher emotional intelligence. They are better able to gather meaning from another person's face.[708] Females have more activation in the superior temporal sulcus, the area of the brain responsible for understanding the mental states of others.[727] This is consistent with females having better empathy.[26, 338] During deceptive communication of personal information, males have more activation in the left middle frontal gyrus, indicating that it takes more effort for males to deceive about personal information.[428] This makes sense because females more commonly communicate about personal information.[97, 384]

The entirety of communication is important to consider. Asking someone to recall a story out of order is difficult if the story is a lie, which would be memorized from beginning to end. Start in the middle and work your way to the beginning. If you want to find out what someone did last night, and they said they met friends, went out to eat, and then saw a movie, ask what everyone ate and when everyone arrived. Additionally, do not rely upon only one nonverbal behavior to make large conclusions. For instance, just because someone touches their nose does not mean that they are lying, maybe their nose just itched.[4, 260] People can improve upon their accuracy of detecting deception by improving upon their ability to recognize micro-expressions.[328] It is important to always consider the entirety of verbal and nonverbal messages communicated.

CONCLUSION

Humans have a need for stability, especially in a relationship. The health of a relationship is often dependent upon it. Open communication can help achieve relationship stability. However, open communication differs between males and females. Difficult discussions are a necessary component of any relationship. It is the timing of these discussions that is important. Females need these difficult discussions completed much sooner than males, and the specific context is also of upmost importance. Understanding a relational partner can help create open communication, stability, and a healthy relationship.

PART 8

GENERAL ISSUES AND TOPICS.

CHAPTER 20

HER HOBBIES, HIS HOBBIES

EARLY CHILDHOOD HOBBY DIFFERENCES
With evidence of gender differences found throughout the entire brain, one would expect hobby and activity interest differences as well.[712] Play differences by gender have been found with children, indicating a biological underpinning for these differences. Often these play and hobby interests are dependent upon natural abilities; for example, boys as young as four months perform better at object tracking.[701] When looking at objects, males focus more attention on spatial aspects of the object; females pay more attention to details of the object, such as color tone details and semantic associations with each object. This helps them develop social skills and interests later in life.[441, 614]

Sex hormonal differences can help explain hobby and interest differences.[283] Prenatal androgen exposure influences activity interests. Normally, males have much higher levels of testosterone prior to birth than females.[486] Females born with congenital adrenal hyperplasia have much higher levels of androgen exposure and perform much better on spatial tasks than females born with normal levels.[267]

Prenatal androgen exposure can be isolated as majorly influencing activity interests; females with congenital adrenal hyperplasia are exposed to high levels of androgens and have similar activity interests as males, who usually have similar levels of androgen exposure.[53] Prenatal sex hormones influence toy selection for boys and girls.[54]

Postnatal androgen surges have also been found to influence toy selection for boys. The time between birth to three months is referred to as mini-puberty. This involves a surge of androgens for boys. This masculinization increases their penile size and will impact masculine activities later in life, such as at four years of age.[500] Lamminmäki, Hines, Kuiri-Hänninen, Kilpeläinen, Dunkel, and Sankilampi, (2012) found infants as young as seven days had toy preference behaviors predictably associated with testosterone levels, such as boys playing with a train and girls with a doll. Additionally, as testosterone levels for boys were lower, they were more likely to play with a doll, while girls with higher levels of testosterone were more likely to play with a train. In a different study, it was found at ages twelve, eighteen, and twenty-four months, boys looked significantly more at trucks than girls, and girls looked significantly more at dolls than boys. These findings are consistent with non-human primates.[311]

Todd, Barry, and Thommessen (2017) have consistent supporting evidence. They did an independent research study allowing children to choose their own toys while there was no parent present. They found that boys played with male-typical toys and girls played with female-typical toys at age ranges nine to seventeen months, eighteen to twenty-four months, and twenty-four to thirty-two months. This early preference by boys for traditionally masculine toys is not from watching television, movies, and certainly not from reading books or magazines. Rather, it is due to biological tendencies.[25]

Testosterone is associated with aggression and strength.[179, 205] Playing actively with cars and trucks by crashing them serves as a release of boys' aggression, while playing sports can serve a need for social status. It also aligns with their natural strengths of spatial ability and object rotation.[268, 392] Males consistently outperform females for various visual tasks involving spatial and motion perceptions.[608] Part of this is due to paying more attention to spatial information when attending to objects.[441]

Evidence of gender differences is present with middle school science and technology scores that involve spatial abilities.[225] Spatial ability performance is related with androgen levels, a typical male sex hormone, for both males and females. The more androgen exposure a person has, the better their spatial ability performance will likely be.[640]

I have heard of several personal stories from others where a mother hands a boy a doll, and rather than nurturing and talking with the doll like many young girls do, the young boy often uses it as a weapon. He did not learn this from society, but it is the higher levels of testosterone related to aggression and lower levels of empathy that influences these actions.[186, 689] This section clearly indicates that gender differences with toy interests and play activities are present at an early age, long before popular culture and parenting influence such behaviors.

ADULT HOBBY DIFFERENCES

Gender differences with play activities as children extend into adulthood. This can be observed through shopping behaviors. Observe shopping behavioral differences between males and females at one of the few malls left in the United States. Males with their compartmentalized brain tend to be topic and task-focused.[99] As a result, they are likely to go directly to the destination for the item for which they came to the mall. On the other hand, females with a more integrated brain enjoy more social interaction due to higher levels of oxytocin, and are likely to have different observed shopping behaviors.[97, 419, 606]

Females find other people's faces—an important part of socializing—exciting.[536, 538] Females have up to 20 times more estrogen, which contributes to their superior language abilities.[338, 620] Males have up to 20 times higher testosterone levels, which hinders their language abilities.[365] Prior to birth, testosterone levels of boys have been found to inversely impact their language abilities at age two.[293] Females are much better with semantic labeling of objects.[268] Females divert more attention to semantic associations of an object when looking at it.[441]

Furthermore, females have a more active resting state connectivity, involving memories, language, and action.[347, 703] Cortisol—stress hormone—levels also negatively impact the female's ability to rest by activating more of her brain.[347] Taken together, women can experience a level of stress relief and restfulness from shopping that is likely to activate positive past memories and help them communicate with others, while the physical exercise of walking can help lower stress levels.

Females are more likely to shop in groups with other females and interact with customer service employees. For males, it is about accomplishing the task of gathering a necessary resource, while for women it can be a stress-relieving adventure that involves socializing with others, collecting items that increase their social attractiveness, even if they were not on the list, and feeling the excitement of an unplanned adventure. The importance of social relationships with others for females extends virtually as well. Females are more involved with social media as a means to maintain and develop their real-life relationships.[579]

SEX HORMONES AND HOBBIES

Males and females often have different experiences from the same activity; this is due to sex hormonal differences.[1] Oxytocin and testosterone have opposite effects in some regard. Oxytocin promotes sociable interests with others, while testosterone is related with self-oriented behaviors.[129] Furthermore, estrogen interacts with oxytocin to increase social understanding.[481]

Males have lower brain activity and less heart rate variability when resting.[202, 703] Higher levels of testosterone in males also allows for more emotional stability of staying in the resting state for long periods of time during an activity.[15, 206, 510] Males are much better equipped to tune out distractions during an activity they find restful. The activities that males find restful and fun often involve action and motion.

As was previously described in an earlier chapter, early high amounts of androgen exposure helps explain male superior spatial abilities.[392] Males having more magnocellular-projecting ganglion cells (M-GCs) in their retinas enables them to take in more information involving visual motion.[17, 698] As a result, males are more likely to remember these spatial activities.[684] Observing and participating in spatial activities often involve less conversations than more social activities.

CONCLUSION

Biological sex differences account for gender differences with hobbies and interests.[39] It becomes important to recognize that males and females have different needs and conditions to relax. Recognizing this can lead to understanding why men and women occasionally need separate nights out, informally referred to as guys' night out or girls' night out.

CHAPTER 21

I WANT A BABY, AND ANOTHER...

It often does not take long for a woman of reproductive age to start desiring a baby of her own after holding someone's else's baby. This can be especially true when she's in a long-term relationship, within the reproductive timeframe, financially stable, and her friends and family members have babies, which she holds.

EVOLUTIONARY BABY DESIRES

These experiences and desires that women go through are not the same for men. There are biological explanations for these differences that can be traced back through many generations to our ancestors. For instance, much higher levels of testosterone in males is associated with more individualistic behaviors and less concern for bonding with others.[129] The detrimental effects of increasing testosterone levels for a man can occur when he feels stressed.[11]

During primitive times, the woman stayed back at the cave to raise the children while the man went out to hunt.[25] Therefore, the reproductive success of the offspring depended to a great deal upon the mother's nurturing abilities. These traits have stayed consistent with today's modern women having more prosocial behaviors and becoming more dependent upon others during the luteal phase of their menstrual cycle. She will be much further along in her pregnancy at this time in her cycle if it were to occur, and building social alliances becomes important.[634] Women also have better perception through the use of touch.[3] Touch between a mother and her child plays an important bonding role for physiological, psychological, and immune system developments.[448] Infants experience the same emotional state as their mother through touch.[690]

Higher levels of testosterone are associated with new fathers having lower father-infant mimicry and synchrony, and also a negative relation between oxytocin and affectionate touch of their newborn. However, for new mothers, higher levels of testosterone are associated with increased levels of oxytocin from touching their new infant.[244] These indicate hormonal differences for infant bonding between mothers and fathers when holding babies. Mothers who have higher levels of oxytocin have better attachment styles with their newborns.[641] Importantly, the more aligned the oxytocin levels are between mother and newborn, the more aligned are the emotional states of both.[196]

From an evolutionary communicative perspective, offspring who had these positive emotional experiences had increased chances of surviving and passing their mother's genetics to future generations. Those mothers who did not have these positive emotional experiences from touching their offspring were less likely to pass their genetics to future generations. If it feels good for her holding someone else's baby, just think how good life will feel when having her own baby full-time.

PREGNANCY

In order for a woman to have a baby, pregnancy must first occur. The lifestyle of both partners can influence how DNA of their offspring functions.[372] For example, the Mediterranean diet for women has been found to increase the likelihood of a successful pregnancy and live births.[332] Vitamins have also been found to improve female fertility.[103] The male partner's lifestyle can also play a factor in pregnancy. For males, saturated fats, alcohol, and cannabis hinders sperm quality while walnuts can help for increased chances of pregnancy.[35, 563] These lifestyle choices should be considered by both parents at least four months prior to conception, along with stress, sleep, exercise, and exposure to carcinogens.[372]

The hip size of a woman helps determine her attractiveness to potential mates.[380] A waist-to-hip ratio of .7 is visually processed quickly in the brain, and is perceived attractive by men instinctually, because it implies that the woman is more likely to have a successful birth and is healthy.[149] There is somewhat of a biological conundrum regarding what females look for in a mate. Females tend to perceive strength as more attractive for potential male partners, but strength is related to lower ejaculate quality.[213]

For humans, often the crucial caregivers are mothers. This is not by chance, but rather from genomic imprinting from the mother that takes place with the female embryo, preparing it for the next generation of motherly caregiving responsibilities.[339] During pregnancy, a woman's body goes through many changes to help with these new demands.[128] It has been consistently found that females have more mimicked and synchronized behaviors with others, indicating a strong desire for relationship-building.[224, 682]

Synchronized and mimicked behaviors have also been linked to a more pro-social communication orientation, stronger relationship bond, better understanding of each person in the relationship, more prosocial behaviors, and more positive emotions.[413, 451] Synchronized and mimicked behaviors help with activating shared cognitive circuits that transform two individuals into one.[301] Therefore, these changes are often a means to synchronize the woman and baby during gestation.

During pregnancy, the mother's brain physically changes to better adapt to meeting the needs of her baby.[343] A pregnant mother's brain volume decreases by 8%.[479] These changes help her enhance her social abilities to better understand communication from her baby, identify social threats from others, and enhance bonding with the baby for greater empathy, warmth, and care. After giving birth, these brain changes are still observable for a long period of time.[178, 288, 343]

The mother also helps the fetus acquire valuable survival information during brain development. Genomic imprinting and epigenetic information help the developing brain of the fetus acquire valuable information for the changing future environment encountered after birth.[78] Other factors prior to birth that have after birth effects are the age of the mother and season at time of conception.[94] Another physical change with a pregnant woman is handgrip strength. Pregnant women have a decrease in hand strength. However, women with a stronger hand strength during pregnancy are more likely to have a baby boy, and this can also be predictive of the baby's weight after controlling for the baby's sex.[726]

While physical changes such as her brain and grip strength may occur, internal workings that are often less visible are also changing. Hormones can lead to physiological changes for women.[291] Hormonal changes can also influence mood swings. The hormone serotonin helps positive emotional feelings, but this decreases as pregnancy advances.[34]

With women already having a heightened and more complex sense of smell, one can easily understand how hormonal fluctuations can affect these areas.[627] A large portion of food tastes come from smell.[629] Taste is often more intense for women, and they have a greater ability to distinguish different tastes.[227,631] Food cravings for pregnant women can become erratic, from increasing their energy intake and the craving for sweet foods.[282] As a result, her dietary and emotional state can become less stable from these hormonal changes.

POST-PREGNANCY

After-birth experiences for a newborn can impact their psychological and physical health.[372] Female infants show more attention to faces than do males, which helps develop social understanding of their offspring later in life.[441] Mothers display more attention to infants than men do.[499] The need for bonding for a newborn baby is present before birth. Fetuses show cognitive attention toward three circles that resemble a face but do not have this activation for three circles that do not resemble a face.[549]

Body odors also play an important role with bonding, although these are not consciously noticeable.[409] This can occur from the mother lactating, as well as milk production and transfer. Numerous odorous substrates are emitted from the arcolar glands. This area of the mother's breast is quite active when interacting with the newborn baby.[163] Breastfeeding also helps enhance the bond between the mother and child, along with her ability to attend to the baby's needs.

During the first postpartum month, the baby's cry leads to more activation in the mother's right superior frontal gyrus and amygdala in mothers who breastfeed their infant. Greater activation in the right superior frontal gyrus and amygdala is associated with more sensitivity to their infant's needs, such as better empathy.[342] Bonding between the mother and infant is necessary because it helps with cognitive and emotional processing by decreasing amygdala activity in the infant's brain, which involves the threat response for stress and fear.[643]

Quality of the bond between the mother and baby is what matters for infant mental health and development. The mother's more interconnected brain enables her to communicate and be better equipped for bonding with her offspring.[305] Synchronized biology and mimicked behaviors is necessary for a healthy bonding to develop between mother and child; this is referred to as biobehavioral synchrony.[192] Important parts of the social brain are coupled between the mother and child during synchronous and mimicked interactions.[193]

Atzil, Hendler, and Feldman (2011) investigated mother interactions with their infants for synchronous and mimicked behaviors, and the relation with mother intrusiveness indicating normative and high-risk parenting, depending on the intrusiveness levels. Brain and hormonal influences of mothers who interacted with their infant in a healthier way through mimicked behaviors or synchronization were found to be different from mothers who were more intrusive and displayed fewer synchronized behaviors.

Mothers who were more synchronized with their infant had more activation in the left nucleus accumbens (NAcc) than the right amygdala when viewing their infant's cues. The left (NAcc) and right amygdala activation levels for these mothers were correlated with emotion regulation and empathy. This activation of the (NAcc) indicates that synchronous mothers are motivated by rewarding experiences with their infant, rather than stress of the infant needing attention that is indicated by right amygdala activation. The left (NAcc) activation and amygdala activation also revealed better coordination of the brain between the different areas needed for understanding and interacting with her baby.

The right amygdala for this group was functionally more connected with the mirror system activations, indicating a better understanding of their infants, especially regarding fear and stress, and in turn responding with mimicked and synchronized behaviors. The oxytocin levels for these mothers were also highly related with the activation of the (NAcc) and right amygdala, expressing motivation stemming more from the bonding relationship with their infant and less from the distress need to attend to the infant. The synchronized mothers have more reward-related motivation for infant interaction that is characterized by a more cohesive neural activity with affiliative hormones.

On the other hand, mothers who were characterized as intrusive displayed more excessive mothering behaviors that were less synchronized with their infants. They had more activation in the right amygdala than the (NAcc) and had more association between the activations of the (NAcc) and right amygdala with pro-action areas. This indicates that their motivation was to address the fear and anxiety needs of the infants, and less so the enjoyment of bonding. It can also indicate less control of their behaviors and less mental understanding of their infant's needs. The intrusive mothers also had less unified coordination between neural networks and affiliative hormones needed for understanding and interacting with their newborn.

Taken together, the synchronized mother behaviors are associated with rewarding motives, while intrusive mother behaviors are from stress. These areas are necessary to understand for improved empathy of the infant's state, behaviors from prior experiences, and anticipation of parental behaviors. These can have future physical health, mental health, and developmental outcomes for the infant. To further illustrate the power of synchronized behaviors between mother and child for bonding, heart rhythms have also been found to synchronize to their behaviors.[197]

Females are much better at interpreting faces, especially if there is a lack of other informational cues about the face.[538] They also are able to process faces quicker by using more areas of their brain.[239] Females have a natural bias for attention to details, such as in faces and through exploratory face scanning abilities, which enables them to take in and interpret more emotional cues.[126, 268, 441] The activation in the fusiform face area of the female brain is responsible for processing facial features when viewing emotional faces and is an advantage with understanding her infant's needs.[402, 434] This superior face processing ability is one contributing factor to females having a better memory for faces.[259]

Facial perception abilities enable a superior ability for mothers to read the emotional state of their infant, which is aided by a better mirror neuron system than males. This enables females to recognize emotions and empathize with their infant through sight.[455] New mothers have larger pupil sizes when they see a newborn's negative facial expression compared with a positive one, because they sense their infant is in distress and need to take in more sensory information.[719] This makes sense because dilated pupils are a sign of arousal that the newborn needs attention, with the dilated pupils allowing for more light and sensory information for the new mother.[373]

New mothers have an automatic parental care activation system when viewing their infant's face.[181] Particular areas of her brain are activated when viewing her own infant's face, which differs from viewing the face of other infants. When viewing her own infant's face, she has more cerebral activation in the cortical and subcortical regions that are involved with maternal caregiving motivations.[558] Mothers of newborns who are considered highly sensitive have a visuo-perceptual strategy that enables them to process their own newborn's face differently than faces of other newborns, allowing them to better understand their newborn's facial cues. In turn, this creates a better-quality mother-and-newborn interaction and relationship.[452]

Face interpretation is not the only source of information that mothers gather from a baby. Females have more auditory connections for word processing.[157] They have a superior hearing ability that is strongly related to estrogen levels. Females have up to 20 times more estrogen, and it helps protect hearing loss as well as enhance hearing ability.[613, 620] Surely, the correlation between estrogen and hearing ability and protection is not coincidental, but rather evolutionary underpinnings at work. It just so happens that estrogen levels are higher and hearing ability is better when women are of reproductive age, but estrogen levels decrease during menopause when hearing their offspring becomes less pertinent. This heightened ability by mothers was not brought on by social forces but is observed early in childhood as girls recognizing and reacting to emotional facial expressions.[100]

DEPRESSION

Women are twice more likely than men to be diagnosed with depression.[178] Depression related to pregnancy increases the chances of developing fibromyalgia syndrome, which is characterized as more prevalent pain and more sensitivity to pain throughout the central nervous system.[34] Changes in the mother's brain continue even after birth, during the time period labeled as postpartum.[343] This depression vulnerability for women does not stop with pregnancy because postpartum depression can take place for a woman after giving birth, and affects 15-20% of mothers.[228, 396]

Major causes of postpartum depression are stress and worry.[215, 697] The added stress of a newborn baby can affect mothers who have lower levels of oxytocin with becoming more at risk for relationship termination with their partner by the time the newborn is a toddler.[644] Some behavioral signs of postpartum depression are decreased social interaction with others, less interest in the infant, and other interpersonal difficulties.[509]

Postpartum depression is a serious issue that not only affects the mother but the health and development of the child as well.[323, 679] Pregnancy, along with giving birth, can be stressful experiences for the mother. Women are more affected by the stress reaction chemical cortisol that directs energy to attend to a stressful event, which can impact the amygdala, hippocampus, and anterior cingulate cortex.[454, 473] In turn, this can negatively impact memory and emotional regulation, resulting in women becoming more vulnerable to mood disturbances and negative information due to sex hormonal changes in the brain.[16, 273]

Postpartum depression is often associated with lessened neural responses in the emotion regulation circuits. Females have been found to have larger orbitofrontal areas.[22] Regions such as orbitofrontal and temporal cortices can become less adaptive and capable of responding to the new and complex situations of motherhood. Negative emotional stimuli and child distress cues become less noticeable to the mother resulting in mother insensitivity.[343] However, intranasal injections of oxytocin can help a mother become more aware of her infant's facial cues.[508] Estrogen has been found to intermingle with oxytocin in the brain for better social understanding.[481]

Higher levels than normal of estrogen following pregnancy can cause depression as well, thus finding the right level of estrogen is important for understanding post-partum depression.[15] There is an equilibrium of estrogen—not too high and not too low—needed after a woman gives birth in order to reduce the onset of depression.[422] Often, antidepressants are not effective with treating depression during pregnancy and also during postpartum, which can also be dangerous to the child.[79, 144] Perhaps postpartum depression has more to do with physical brain changes and sex hormone changes that antidepressants do not adequately address.

CONCLUSION

The perpetuation of the human species is dependent upon women desiring to reproduce. One way this desire comes about is through the positive experiences a woman has when interacting with a baby. Pregnancy is a complicated life experience both during a pregnancy and after. The mother's body goes through many biological and psychological changes, often from the adjustment to motherhood. It is important to understand these changes for the health of both the mother and her offspring.

The father needs to understand that the mother physically and psychologically changes to direct her attention toward nurturing the new baby. The mother only has a certain amount of energy, which must now be greatly focused on the needs of the baby. The mother diverting less attention toward the father is not necessarily a result of relationship problems. On the contrary, her attention to the new baby ensures the genetics of both parents survive. The father needs to be understanding that the new mother can no longer give him the same amount of attention toward him and their relationship because the new baby becomes a top priority.

CHAPTER 22

THE FAMILY

CHILDREN & GENDER

As has been covered extensively throughout this book, males and females are born biologically different.[605] These dissimilarities impact gender differences regarding communication, behaviors, perception, skills, and interests to mention some of the areas stemming from biology.[654, 712] As reliably evidenced, these differences are found early on in life before long periods of exposure to societal influences and social learning.[25, 283] Additionally, as has been previously covered, hormonal levels can increase or decrease these differences.[278]

BOYS

Boys see the world differently than girls.[17, 441] Boys have their own particular interests.[654] They pay more attention to spatial aspects of objects they look at.[441] The role of testosterone should be recognized for boys in the family. Boys have much higher levels of prenatal androgen exposure than girls.[311] Postnatal androgen surges for boys occur from birth to three months, known as mini-puberty, which influences their masculine activity interests later in life.[500] The extreme high levels of testosterone are associated with aggression and competition, which leads to their hobbies and interests before social learning takes place.[54, 283, 376]

Testosterone levels are specifically related to status-seeking behaviors in males.[165] That explains why boys have interest in participating in competitive sports. Adolescence is a time for boys to figure out how to compete for resources and status by using their strength and spatial ability skills. However, when there is more than one boy growing up in the same household, this must be recognized and reigned in. Without parental oversight and control uncontrollable conflict can arise between the boys growing up as a means to show status dominance and gain resources, such as parental attention.

Often is the case that the older boy was accustomed to getting parental attention by themselves early in life. The parents need to explain to the older boy that a new baby boy also has needs for attention and should not be viewed as a competitor but as a family member. The play between the boys can be healthy, usually resulting with the younger one upping his abilities to compete with the older boys. However, too much competition and aggressing between male siblings can result in family turmoil. This sibling competition can extend later in life. If a man's partner is unfaithful with his brother, it will be more hurtful than if it was with a stranger, perhaps due to the competitiveness between the siblings.[354]

It should be recognized that boys are not born with the same language and social skills as girls. Testosterone levels are negatively associated with language development as early as one month of age.[365, 586] Even testosterone levels prior to birth negatively impact boys' language abilities later in life.[293] Parents need to understand that teaching and listening to a boy about problems is different from that of a girl.

The assertive communication style for boys does not lend to volunteering deep personal information.[97] Rather, parents should look for behavioral indications of what is occurring in a boy's life. A parent should inquire through conversation when engaging in an activity with a boy, rather than an uncomfortable private sit-down conversation.[99, 392] Engaging in an activity such as throwing a ball or fishing can help create that bond and trust for the boy to self-disclose more personal information.

GIRLS

Girls have different needs and abilities than boys in the family. Girls perceive the world around them differently.[17, 441] They divert more attention toward details and semantic associations of objects they look at, which helps with the development of their social skills.[441] Estradiol is associated with language development, which girls have much higher levels.[586] The way girls play emphasizes the value they place on socializing and relationships.[654] The lower levels of testosterone for girls influences their interests and play behaviors.[54, 283, 376]

The more advanced language ability and need for social connections with others, often brought on by the rising estrogen levels in girls, creates a different type of competition.[338] This can be less of a competitive sport and derive from attention accomplished through social status.[419, 606] For example, women who have recently started a relationship or have become engaged will use these things to increase their social status. As a result, females over generations have developed heightened social abilities, such as the ability to better understand social information derived from the faces of others, and this is evident from childhood.[100, 538]

One way females accomplish facial emotional recognition is by scanning more of the face for information and by having more activation in the fusiform face area of the brain when viewing emotional faces.[126, 402, 434] This enables females to process faces quicker.[239] The woman's menstrual cycle influences her relationships with others; the luteal phase prepares her for pregnancy but is also related with more important prosocial behaviors, thus creating the necessary bonds with others to have in the event of pregnancy.[634] Furthermore, the menstrual cycles of women who live together often synchronize. This indicates the importance that relationships have with women biologically. Thus, they are better able to understand the women that they live with, and other close relationships, through coordinated biological functioning.[201]

Female social status can come from friendships, relationships, and attention she receives from others. This is often accomplished through forming friend alliances to become popular. Those early relationships a girl forms with her sister(s) and mother are biologically innate from the need of her ancestors to form social ties for survival.[129]

Her appearance plays a much larger role in gaining attention and obtaining social status than it does with males.[687] As was covered previously in this book regarding evolutionary influences on gender communication, the female's ability to reproduce and have their offspring survive relied upon belonging to groups that assisted with their needs.[25] It was not possible for a woman to have a baby within her for nine months and still be able to hunt and gather resources, while also protecting herself and the unborn baby. After birth, it became just as essential to receive assistance from others in order to nurture the baby with adequate attention without needing to run around and forage for food. They accomplished this through communication with others that today translates to modern superior language abilities and nonverbal communication skills.[338] Spatial skills were less needed as a survival trait for females in primitive times, and are still often lacking, compared with boys starting at an early age.[392]

FAMILY UNIT

The old adage that it takes a village to raise a child may not be that far off. Having two parents in the home helps the development of the child more than having a child raised by a single parent.[355] There are different biological parenting activations for fathers and mothers that elicit caregiving behaviors.[545, 559] Sex hormone differences are responsible for brain synaptic sex differences that ultimately lead to parenting differences.[303] However, even though these biological reactions can activate automatically, each parent still has to make a conscious effort when exhibiting parenting behaviors.[181, 194]

As has been covered in a previous chapter, mothers undergo hormonal changes during and after pregnancy.[291, 473] Mothers experience oxytocin sensations when contractions occur during labor and also when nursing the baby.[559] Estrogen interacts with oxytocin in the brain for better social understanding of others.[481] Prolactin is a hormone that is associated with nurturing behaviors and has been found to increase at the beginning of pregnancy, after beginning interactions with the newborn, and also during nursing.[252] However, fathers can also undergo hormonal changes from interacting with their pregnant partner, or after birth when interacting with their lactating partner and new baby.[545] Prolactin levels of fathers has been related with mimicked and synchronized play behaviors with their infant.[246]

Both parents are capable of experiencing increased levels of oxytocin when physically interacting with their child. However, when mothers experience increased levels of oxytocin when interacting with their infants, they display more affectionate behaviors; fathers display more play stimulation touch, but not affectionate touch.[196] This is consistent with what has been previously addressed in an earlier chapter; males communicate more through movement than females.

Both parents with higher levels of oxytocin while interacting with their child in the first six months is associated with the child having higher levels of oxytocin and better social development.[195] Additionally, oxytocin enables neural responses in mothers that allow them to understand the emotional state from their baby's faces.[508] However, testosterone, which is found in much higher levels within males, has opposite effects of oxytocin.[129] For males, higher levels of testosterone are associated with mating behaviors, while lower levels are associated with caregiving.[545] Not surprisingly, males with children have lower levels of testosterone than childless males.[253]

The interactions of oxytocin and testosterone are different for mothers and fathers. For mothers, when testosterone levels are high, it is transformed to estradiol, which works coordinately with oxytocin, assisting with bonding between mother and infant.[69] There is an association with oxytocin and affection infant touch, but high levels of testosterone for fathers creates a negative association between oxytocin and affection touch.[244] However, closer proximity to the mother and more contact with the infant or distress of the infant can lead to decreased testosterone levels for fathers.[366, 584]

It has also been found that testosterone levels increase for adult males when competing in a competitive sport.[130] Stress can also be a major contributor to increasing male testosterone levels.[11] Therefore, reducing stress for a father can help reduce his testosterone levels and enhance caregiving behaviors. Oxytocin helps family members empathize with each other, comply with family norms, increase trust and cooperation, and protect against family threats.[145]

As has been extensively covered throughout this book, males and females have strengths and weaknesses that can complement one another during parenting.[194] For example, women have a superior mirror neuron system along with activation in particular areas of their brains responsible for maternal caregiver motivation when viewing their own baby, which enables better empathy, interpersonal sensitivity, and emotion recognition.[455, 558] Males have superior spatial and motion abilities starting at an early age.[392, 701] One can easily see how these different strengths can complement one another in parenting. These parental differences can help teach the child about each parent's area of strength. The child can also learn from observing parental behaviors. Therefore, instead of modeling after one parent who is their same biological sex, the child can develop more completely by learning the different strengths of each parent.

The multifaceted approach to raising a child does not end with the parents. The family is often dependent upon others for assistance. Extended family members and friends can also be of assistance. This can come in the form of babysitting or taking the child to activities when the parents are unavailable.

CLOTHING

The clothing we wear often reflects the biological survival strategies of our ancestors. The business suit on a man is attractive to women because it indicates ability to gather resources and gain power.[687] Instead of clubbing a wild game over the head and bringing it back for the family to eat, the suit indicates the ability to pay someone else to do the clubbing and cooking for him and his family at a restaurant. Lingerie on a woman helps to emphasize reproductive youth and health.[687] Men feel a greater positive sensation from sexual images than women, and also from a greater functional connection between the nucleus accumbens and the right lateral occipital cortex, which are areas of the brain responsible for visual rewards. Additionally, these specific areas are modulated by plasma testosterone levels.[388]

LATER YEARS

Males and females age differently, as do their brains. Grey matter volume of the caudate nucleus and putamen, areas of the brain responsible for body movements, decrease at a much faster pace as males age.[345] It has also been found that visuospatial processing deteriorates much more quickly for males as they age.[700]

Furthermore, older adults have smaller anterior hippocampi that is less active and hinders language ability related to memory. These deteriorating aging effects related to the anterior hippocampi worsen more for males.[475] Lower levels of testosterone found with older males are thought to play a role with decreased memory capabilities.[605] Hence, the language ability gap widens between males and females as they progress in age.

Sex hormones eventually move more in the direction of convergence in the later years with men having lower testosterone levels in older age, while women have lower estrogen levels after a certain age.[16, 543] Males experience a decrease in levels of testosterone at about age twenty, while females start to notice decreases in their estrogen levels around age forty.[480]

Females have superior hearing abilities that extend into adulthood.[592] Estrogen levels are related to hearing ability as well as sustaining hearing skill levels. As post-menopausal estrogen levels fall, hearing ability and protection do as well. However, women still have more protection from hearing loss that comes with age than men as a result of still having higher levels of estrogen.[613] Males decline on nearly every ability of subcortical auditory processing with age, while females decline on only a few.[360]

While females may have an upper hand with slower brain deterioration and better senses such as hearing, hormonal influences on emotions often play a larger role for females. Menopause is a highly hormonal time in a woman's life with decreases in estrogen levels leading to neural and cognitive declines, while increasing these low estrogen levels can help offset these effects.[276] As was previously covered in an earlier chapter, females are much more susceptible to depression.[283, 683]

Some precision can be drawn about the susceptibility for a woman to develop depression as she ages. Jung, Shin, and Kang (2015) found that the risk for depression increases after a woman begins menopause. Additionally, having more pregnancies and exogenous hormone use also increases depression risk for women. A factor that reduces the likelihood of women developing depression is having more years with the physical capability to reproduce, such as past age 35. Beginning menopause after age 52 can decrease depression onset compared with women beginning menopause at an age younger than 46.

CONCLUSION

Biologically, boys and girls start life differently, which influences later behaviors and decisions. These should be recognized to better understand sex differences in physical and psychological development. Assuming that there are not any gender developmental differences is reckless. Men and women also enter into their later years differently. Cognitively, males tend to deteriorate much more quickly. On the other hand, women tend to have more emotional issues, such as depression. The hormones of each sex tend to converge in the later years with male testosterone levels decreasing and female estrogen levels decreasing. Life seems to resemble a gender circle of life.

CHAPTER 23

LET'S EAT

GENDER FOOD PERCEPTIONS

Males and females differ in their abilities and sensitivities to tastes. In the presence of food stimuli, females have more brain activation.[105] A large portion of our recognition of taste comes from smell.[629] Females have a better ability to smell, such as perceiving smells at a much lower concentration, recognizing and labeling a particular smell, and recognizing when two smells are different.[627]

Females have a greater ability to distinguish different tastes.[227] Often, taste is more intense for females.[631] Females are also more sensitive regarding when they eat. Females are affected in the areas of digestive well-being, fullness, anxiety, and mood when not eating at their regularly scheduled time of day, while males have no such differences in these areas when they eat off schedule.[432] Thus, females are often more sensitive to food than males. This may give some insight into why males and females have differing preferences for food. Often, females tend to eat healthier foods, such as fruits and vegetables, and lower intakes of fat and salt.[29]

INSULA SEX DIFFERENCES AND FOOD

Sex biological differences contribute to eating differences. Males and females have different reasons for the food they choose to eat.[381] Brain activity sex differences related to food provides some explanation for these differences.[264] The insula plays a major role with brain activation from food cues.[261, 650] Females have a larger insula that also contains more gray matter and tends to have higher levels of activation to stimuli such as food when compared with males.[302, 341, 406, 578]

Females also have more activation in the insula, from emotional reward sensations, when viewing food cues that go beyond only satisfying nutritional needs.[389] Treatments that can lower these brain activity reactions to food cues can lead to successful weight loss.[314, 463] For example, naltrexone and bupropion have been found to help reduce food cravings and improve weight loss.[58] Systematic desensitization—meaning that exposure to the same stimuli lessens its effects—can help with viewing food images without consumption by making the subject become less physiologically reactive to food images.[218]

SEX HORMONE FOOD DIFFERENCES

Sex hormonal dissimilarities also contribute to gender food preference differences by interacting with neurotransmitters and the gastrointestinal system.[264] According to Hallam, Boswell, DeVito, and Kober (2016), different phases of the female menstrual cycle fluctuates food cravings. The beginning of the follicular phase is usually attributed as the start of menses (0-14 days) with low estrogen and progesterone levels. Estrogen levels increase as the follicular phase advances. This increase comes in preparation for ovulation during the mid-cycle (days 14-17) with estrogen increasing and ovulation occurring. After ovulation occurs the luteal phase (days 17-28) begins with low levels of estrogen. Low levels of estrogen in the luteal phase are associated with more food consumption.[33, 571]

During the mid-luteal phase, women were found to have their highest protein cravings and intake, but the late-luteal phase was found to have their largest appetite, highest cravings for sweets such as chocolate, and also salty flavors.[247]

Estrogen and progesterone have opposite effects on appetites during a woman's menstrual cycle. As estrogen increases, food cravings decrease and sexual desire increases; as progesterone increases, food cravings increase and sexual desire decreases.[571] Reducing food intake during the luteal phase each month over a span of several months will result in weight loss.[264]

EATING DISORDERS AND GENDER

Health professionals have recognized that eating disorders are more likely to occur with females.[596, 642] This cannot be contributed only to societal beauty images seen in popular culture. Females have been found at times to choose high calorie foods more than males.[426] Stress changes the eating dynamic with females eating higher calorie foods under stress, particularly sweet foods.[673]

Females are more vulnerable to eating disorders than males when their stress is interpersonally related, such as with social rejection.[115] This highlights an important link between psychological processes and eating, well beyond merely satisfying a physiological need for food. Along this line of thinking, a likely contributing factor to eating disorders with females is emotions. Females have been found to have more eating disorders and rumination; this is due to the emotional irregularity of focusing on negative experiences, problems, and worries, along with negative possible outcomes.[485]

CONCLUSION

Males and females differ in food cravings and intake for a variety of reasons. One reason is female sensitivity to smell and taste. There are also biological sex differences that help explain these food preference differences, such as the insula and sex hormones and their fluctuations. These differences need to be understood when treating eating disorders and maintaining a healthy body weight.

CHAPTER 24

WORKPLACE

GENDER PAY GAP

Diana Fleischman, evolutionary psychologist, writes, "If we keep saying differences in what men and women choose are because of sexism, nobody is going to end up happy. We're going to keep making laws to remedy what is actually the result of freedom." (Twitter: @sentientist 10-16-19). Information that is disseminated in gender communication classes comes into question regarding careers and the workplace.

It is popularly understood in our society that there is a gender pay gap. Major sources of this information are gender communication classes, which inform students women are paid about seventy-nine cents for every dollar a man is paid for the same job. A loosely related statistic is actually more of a guess than fact and comes from the U.S. Census Bureau stating in 2014 median annual income for males and females based only from data they were able to collect.[151]

A major issue with this popular statistic is that virtually nobody who cites the pay gap knows where exactly the statistic comes from. The instructors who teach this statistic in gender communication classes often do not properly state how that information is calculated or who calculated that statistic. Most likely all students who recite this statistic after hearing it cannot state the source or how it was calculated. The calculation is nearly impossible to perform.

What constitutes the same job? Doing the exact same thing every day at the same place or at any organization? Does location of the organization matter? Do years of experience matter, education, or do achievements enter into the calculation? Most likely the statistic is miscommunicated intentionally or unintentionally from the previously cited U.S. Census Bureau. The one popular statistic about the gender pay gap is based upon a broad assessment regarding the income from only the men and women that they received information from and does not take into account job types and differences.[324]

GENDER DISCRIMINATION

It is commonly taught and accepted implicitly that one's gender should be taken into consideration when making hiring decisions.[420] It becomes problematic when determining how many men working at one organization constitutes too many, or why a candidate should be at a disadvantage due to factors they cannot control, such as their gender.

BASIC BIOLOGICAL WORKPLACE INFLUENCES

"We are all biological creatures and our biology affects all aspects of our behavior, including our work." (p. 22).[474] The human brain has internal stable continuous activity derived from internal production that leads to exhibiting consistent behaviors, rather than merely reacting to the workplace environment.[76] Consistent with this position is what was previously covered in this book about communibiology, estimating that between 60-80% of a person's communication is influenced by their biology.[49]

Comparably, Nofal, Nicolaou, Symeonidou, and Shane (2018) estimate that a person's behaviors in the workplace are 20-60% influenced by biology. Their research article addresses genetics, physiology, and neuroscience to more completely understand how biology influences employee behaviors. Not only do these biological factors influence behaviors at work, they are present and influential long before one's first job.

Prenatal sex hormones influence career choices.[54] Often performance abilities are closely linked with interests and hobbies, such as boys having better object tracking abilities beginning as young as four months.[701] Males also pay more attention to spatial aspects of an object than females.[441] Toy preference differences between boys and girls have been found as early as nine months of age.[654] In infancy, testosterone plays a huge role with toy preferences for both boys and girls; more testosterone is associated with the desire to play with a train, and lower levels of testosterone are associated with a greater tendency to play with a doll.[376] Boys experience a mini-puberty from birth to three months of age in which they proceed through an androgen surge and then later in their life show more masculine play interests as a result.[500]

Girls with a condition known as congenital adrenal hyperplasia are exposed to high levels of androgens prior to birth, and tend to have the same play interests as boys who usually have around the same level of androgen exposure.[53]

With sex hormones having an early influence with play interests, it is no surprise that sex hormones also influence interests later in life as well, such as career choices. Sex hormones contribute to career interests and choices because the same sex hormone can have consistent results in these areas. For example, the male superior spatial abilities are evident in middle school science and technology classes that emphasize spatial abilities finding boys having better scores in these classes.[225] The middle school years are a time when people begin to consider career choices based upon their interests and successes.

Girls with congenital adrenal hyperplasia are exposed to high levels of androgen early in life and have similar interests and activities as boys that have about the same level of androgen exposure.[53] As adults, females with congenital adrenal hyperplasia choose to work in more male-dominant occupations.[220] Spatial gender performance differences from sex hormones show that larger differences in spatial performance occurs after age thirteen, when male and female sex hormone differences increase.[469]

Males and females even communicate differently regarding spatial tasks. Males are better with cardinal direction tasks (North, South, East,

West) and females do the same or sometimes even better with landmark spatial tasks (turn left at the third stoplight, then turn right when you see the big lavender sign).[441] Understanding these spatial gender differences is important in the workplace in order to have a clear understanding for all involved with visual aids used during presentations and development of new products, and to ensure everyone shows up to the correct place to meet.[723]

From a biological perspective it's important to understand why some professions and organizations have more females and others have more males. It is inadequate to recognize these differences and then look for explanations in society that may not even be related, and certainly are not from a single cause. Society contains too many different variables for one to isolate a single or only few social variables for gender career differences. That is why it is necessary to also consider biology as a factor.

BIOLOGICAL ENVIRONMENTAL RESPONSES

It is shortsighted to try to understand males and females as the same biologically and psychologically.[178] Males and females have different consistent psychophysiological responses to their environment.[1] For example, females pay more attention to, and are also more impacted by, rewards and punishment. This comes from women having more activation in the dorsal attention network, while having more suppression in the default mode network.[170] Perhaps these findings of female sensitivity to resource distribution is present early in life, with girls having a more egalitarian approaches than boys in childhood.[52]

Many sex differences in abilities can be attributed to evolutionary means.[25] Males and females tend to pursue different careers due to different academic abilities.[148] As was previously covered in this book, males tend to have superior spatial and object rotation abilities compared with females.[268, 392] This is evident early on in life and continues throughout adulthood involving various tasks of spatial and motion perceptions and reaction times.[608]

Males are less distracted by irrelevant information and respond more quickly after a mistake when performing spatial tasks.[185, 637] Males and females also use different areas of the brain when performing object rotation problems.[307, 368] This comes from structural brain differences and sex hormonal differences.[121, 522] As a person has higher levels of androgen exposure, male typical sex hormone, their spatial ability performance improves.[640]

Females born with congenital adrenal hyperplasia are exposed to much higher levels of androgens than most girls and also perform better on spatial tasks than most girls.[267] With these spatial and object rotation differences observed early on in life, but also related to sex hormonal differences, it is easy to infer how more males would consider careers that these skills play a large role.[37] Therefore, females are less likely to pursue careers in these fields.[713]

Sex hormones associated with superior performance with spatial abilities and object rotation, such as testosterone, tend to be much more present in males.[186] The huge surge of testosterone that males experience in their teens coincides at a time in their life when they are also considering colleges to attend, majors to specialize in, and career paths.[564] Some of the careers that emphasize spatial ability and object rotation are medicine, engineering, physics, mathematics, computer science, and architecture, to mention a few.[90]

The sports industry is another good example of how biology influences male and female career paths. It is more common for males to have roles of play-by-play broadcasting, and for females to conduct interviews with players and coaches. As has been addressed in a previous chapter citing Case and Oetama-Paul (2015), males have a tendency to use 'assertive' talk involving the topics and facts and less emphasis with relationships and emotions. Having a male do play-by-play is consistent with most males' natural communication style. Likewise, having a female conduct interviews with players and coaches is consistent with most females' communication style of 'affiliative' that builds a social connection with others and interjects some emotion during the communication. These female communication skills make interviews more interesting beyond only each person robotically stating facts.

LANGUAGE CAREER SKILLS

Having more connections to different areas of a female's brain enables better social skills.[305] Females have been consistently found to outperform males in language tasks and social awareness beginning at an early age, such as infancy.[514, 586] Females have more interest in semantics, such as with associating objects with letters.[441]

As young as one month of age, boys have much higher levels of testosterone, which hinders male language development observed later in life.[365] Furthermore, prior to birth, testosterone levels can hurt language abilities of boys years later.[293]

Females have much higher levels of estrogen on the other hand, which facilitates better language performance and social awareness.[26, 338, 481] This outperformance of language and social awareness by females continues into adulthood.[334, 338, 640] Females have more selective attention during language tasks.[637] Consistent with these findings, females have more interest in social interactions, as is indicated by their higher levels of physiological arousal.[536]

Another additional strength females have over males is attentiveness to detail, which can be inanimate objects in the environment, or recognizing and remembering details of conversations, or subtle behaviors and micro facial changes exhibited by other people.[97, 277, 358] An advantage that females have regarding detail recognition is a better ability to distinguish different hues of colors and describe different color tones.[5, 614] Not only do they have the ability to visually distinguish different colors, they pay more attention to, and have a larger vocabulary for, colors.[268]

Brain structural sex differences help shed light on language performance and social awareness differences.[345] Sex hormonal differences have also been found to contribute as well.[481] Estrogen has specifically been found to improve language performance.[338] Females have up to 20 times more estrogen than males.[620] Females also have a larger increase in oxytocin when communicating with others, which makes it more rewarding to have social interactions and increase their social cognition, along with their memory of such events.[419, 606] Oxytocin and estrogen interact in the brain for better social awareness of others.[481]

The large increase in estrogen for females during adolescent development coincides with the time in their life when they are making choices that determine their future career, such as what education and skills are necessary to acquire for their desired career path.[564] This influence from estrogen helps to explain why some professions have more females than males.[148]

GENDER COMMUNICATION APPLIED IN THE WORKPLACE

It becomes essential to recognize and understand gender communication differences for the betterment of each organization. This understanding helps shed light on why certain careers have more males and others have more females. To ignore these differences can be costly to organizations financially and productively, and impact employee physical and psychological health.

Employees do not work in isolation in organizations. Rather, organizations are comprised of employees who are interdependent and interconnected with each other creating the whole organization together.[569] The communication of one person can vastly influence other employees and in turn, the entire organization. One can easily understand from this perspective the necessity to have accurate communication amongst its employees, which includes gender communication.

Gender communication differences stemming from biology do not end as one leaves the house and arrives at work. Rather, gender communication is amplified in the workplace due to the nearly unlimited different possibilities in gender communication interactions, such as the number of individuals involved and ratios of male to female.

Case and Oetama-Paul (2015) clearly lay out biology and neuroscience research that supports the notion of gender communication differences. They point out the different goals language is used to achieve: males for power and objects, and females for personal relational goals. They also highlight that males and females have different strengths to offer, such as the ability to understand from completely different perspectives. Females have a natural ability for a person-centered approach to problem-solving along with awareness of details within the environment. As has been previously outlined, females have a more complicated approach to decision-making. This is due to more interconnectedness across hemispheres of their brain, which link together incoming factual data with memories, relational aspects with other people, and emotions, while using discourse with others to reach decisions. Females often use communication to maintain relationships and coalitions, and they also contribute more in teamwork, such as encouraging different viewpoints before acting on one they see as a solution.

Evidence of this is found with females displaying more mimicked and synchronized behaviors during conversations.[224, 682] A pro-social orientation to communication is associated with more mimicked and synchronized behavioral displays.[413] Mimicked and synchronized behaviors transform two individuals into one by activating the same cognitive circuits.[301] As a result, the relationship bond between the individuals is perceived to be stronger, more prosocial behaviors occur, a better understanding of each person increases, and more positive emotions are experienced.[451] This communication approach is vastly different from many organizations that take on a more masculine style focused on the end result. Comparatively, males use a more compartmentalized approach to decision-making, focusing on the incoming data while keeping emotions and relations with others essentially separated. Males are more competitive by challenging ideas to find the best one, depending more upon linear thinking and wanting to go with the plan they see as an immediate solution before exhausting perspectives from others. However, exhibiting too much or too little assertiveness is often perceived as an inferior communication style approach.

GENDER SPECIFIC ADVANTAGES AND DISADVANTAGES

Both male and female communication styles have their advantages and disadvantages regarding decision-making, leadership, problem-solving, and working relationships. Expanding upon what was previously covered in this chapter regarding workplace skills gender differences, organizations should recognize these gender differences when making policies along with creating workplace norms, roles, and working relationships.

The male communication style, which involves finding solutions for problems with less regard for relationships, can benefit efficiencies in some cases. It is not possible to please every employee with every decision and to even take the time to ask for employee input for every decision. Therefore, when a quick decision needs to be made without the need to consult a lot of other employees a male employee taking that role can be beneficial.

Additionally, organizations need to understand that overall males are better equipped biologically with spatial skills and object rotation due to higher levels of testosterone. This can help organizations realize that hiring more males for these types of job roles is not intentionally biased against women.

Women in organizations also bring their own superior unique skills, often involving social awareness, relationship interactions, and attention to details. When an organization has an interpersonal job task, a woman should be considered for that role. One example is meeting with clients to build a new working relationship and remembering the facial expressions of the clients during the meeting.

Women can also lead team tasks, in which collaboration is essential. They can help make everyone feel included and socialize with the rest of the team members. As was previously covered, women have superior non-verbal skills. Organizations would do well to value this in hiring decisions by having a woman in the position to interact with interviewees during the interview process to more completely understand the whole person beyond what they are saying.

Females also are superior with attention to details. As has been previously described in this book as a sixth sense, they have unique biological abilities to see things in ways beyond the biological perception limitations of men. This can help with designing the workplace, such as the aesthetics and colors of furniture, art work, and other parts of the workplace environment. Women can also provide valuable insight into setting company dress code policies through their attention to details.

CONCLUSION

It becomes essential to recognize the abilities that each of us have, and understand that social learning can only change these talents, skills, and limitations so far. This is essential to understand when deciding upon a career, along with understanding one's strengths and weaknesses once they begin employment. It is a combination of our natural strengths along with our interests that are strong influences with career choices to pursue.

CHAPTER 25

WHERE DO WE GO FROM HERE?

In order to effectively understand and treat mental and physical health, one must recognize the differences in males and females.[22] As has been covered extensively throughout this book, hormones play a vital role in all of our lives.[283] In particular, hormones can have sex-specific influences on how we communicate with others.[430] This has been found in brain synapses changes that lead to different reactions, emotions, and behaviors due to different hormone levels.[303] Therefore, we must have a better understanding about the individual effects regarding communication, perception, and relationships with others that occur from medically altering hormone levels.

HORMONE THERAPY

Medically changing a person's hormone levels can have drastic outcomes, not only for that individual, but also for future generations. Evolutionary changes in humans go well beyond simple natural selection to also include developmental tinkering, by-product evolution, and other genetic changes.[676] If one is still not convinced about the seriousness of hormone levels, which mates women find attractive to pursue fluctuates based upon their menstrual hormonal changes.[233] Therefore, artificially changing hormones can literally change the human gene pool.

Changes in hormones have ramifications for the physiology of the entire person.[605] In order for hormone therapy to be effective, one must first acknowledge the baseline hormone levels of each sex. To assume that males and females are basically the same—especially hormonally—is reckless and irresponsible. Males are born with 20-25 times more testosterone, while females are born with around 20 times more estrogen.[80, 127, 186, 481, 620] These sex hormones often have much different, and sometimes opposite, effects on an individual. These hormones should not be understood in isolation, but rather as affecting, and being affected by, other hormones of the entire body system.

WOMEN

The powerful influence of hormones for women is observed during major hormonal changes. These fluctuations impact their physiological abilities. Estrogen physically changes the hippocampus.[45] Women also have better listening abilities at the beginning of their menstrual cycles.[298] This is consistent with findings that estrogen helps listening abilities for women.[613]

Menopause and post-menopause also consist of major hormonal changes that can greatly impact a woman's communication. Menopause is associated with dramatic decreases in circulating levels of estrogen from the ovaries.[268] Women tend to experience decreasing levels of estrogen at around age forty.[480] Hormone therapy can help hormonal changes activated by menopause and also with postmenopausal women, such as depression and cognitive decline if implemented early enough.[243, 276]

Hormone therapy is much more effective for women when administered early in menopause, rather than during middle or late stages.[268] Menopausal hormone therapy has been associated with cognitive deterioration for women over age sixty-five. However, for women who are younger in the postmenopausal stage, cognitive decline was not found with hormone therapy. Therefore, the use of hormone therapy to increase estrogen levels for younger women just entering the postmenopausal phase can be helpful with emotional improvement, while not inversely impacting cognitive abilities.[237] Furthermore, an estrogen hormone therapy patch can help reduce depression that was brought on by menopause.[243]

Menopausal women experience skeletal muscle loss due to inadequate hormone functioning, but hormonal therapy with estrogen can help menopausal women with their muscle mass, bone density, verbal memory, and sexual problems.[38, 371, 493, 611, 622] Hormonal therapy for women involving estrogen has been found to help them remember words.[729] Hormonal therapy involving other hormones can also be beneficial; a single dose of testosterone to women has been found to improve spatial cognition.[521] However, there are added risks for women undergoing hormone therapy for problems associated with menopause, such as an increased chance of hearing loss or stroke, and developing cancer.[95, 136, 294]

Much caution should be made concerning the complicated and serious medical procedures involved with a biological male transitioning to female.[594] For a male transitioning to female through hormonal treatment, their resting-state functional connectivity differs from that of both men and women, indicating that sex hormone therapy can alter other parts of the body beyond hormones.[116, 458] It can be a complicated process, and much more needs to be understood and communicated about the post-treatment health risks.[133, 330] It is recommended for males who transition to female to be screened for breast cancer and also for meningioma.[544, 636]

MEN

Hormone levels play an intricate part in men's lives as well. Starting in young adulthood, as men age, their testosterone levels decrease.[622, 728] Males tend to experience decreasing testosterone levels at around age twenty.[480] Lower testosterone levels are associated with cognitive decline in aging men, and often hormone testosterone therapy cannot substantially improve cognitive abilities.[292]

Testosterone is related to muscle mass, strength, sexual desire, sexual activity, erectile functioning, and body composition. Hormone therapy can be beneficial in these areas for men.[605, 622, 657] Testosterone is also associated with sexual motivation for men, clearly highlighting another major problem with lower testosterone levels.[80, 127, 186] Hormone therapy using testosterone can be beneficial for treating men with sexual problems, along with improving mood while reducing depression.[123, 622]

However, changing a man's testosterone levels to solve sexual problems can alter which facial characteristics the man will desire in a woman.[60] Changing testosterone levels can also alter talkativeness and openness to experience.[11] Participating in hormone therapy can be a serious issue for men because it may lead to increased chances of cardiovascular disease, prostate cancer, luteinizing hormone suppression, and becoming overweight.[12, 466, 494] Testosterone hormone therapy is a complex issue that needs to be monitored through regular testing of hormone levels.[462]

Men have consistently been found to have better spatial abilities due to their higher levels of testosterone.[266] Lowering a man's testosterone levels can be effective for treating prostate cancer. However, spatial ability has been found to decline for men whose testosterone levels were lowered from hormone therapy.[108] Additionally, a higher risk for depression for both the man and his partner can also occur as an outcome of sexual problems.[162]

A man's perception and focus can also be altered by hormonal therapy. Pletzer, Petasis, and Cahill (2014) investigated the link between how testosterone and progesterone cause people to perceive details (local) versus the big picture (global) of a stimulus. Global focus of attention was related with testosterone and negatively with progesterone. Global focus of attention has been found to increase the ability to solve object rotation problems.[368]

Biological females transitioning to become male using testosterone treatment will experience muscle mass increases from the treatment.[199, 670] Often, biological females using testosterone treatment to transition to male will experience much higher levels of acne as a result.[497] This, in turn, can lead to a higher risk for depression and be a contributing factor for suicide.[456] Females transitioning to a male using testosterone treatment increase their risks for cardiovascular complications, central serous chorioretinopathy, polycythemia, and venous thromboembolism.[466, 513]

A major factor influencing the perceived success of using testosterone to transition from female to male is a more masculine voice.[691] This indicates that the hormone treatment influences more than their hormone levels. Additionally, the high levels of artificially-induced testosterone required to transition from a female to a male decreases gray matter in the Wernick's and Broca's areas of the brain that are responsible for language performance.[263]

PSYCHOLOGICAL EFFECTS

Whenever major medical treatments occur, one should not stop at the physical outcomes, but also consider the psychological effects. The body is a system, with the brain serving as a central hub to direct the rest of the body. Physical activations on the brain from medical procedures can have psychological effects that are sex-dependent.[56] Sex hormone changes can have psychological effects, such as with depression.[356] Furthermore, having major changes to one's body is often stressful. This induced stress can have effects of its own. Stress can lead to depression.[15, 206, 336] Additional risks that should be considered when hormone therapy is used to transition to another gender are cancer, thromboembolism, diabetes, cardiovascular disease, and suicide.[696]

CONCLUSION

Sex hormones play a powerful role with humans. Males and females have different levels of sex hormones. Therefore, these must be adequately understood before artificially changing hormone levels through medical procedures. The human body is a complicated system, and changing hormone levels can alter the entire system. We have yet to fully understand the long-term effects of hormone therapies done today. We can only speculate what medically-induced hormone changes today may affect years, decades, or even generations into the future.

CHAPTER 26

'10 LIFE LESSONS'

1. All communication starts in the brain.
2. There are brain structural sex differences in areas that are responsible for communication.
3. Sex hormones influence gender communication, sometimes even more so than brain structures or society.
4. Gender communication differences impact mental and physical health.
5. Gender communication differences are evident early in life. These differences change as sex hormones and other biologicals factors change throughout one's life.
6. Communication, behaviors, and emotional feelings all can be observed to gain insight into hormone levels.
7. Gender communication differences impact all areas of life, which include relationships, family, hobbies, parenting, workplace etc.
8. Artificially induced hormonal changes long-term effects are unknown.
9. Gender communication differences should be understood both when sending and receiving messages.
10. More knowledge on a topic is better than less.

REFERENCES

1. Abad-Tortosa, D., Costa, R., Alcreu-Crespo, A., Hidalgo, V., Salvador, A., & Serrano, M. (2019). Hormonal and emotional responses to competition using a dyadic approach: Basal testosterone predicts emotional state after a defeat. *Physiology & Behavior, 206,* 106-117.
2. Abbruzzese, L., Magnani, N., Robertson, I., & Mancuso, M. (2019). Age and gender differences in emotion recognition. *Frontiers in Psychology, 10* doi:10.3389/fpsyg.2019.02371
3. Abdouni, A., Vargiolu, R., & Zahouani, H. (2018). Impact of finger biophysical properties of touch gestures and tactile perception: Aging and gender effects. *Scientific Reports, 18*: 12605. DOI:10.1038/s41598-018-30677-2
4. Abouelenien, M., Burzo, M., Perez-Rosas, V., Mihalcea, R., Sun, H., & Zhao, B. (2019). Gender differences in multimodal contact-free deception detection. *Ieee Multimedia, 26,* 19-30.
5. Abramov, I., Gordon, J., Feldman, O., & Chavarga, A. (2012). Sex and vision II: Color appearance of monochromatic lights. *Biology of Sex Differences, 3,* 21-21.
6. Abreu, R., Leal, A., & Figueiredo, P. (2018). EEG-informed fMRI: A review of data analysis methods. *Frontiers in Human Neuroscience.* 12: 29. doi: 10.3389/fnhum.2018.00029
7. Adani, S., & Cepanec, M. (2019). Sex differences in early communication development: Behavioral and neurobiological indicators of more vulnerable communication system development in boys. *Croatian Medical Journal, 60,* 141-149.
8. Adenzato, M., Brambilla, M., Manenti, R., De Lucia, L., Trojano, L., Garofalo, S., Enrici, I., & Cotelli, M. (2017). Gender differences in cognitive Theory of Mind revealed by transcranial direct current stimulation on medial prefrontal cortex. *Scientific Reports, 7,* 41219.
9. Aerts, A., Mierlo, P., Hartsuiker, R., Santens, P., & Letter, M. (2015). Sex differences in neurophysiological activation patterns during phonological input processing: An influencing factor for normative data. *Arch Sex Behav, 44,* 2207-2218.
10. Afifi, W., & Burgoon, J. (2000). The impact of violations on uncertainty and the consequences for attractiveness. *Human Communication Research, 26,* 203-233.
11. Afrisham, R., Sadegh-Nejadi, S., SoliemaniFar, O., Kooti, W., Ashtary-Larky, D., Alamiri, F., Aberommad, M., Najjar-Asl, S., & Khaneh-Keshi, A. (2016). Salivary testosterone levels under psychological stress and its relationship with rumination and five personality traits in medical students. *Psychiatry Investigation, 13,* 637-643.
12. Aghazadeh, Y., Zirkin, B., & Papadopoulos, V. (2015). Pharmacological regulation of the cholesterol transport machinery in steroidogenic cells of the testis. *Vitamins and Hormones, 98,* 189-227.
13. Akman, O., Moshé, S., & Galanopoulou, A. (2014). Sex-specific consequences of early-life seizures. *Neurobiology of Disease, 72,* 153–166.
14. Aknin, L., & Human, L. (2015). Give a piece of you: Gifts that reflect givers promote closeness. *Journal of Experimental Social Psychology, 60,* 8-16.

15. Albert, P. (2015). Why is depression more prevalent in women? *Journal of Psychiatry & Neuroscience, 40,* 219-221.
16. Albert, K., & Newhouse, P. (2019). Estrogen, stress, and depression: Cognitive and biological interactions. *Annu. Rev. Clin. Psychol., 15,* 399-423.
17. Alexander, G. (2017). Sex Differences in Visual Pathways: A Comment on Handa and McGivern (2015). *Current Eye Research, 42,* 653-654.
18. Alexander, B., Barnes, H., Trimmer, E., Davidson, A., Ogola, B., Lindsey, S., &Mostany, R. (2018). Stable Density and Dynamics of Dendritic Spines of Cortical Neurons Across the Estrous Cycle While Expressing Differential Levels of Sensory-Evoked Plasticity. *Front. Mol. Neurosci., 1:* 83. doi: 10.3389/fnmol.2018.00083
19. Al-Shawaf, L., Conroy—Beam, D., Asao, K., & Buss, D. (2015). Human Emotions: An evolutionary psychological perspective. *Emotion Review, 8,* 173-186.
20. Alvergne, A., & Lummaa, V. (2010). Does the contraceptive pill alter mate choice in humans? *Trends in Ecology & Evolution, 25,* 171-179.
21. American Psychological Association (2019). https://www.apa.org/index.aspx
22. Anderson, N., Harenski, K., Harenski, C., Koenigs, M., Decety, J., Calhoun, V., & Kiehl, K. (2019). Machine learning of brain gray matter differentiates sex in a large forensic sample. *Human Brain Mapping, 40,* 1496-1506.
23. Annette, H., & Murachver, T. (2007). Gender preferential responses to speech. *Journal of Language and Social Psychology, 26,* 274-290.
24. Anto-Ocrah, M., Bazarian, J., Lewis, V., Jones, C., Jusko, T., & Van Wijngaarden, E. (2019). Risk of female sexual dysfunction following concussion in women of reproductive age. *Brain Injury, 33,* 1449-1459.
25. Archer, J. (2019). The reality and evolutionary significance of human psychological sex differences. *Biological Reviews*: DOI https://doi.org/10.1111/brv.12507
26. Archey, M., Goldey, K., Crockett, E., & Boyette-Davis, J. (2019). An investigation of the effects of testosterone and behavioral expressions of pain on Sex/Gender differences in pain perception. *Psychological Reports, 122,* 826-840.
27. Arcos-Romero, A., & Sierra, J. (2020). Factors associated with subjective orgasm experience in heterosexual relationships. *Journal of Sex & Marital Therapy, 46,* 314-329.
28. Arelin, K., Mueller, K., Barth, C., Rekkas, P., Kratzsch, J., Burmann, I., Villringer, A., & Sacher, J. (2015). Progesterone mediates brain functional connectivity changes during the menstrual cycle–a pilot resting-state MRI study. *Frontiers in Neuroscience, 9 (44),* 1-11.
29. Arganini, C., Turrini, A., Saba, A., Virgili, F., & Comitato, R. (2012). "Gender differences in food choice and dietary intake in modern western societies," in *Public Health—Social and Behavioral Health,* ed. J. Maddock (Rijeka: InTech OpenAccessPublisher), 85–102.
30. Arnocky, S., Carre, J., Bird, B., Moreau, B., Vaillancourt, T., Ortiz, T., & Marley, N. (2018). The facial width-to-height ratio predicts sex drive, sociosexuality, and intended infidelity. *Arch Sex Behav, 47,* 1375-1385.
31. Arnold, A. (2017). A general theory of sexual differentiation. *Journal of Neuroscience Research, 95,* 291-300.
32. Arnold, A., Reue, K., Eghbali, M., Vilain, E., Chen, X., Ghahramani, N., Itoh, Y., Li, J., Link, J., Ngun, T., & Williams-Burris, S. (2016). The importance of having two X chromosomes. *Philos Trans R Soc Lond B Biol Sci, 371:* 20150113. doi: 10.1098/rstb.2015.0113.
33. Asarian, L., & Geary, N. (2013). Sex differences in the physiology of eating. *Am J Physiol Regul Integr Comp Physiol., 305,* R1215–R1267.
34. Atasever, M., Kalem, M., Sonmez, C., Seval, M., Yuce, T., Aker, S., Koc, A., & Genc, H. (2016). Lower serotonin level and higher rate of fibromyalgia syndrome with advancing pregnancy. *The Journal of Maternal-Fetal & Neonatal Medicine, 30,* 2204-2211.
35. Attaman, J., Toth, T., Furtado, J., Campos, H., Hauser, R., & Chavarro, J. (2012). Dietary fat and semen quality among men attending a fertility clinic. *Human Reproduction (Oxford, England), 27(5),* 1466-1474.
36. Atzil, S., Hendler, T., & Feldman, R. (2011). Specifying the neurobiological basis of human attachment: Brain, hormones, and behavior in synchronous and intrusive mothers. *Neuropsychopharmacology: Official Publication of the American College of Neuropsychopharmacology, 36,* 2603-2615.

37. Auyeung, B., Knickmeyer, R., Ashwin, E., Taylor, K., Hackett, G., & Baron-Cohen, S. (2012). Effects of fetal testosterone on visuospatial ability. *Arch Sex Behav, 41,* 571-581.
38. Baber, R., Panay, N., Fenton, A., & IMS Writing Group. (2016). 2016 IMS recommendations on women's midlife health and menopause hormone therapy. *Climacteric, 19,* 109-150.
39. Baker, M., & Cornelson, K. (2018). Gender-based occupational segregation and sex differences in sensory, motor, and spatial aptitudes. *Demography, 55,* 1749-1775.
40. Bale, T., & Epperson, C. (2015). Sex differences and stress across the lifespan. *Nature Neuroscience, 18,* 1413-1420.
41. Balon, R. (2015). Is infidelity biologically determined? *European Psychiatry, 30,* 72.
42. Bangasser, D., Eck, S., Telenson, A., & Salvatore, M. (2018). Sex differences in stress regulation of arousal and cognition. *Physiology & Behavior, 187,* 42-50.
43. Barjaktarovic, M., Korevaar, T., Jaddoe, V., Rijke, Y., Visser, T., Peeters, R., & Steegers, E. (2016). Human chorionic gonadotropin (hCG) concentrations during the late-first trimester are associated with fetal growth in a fetal sex-specific manner. *Eur J Epidemiol, 32,* 135-144.
44. Barnacle, G., Tsivillis, D., Schaefer, A., & Talmi, D. (2017). Local context influences memory for emotional stimuli but not electrophysiological markers of emotion-deception attention. *Psychophysiology, 55,* 1-14.
45. Barth, C., Steele, C., Mueller, K., Rekkas, V., Arélin, K., Pampel, A., et al. (2016). In-vivo dynamics of the human hippocampus across the menstrual cycle. *Scientific Reports, 6(1),* 32833. doi:10.1038/srep32833.
46. Barth, C., Villringer, A., & Sacher, J. (2015). Sex hormones affect neurotransmitters and shape the adult female brain during hormonal transition periods. *Frontiers in Neuroscience, 9,* 37.
47. Baucom, B., Dickenson, J., Atkins, D., Baucom, D., Fischer, M., Weusthoff, S., Hahlweg, K., & Zimmermann, T. (2015). The interpersonal process model of demand/withdraw behavior. *Journal of Family Psychology: JFP: Journal of the Division of Family Psychology of the American Psychological Association (Division 43), 29,* 80-90.
48. Beatty, M., & McCroskey, J. (1998). Interpersonal communication as temperamental expression. In J. McCroskey, J. Daly, M. Martin, & M. Beatty (Eds.), *Personality and communication: Trait perspectives* (pp. 41-67). NewYork: Hampton Press.
49. Beatty, M., & McCroskey, J. (2000). A few comments about communibiology and the nature/nurture question. *Communication education, 49,* 25-28, DOI: 0.1080/03634520009379189
50. Beatty, M., & McCroskey, J. (with Valencic, K.). (2001). *The biology of communication: A communibiological perspective.* Cresskill, NJ: Hampton Press.
51. Beatty, M., McCroskey, J., & Heisel, A. (1998). Communication apprehension as temperamental expression: A communibiological paradigm. *Communication Monographs, 65,* 197-219.
52. Benenson, J., Durosky, A., Nguyen, J., Crawford, A., Gauthier, E., & Dubé, É. (2019). Gender differences in egalitarian behavior and attitudes in early childhood. *Developmental Science e12750* https://doi.org/10.1111/desc.12750
53. Berenbaum, S. (2018). Beyond pink and blue: The complexity of early androgen effects on gender development. *Child Development Perspectives, 12,* 58-64.
54. Berenbaum, S., & Beltz, A. (2016). How early hormones shape gender development. *Current Opinion in Behavioral Sciences, 7,* 53-60.
55. Berger, C., & Calabrese, R. (1975). Some explorations in initial interaction and beyond: Toward a developmental theory of interpersonal communication. *Human Communication Research, 1,* 99-112.
56. Bertossi, E., Peccenini, L., Solmi, A., Avanti, A., & Ciaramelli, E. (2017). Transcranial direct current stimulation of the medial prefrontal cortex dampens mind-wandering in men. *Scientific Reports, 7(1),* 16962-10. doi:10.1038/s41598-017-17267-4.
57. Bhat, A., Hoffman, M., Trost, S., Culotta, M., Eilbott, J., Tsuzuki, D., & Pelphrey, K. (2017). Cortical activation during action observation, action execution, and interpersonal synchrony in adults: A functional near-infrared spectroscopy (fNIRS) study. *Frontiers in Human Neuroscience, 11,* 431-431. doi:10.3389/fnhum.2017.00431
58. Billes, S., Sinnayah, P., & Cowley, M. (2014). Naltrexone/bupropion for obesity: An investigational combination pharmacotherapy for weight loss. *Pharmacological Research, 84,* 1–11.

59. BioSante Pharmaceuticals. (2011). BioSante Pharmaceuticals announces results from LibiGel efficacy trials. *Women's Health Weekly, 42.*
60. Bird, B., Welling, L., Ortiz, T., Moreau, B., Hansen, S., Emond, M., Goldfarb, B., Bonin, P., & Carré, J. (2016). Effects of exogenous testosterone and mating context on men's preferences for female facial femininity. *Hormones and Behavior, 85,* 76-85.
61. Birnbaum, G., & Finkel, E. (2015). The magnetism that holds us together: Sexuality and relationship maintenance across relationship development. *Current Opinion in Psychology, 1,* 29-33. doi:10.1016/j.copsyc.2014.11.009
62. Bitan, T., Lifshitz, A., Breznitz, Z., & Booth, J. (2010). Bidirectional connectivity between hemispheres occurs at multiple levels in language processing but depends on sex. *The Journal of Neuroscience, 30,* 11576-11585.
63. Blackburn, K., Brody, N., & LeFebvre, L. (2014). The I's, we's, and She/He's of breakups public and private pronoun usage in relationship dissolution accounts. *Journal of Language and Social Psychology, 33,* 202-213.
64. Blake, R., & Mouton, J. (1964). *The managerial grid: Key orientations for achieving production through people.* Houston, Tex: Gulf Pub. Co.
65. Blum, K., Chen, L., Giordano, J., Borsten, J., Chen, T., Hauser, M., Simpatico, T., Femino, J., Braverman, E., & Barh, D. (2012). The addictive brain: All roads lead to dopamine. *Journal of Psychoactive Drugs, 44,* 134–143.
66. Bodie, G., Cannava, K., Vickery, A., & Jones, S. (2016). Patterns of nonverbal adaptation in supportive interactions. *Communication Studies, 67,* 3-19.
67. Bogaert, A., Visser, B., & Pozzebon, J. (2015). Gender differences in object of desire self-consciousness sexual fantasies. *Archives of Sexual Behavior, 44,* 2299-2310.
68. Borráz-León, J., Cerda-Molina, A., & Mayagoitia-Novales, L. (2017). Testosterone level changes after perceiving the body odour of a possible rival in human males: The role of facial symmetry. *Behaviour, 154,* 677-691.
69. Bos, P., Hermans, E., Montoya, E., Ramsey, N., & Van Honk, J. (2010). Testosterone administration modulates neural responses to crying infants in young females. *Psychoneuroendocrinology, 35,* 114-121.
70. Boucher, O., Rouleau, I., Lassonde, M., Lepore, F., Bouthillier, A., & Nguyen, D. (2015). Social information processing following resection of the insular cortex. *Neuropsychologia, 71,* 1–10.
71. Boucher, O., Turgeon, C., Champoux, S., Menard, L., Rouleau, I., Lassonde, M., Lepore, F., & Nguyen, D. (2015). Hyperacusis following unilateral damage to the insular cortex: A three-case report. *Brain Res., 1606,* 102–112.
72. Boudesseul, J., Gildersleeve, K., Haselton, M., & Bègue, L. (2019). Do women expose themselves to more health-related risks in certain phases of the menstrual cycle? A meta-analytic review. *Neuroscience and Biobehavioral Reviews, 107,* 505-524.
73. Bowers, J., Perez-Pouchoulen, M., Edwards, N., & McCarthy, M. (2013). Foxp2 mediates sex differences in ultrasonic vocalization by rat pups and directs order of maternal retrieval. *The Journal of Neuroscience: The Official Journal of the Society for Neuroscience, 33,* 3276-3283.
74. Boyacioglu, I., Akfirat, S., & Yılmaz, A. (2017). Gender differences in emotional experiences across childhood, romantic relationship, and self-defining memories. *Journal of Cognitive Psychology, 29,* 137-150.
75. Bozzolino, C., Vaglio, S., Amante, E., Alladio, E., Gerace, E., Salomone, A., & Vincenti, M. (2019). Individual and cyclic estrogenic profile in women: Structure and variability of the data. *Steroids, 150,* 108432. doi:10.1016/j.steroids.2019.108432
76. Braeutigam, S., Lee, N., & Senior, C. (2019). A Role for Endogenous Brain States in Organizational Research: Moving Toward a Dynamic View of Cognitive Processes. *Organizational Research Methods, 22,* 332-353.
77. Brecht, M., Lenschow, C., & Rao, R. P. (2018). Socio-sexual processing in cortical circuits. *Current Opinion in Neurobiology, 52,* 1-9.
78. Broad, K., Rocha-Ferreira, E., & Hristova, M. (2016). Placental, matrilineal, and epigenetic mechanisms promoting environmentally adaptive development of the mammalian brain. *Neural Plasticity, 2016,* 6827135-8. doi:10.1155/2016/6827135.

79. Brown, H., Hussain-Shamsy, N., Lunsky, Y., Dennis, C., & Vigod, S. (2017). The association between antenatal exposure to selective serotonin reuptake inhibitors and autism: A systematic review and meta-analysis. The *Journal of Clinical Psychiatry, 78,* e48-e58. https://doi.org/10.4088/JCP.15r10194.
80. Brzeziński, P., & Martini, L. (2018). Cystic acne in women who present excess of testosterone because of social reasons and not of pathological diseases. An attempt to treat this malaise by natural remedies and the discovery of a suggestive equation to solve to know how many days of treatment are required for remission. *Nasza Dermatologia Online, 9(e),* e2-e2.
81. Burgess Moser, M., Johnson, S., Dalgleish, T., Lafontaine, M., Wiebe, S., & Tasca, G. (2016). Changes in relationship-specific attachment in emotionally focused couple therapy. *Journal of Marital and Family Therapy, 42,* 231-245.
82. Burgoon, J. (1978). A communication model of personal space violations: Explication and an initial test. *Human Communication Research, 4,* 129-142.
83. Burgoon, J., Guerrero, L., & Floyd, K. (2009). (1st Ed.) *Nonverbal Communication.* Pearson.
84. Burkett, J., & Young, L. (2012). The behavioral, anatomical and pharmacological parallels between social attachment, love and addiction. *Psychopharmacology, 224,* 1-26.
85. Burleson, M., Trevathan, W., & Todd, M. (2007). In the mood for love or vice-versa? Exploring the relations among sexual activity, physical affection, affect, and stress in the daily lives of mid-aged women. *Archives of Sexual Behavior, 36,* 357-368.
86. Burman, D., Minas, T., Bolger, D., & Booth, J. (2013). Age, sex, and verbal abilities affect location of linguistic connectivity in ventral visual pathway. *Brain & Language, 124,* 184-193.
87. Bushdid, C., Magnasco, M., Vosshall, L., & Keller, A. (2014). Humans can discriminate more than 1 trillion olfactory stimuli. *Science, 343(6177),* 1370-1372.
88. Butler, S., Smith, N., Collazo, E., Caltabiano, L., & Herbenick, D. (2015). Pubic hair preferences, reasons for removal, and associated genital symptoms: Comparisons between men and women. *The Journal of Sexual Medicine, 12,* 48-58.
89. Cahill, L., & Aswad, D. (2015). Sex influences on the brain: An issue whose time has come. *Neuron, 88,* 1084-1085.
90. Camasso, M., Jagannathan, R., & Bzdak, M. (2019). Private sector inputs into public school preparation for careers in health care and STEM: An examination of cognitive skills development in the Johnson & Johnson Bridge-to-Employment program in the United States. *International Journal of educational Research, 95,* 118-130.
91. Campbell, M., Toth, A., & Brady, N. (2018). Illuminating sex differences in mental rotation using pupillometry. *Biological Psychology, 138,* 19-26.
92. Canan, F., Karaca, S., DÜZGÜN, M., Erdem, A., KARAÇAYLI, E., Topan, N. et al. (2017). The relationship between second-to-fourth digit (2D:4D) ratios and problematic and pathological internet use among Turkish university students. *Journal of Behavioral Addictions, 6,* 30-41.
93. Cappelletti, M., & Wallen, K. (2016). Increasing women's sexual desire: The comparative effectiveness of estrogens and androgens. *Hormones and Behavior, 78,* 178-193.
94. Carpenter, B., Zhou, W., Madaj, Z., DeWitt, A., Ross, J., Grønbæk, K. et al. (2018). Mother-child transmission of epigenetic information by tunable polymorphic imprinting. *Proceedings of the National Academy of Sciences of the United States of America, 115(51),* E11970-E11977. doi:10.1073/pnas.1815005115
95. Carrasquilla, G., Frumento, P., Berglund, A., Borgfeldt, C., Bottai, M., et al. (2017). Postmenopausal hormone therapy and risk of stroke: A pooled analysis of data from population-based cohort studies. *PLoS Medicine, 14(11)* e1002445.
96. Casamento-Moran, A., Hunter, S., Chen, Y., Kwon, M., Fox, E., Yacoubi, B., & Christou, E. (2017). Sex differences in spatial accuracy relate to the neural activation of antagonistic muscles in young adults. *Experimental Brain Research, 235,* 2425-2436.
97. Case, S., & Oetama-Paul, A. (2015). Brain biology and gender discourse. *Applied Psychology: An international Review, 64,* 338-378.

98. Casler, L. (1965). The effects of extra tactile stimulation on a group of institutionalized infants. *Genetic Psychology Monographs, 71,* 137-175.
99. Casto, K., & Edwards, D. (2016). Testosterone, cortisol, and human competition. *Hormones and Behavior, 82,* 21-37.
100. Cattaneo, L., Veroni, V., Boria, S., Tassinari, G., & Turella, L. (2018). Sex differences in affective facial reactions are present in childhood. *Front. Integr. Neurosci. 12*:19. doi: 10.3389/fnint.2018.00019
101. Cengiz, B., Vuralli, D., Zinnuroglu, M., Bayer, G., Golmohammadzadeh, H., Gunendi, Z., & Turgut. (2018). Analysis of mirror neuron system activation during action observation alone and action observation with motor imagery tasks. *Experimental Brain Research, 236,* 497-503.
102. Cerniglia, L., Bartolomeo, L., Capobianco, Lo Russo, M., Festucci, F. et al. (2019). Intersections and divergences between empathizing and mentalizing: Development, recent advancements by neuroimaging and the future of animal modeling. *Frontiers in Behavioral Neuroscience, 13* oi:10.3389/fnbeh.2019.00212
103. Cetin, I., Berti, C., & Calabrese, S. (2010). Role of micronutrients in the periconceptional period. *Human Reproduction Update, 16,* 80-95.
104. Chan, C., & Ye, K. (2017). Sex differences in brain-derived neurotrophic factor signaling and functions. *Journal of Neuroscience Research, 95,* 328-335.
105. Chao, A., Loughead, J., Bakizada, Z., Hopkins, C., Gelliebter, A., Gur, R., & Wadden, T. (2017). Sex/ gender differences in neural correlates of food stimuli: A systematic review of functional neuroimaging studies. *Obesity Reviews, 18,* 687-699.
106. Chekroud, A., Ward, E., Rosenberg, M., & Holmes, A. (2016). Patterns in the human brain mosaic discriminate males from females. *Proc Natl Acad Sci U S A 113*:E1968.
107. Chen, P., & Hong, W. (2018). Neural circuit mechanisms of social behavior. *Neuron, 98,* 16-30.
108. Cherner, M., Aubin, S., & Higano, C. (2009). Cognitive and mood changes in men undergoing intermittent combined androgen blockade for non-metastatic prostate cancer. *Psycho-Oncology, 18,* 237-247.
109. Cherry, J., & Baum, M. (2020). Sex differences in main olfactory system pathways involved in psychosexual function. *Genes, Brain and Behavior, 19(2),* e12618-n/a. doi:10.1111/gbb.12618
110. Chivers, M., Rieger, G., Latty, E., & Bailey, J. (2004). A sex difference in the specificity of sexual arousal. *Psychological Science, 15,* 736–744.
111. Chivers, M., Seto, M., & Blanchard, R. (2007). Gender and sexual orientation differences in sexual response to sexual activities versus gender of actors in sexual films. *Journal of Personality and Social Psychology, 93,* 1108–1121.
112. Christian, J. (1963). The pathology of overpopulation. *Military Medicine, 128,* 571-603.
113. Christov-Moore, L., Simpson, E., Coudé, G., Grigaityte, K., Iacoboni, M., & Ferrari, P. (2014). Empathy: Gender effects in brain and behavior. *Neuroscience and Biobehavioral Reviews, 46,* 604-627.
114. Chung, K., Peisen, F., Kogler, L., Radke, S., Turetsky, B., Freiherr, J., & Derntl, B. (2016). The influence of menstrual cycle and androstadienone on female stress reactions: An fMRI study. *Frontiers in Human Neuroscience, 10*: 10.3389/fnhum.2016.00044.
115. Clauss, N., & Byrd-Craven, J. (2019). Exposure to a sex-specific stressor mitigates sex differences in stress-induced eating. *Physiology & Behavior, 202,* 26-35.
116. Clemens, B., Junger, J., Pauly, K., Neulen, J., Neuschaefer-Rube, C., et al. (2017). Male-to-female gender dysphoria: Gender-specific differences in resting-state networks. *Brain and Behavior, 7(5),* e00691-n/a. doi:10.1002/brb3.69.
117. Clifford, C., Vennum, A., Busk, M., & Fincham, F. (2017). Testing the impact of sliding versus deciding in cyclical and noncyclical relationships: Sliding and deciding in relationships. *Personal Relationships, 24,* 223-238.
118. Cloutier, J., Heatherton, T., Whalen, P., & Kelley, W. (2008). Are attractive people rewarding? Sex differences in the neural substrates of facial attractiveness. *Journal of Cognitive Neuroscience, 20,* 941-951.

119. Colley, S. (2017). Judging on their looks: Understanding pre-service social studies teachers' conceptions of historical agency and gender. *The Journal of Social Studies Research, 41,* 155-166.
120. Colzato, L., Pratt, J., & Hommel, B. (2012). Estrogen modulates inhibition of return in healthy human females. *Neuropsychologia, 50,* 98-103.
121. Constantinescu, M., Moore, D., Johnson, S., & Hines, M. (2017). Early contributions to infants' mental rotation abilities. *Developmental Science, 21,* 1-15.
122. Cooke, P., Nanjappa, M., Ko, C., Prins, G., & Hess, R. (2017). Estrogens in male physiology. *Physiol Rev, 97,* 995-1043.
123. Corona, G., Rastrelli, G., Morgentaler, A., Sforza, A., Mannucci, E., & Maggi, M. (2017). Meta-analysis of results of testosterone therapy on sexual function based on international index of erectile function scores. *European Urology, 72,* 1000-1011.
124. Costumero, V., Barro´s-Loscertales, A., Bustamante, J., Fuentes, P., Rosell-Negre, P., Ventura-Campos, N., & Avita, C. (2015). A new window to understanding individual differences in reward sensitivity from attentional networks. *Brain Struct Funct, 220,* 1807-1821.
125. Coutinho, J., Oliveira-Silva, P., Fernandes, E., Goncalves, O., Correia, D., Mc-Govern, K., & Tschacher, W. (2018). Psychophysiological synchrony during verbal interaction in romantic relationships. *Family Process, X,* 1-18.
126. Coutrot, A., Binetti, N., Harrison, C., Mareschal, I., & Johnston, A. (2016). Face exploration dynamics differentiate men and women. *Journal of Vision, 16 (14),* 1-19.
127. Cox, A. (2016). Testosterone solution improves sexual drive in hypogonadism. *Endocrine Today, 14(4),* 24.
128. Creeth, H., McNamara, G., Tunster, S., Boque-Sastre, R., Allen, B., Sumption, et al. (2018). Maternal care boosted by paternal imprinting in mammals. *PLoS Biology, 16(7),* e2006599. doi:10.1371/journal.pbio.2006599
129. Crespi, B. (2016). Oxytocin, testosterone, and human social cognition. *Biol. Rev., 91,* 390-408.
130. Crewther, B., Kilduff, L., & Cook, C. (2014). Trained and untrained males show reliable salivary testosterone responses to a physical stimulus, but not a psychological stimulus. *Journal of Endocrinological Investigation, 37(11),* 1065.
131. Cuff, B., Brown, S., Taylor, L., & Howat, D. (2016). Empathy: A review of the concept. *Emotion Review, 8,* 144-153.
132. Cummins, R. (2017). Excitation transfer theory. In The *International Encyclopedia of Media Effects* (pp. 1–9). Hoboken, NJ, USA: Wiley. https://doi.org/10.1002/9781118783764.wbieme0080
133. Cunha, F., Domenice, S., Câmara, V., Sircili, M., Gooren, L., Mendonça, B., & Costa, E. (2015). Diagnosis of prolactinoma in two male-to-female transsexual subjects following high-dose cross-sex hormone therapy. *Andrologia, 47,* 680-684.
134. Cunningham, G., Stephens-Shields, A., Rosen, R., Wang, C., Ellenberg, S., Matsumoto, A., Bhasin, S., Molitch, M., Farrar, J., Celta, D., Barret-Connor, E., Cauley, J., Cifelli, D., Crandall, J., Ensrud, K., Fluharty, L., Gill, T., Lewis, C., Pahor, M., Resnick, S., Storer, T., Swerdloff, R., Anton, S., Basaria, S., Diem, S., Tabatabaie, V., Hou, X, & Snyder, P. (2015). Association of sex hormones with sexual function, vitality, and physical function of symptomatic older men with low testosterone levels at baseline in the testosterone trials. *The Journal of Clinical Endocrinology and Metabolism, 100,* 1146-1155.
135. Cupini, L., Corbelli, I., & Sarchelli, P. (2020). Menstrual migraine: What it is and does it matter? *Journal of Neurology,* doi:10.1007/s00415-020-09726-2
136. Curhan, S., Eliassen, A., Eavey, R., Wang, M., Lin, B., & Curhan, G. (2017). Menopause and postmenopausal hormone therapy and risk of hearing loss. *Menopause (New York, N.Y.), 24(9),* 1049.
137. Dainton, M., Goodboy, A. Borzea, D., & Goldman, Z. (2017). The dyadic effects of relationship uncertainty on negative relational maintenance. *Communication Reports, 30,* 170-181.
138. Danneskiold-Samsoe, B., Bartels, E., Bulow, P., & Lund, H. (2009). Isokinetic and isometric muscle strength in a healthy population with special reference to age and gender. *Acta Physiologica, 197(s673),* 1-68.
139. Darwin, C. (1872). *The expression of the emotions in man and animals.* United Kingdom: John Murray.

140. Dawson, S., & Chivers, M. (2016). Gender-specificity of initial and controlled visual attention to sexual stimuli in androphilic women and gynephilic men. *PloS One, 11(4)*, e0152785. doi:10.1371/journal.pone.0152785
141. Dawson, S., Fretz, K., & Chivers, M. (2017). Visual attention patterns of women with androphilic and gynephilic sexual attractions. *Archives of Sexual Behavior, 46,* 141-153.
142. Dean III, D., Planalp, E., Wooten, W., Schmidt, C., Kecskemeti, S., Frye, C., Schmidt, N., Goldsmith, H., Alexander, A., & Davidson, R. (2018). Investigation of brain structure in the 1-month infant. *Brain Structure and Function, 223,* 1953-1970.
143. Decety, J. (2015). The neural pathways, development and function of empathy. *Curr. Opin. Behav. Sci., 3,* 1-6.
144. De Crescenzo, F., Perelli, F., Armando, M., & Vicari, S. (2014). Selective serotonin reuptake inhibitors (SSRIs) for post-partum depression (PPD): A systematic review of randomized clinical trials. *Journal of Affective Disorders 152,* 39–44.
145. De Dreu, C., & Kret, M. (2016). Oxytocin conditions intergroup relations through upregulated in-group empathy, cooperation, conformity, and defense. *Biological Psychiatry, 79,* 165-173.
146. de Groot, J., Smeets, M., Kaldewaij, A., Duijndam, M., & Semin, G. (2012). Chemosignals communicate human emotions. *Psychological Science, 23,* 1417-1424.
147. de Groot, J., Smeets, M., Rowson, M., Bulsing, P., Blonk, C., Wilkinson, J., & Semin, G. (2015). A sniff of happiness. *Psychological Science, 26,* 684-700.
148. Dekhtyar, S., Weber, D., & Helgertz, J., & Herlitz, A. (2018). Sex differences in academic strengths contribute to gender segregation in education and occupation: A longitudinal examination of 167,776 individuals. *Intelligence, 67,* 84-92.
149. Del Zotto, M., Framorando, D., & Pegna, A. (2018). Waist-to-hip ratio affects female body attractiveness and modulates early brain responses. *The European Journal of Neuroscience,* doi:10.1111/ejn.14209
150. DeMaria, A., Sundstrom, B., McInnis, S., & Rogers, E. (2016). Perceptions and correlates of pubic hair removal and grooming among college-aged women: A mixed methods approach. *Sexual Health, 13,* 248.
151. DeNavas-Walt, C., & Proctor, B. (2015). Income and Poverty in the United States: *2014. U.S. Census Bureau, Current Population Reports,* P60-252. Washington, DC: US Government Printing Office.
152. Denes, A. (2015). Genetic and individual influences on predictions of disclosure: Exploring variation in the oxytocin receptor gene and attachment security. *Communication Monographs, 82,* 113–133.
153. Deng, Y., Chang, L., Yang, M., Huo, M., & Zhou, R. (2016). Gender differences in emotional response: Inconsistency between experience and expressivity. *PLoS One, 11,* p. e0158666. Health Reference Center Academic, http://link.galegroup.com/apps/doc/A471019183/HRCA?u=txshracd2565&sid=HRCA&xid=2b98ffd5.
154. Depypere, H., Bolca, S., Bracke, M., Delanghe, J., Comhaire, F., & Blondeel, P. (2015). The serum estradiol concentration is the main determinant of the estradiol concentration in normal breast tissue. *Maturitas, 81,* 42-45.
155. Dictionary.com (2019). www.dictionary.com
156. Dimitroff, S., Kardan, O., Necka, E., Decety, J., Berman, M., & Norman, G. (2017). Physiological dynamics of stress contagion. *Sci Rep 7,* 6168. https://doi.org/10.1038/s41598-017-05811-1
157. Dinga, S., Wu, D., Huang, S., Wu, C., Wang, X., Shi, J., et al. (2018). Neuromagnetic correlates of audiovisual word processing in the developing brain. *International Journal of Psychophysiology, 128,* 7-21.
158. Dixson, B., & Rantala, M. (2016). The role of facial and body hair distribution in women's judgments of men's sexual attractiveness. *Archives of Sexual Behavior, 45,* 877-889. doi:10.1007/s10508-015-0588-z
159. Dogan, M., Kara, U., Emre, R., Fung, W., & Canturk, K. (2015). Two brothers' alleged paternity for a child: Who is the father? *Mol Biol Rep, 7,* 1025-1027.
160. Domes, G., Schulze, L., Bottger, M., Grossmann, A., Hauenstein, K., Wirtz, P., Heinrichs, M., & Herpertz, S. (2010). The neural correlates of sex differences in emotional reactivity and emotion regulation. *Hum Brain Mapp., 31,* 758-69.

161. Donkin, I., Versteyhe, S., Ingerslev, L., Qian, K., Mechta, M., Nordkap, L., Mortensen, B., Appel, E., Jorgensen, N., Kristiansen, V., Hansen, T., Workman, C., Zierath, J., & Barres, R. (2016). Obesity and bariatric surgery drive epigenetic variation of spermatozoa in humans. *Cell Metab., 23,* 369–378.
162. Donovan, K., Walker, L., Wassersug, R., Thompson, L., & Robinson, J. (2015). Psychological effects of androgen-deprivation therapy on men with prostate cancer and their partners. *Cancer, 121,* 4286-4299.
163. Doucet, S., Soussignan, R., Sagot, P., & Schaal, B. (2009). The secretion of areolar (montgomery's) glands from lactating women elicits selective, unconditional responses in neonates. *PloS One, 4(10),* e7579-e7579. doi:10.1371/journal.pone.0007579
164. Doyle, C., Werner, E., Feng, T., Lee, S., Altemus, M., Isler, J., & Monk, C. (2015). Pregnancy distress gets under fetal skin: Maternal ambulatory assessment & sex differences in prenatal development. *Developmental Psychobiology, 57,* 607-625.
165. Dreher, J., Dunne, S., Pazderska, A., Frodl, T., Nolan, J., & O'Doherty, J. (2016). Testosterone causes both prosocial and antisocial status-enhancing behaviors in human males. *Proceedings of the National Academy of Sciences of the United States of America, 113 (41),* 11633-11638.
166. Dreher, J., Schmidt, P., Kohn, P., Furman, D., Rubinow, D., & Berman, K. (2007). Menstrual cycle phase modulates reward-related neural function in women. *Proceedings of the National Academy of Sciences of the United States of America, 104,* 2465-2470.
167. Dubé, J., Corsini-Munt, S., Muise, A., & Rosen, N. (2019). Emotion regulation in couples affected by female sexual Interest/Arousal disorder. *Archives of Sexual Behavior, 48,* 2491-2506.
168. Duff, D., Levine, T., Beatty, M., Woolbright, J., & Park, H., (2007). Testing public anxiety treatments against a credible placebo control. *Communication Education, 56,* 72–88. doi:10.1080/03634520601016186
169. Dulebohn, J., Bommer, W., Liden, R., Brouer, R., & Ferris, G. (2012). A meta-analysis of antecedents and consequences of leader-member exchange- Integrating the past with an eye towards the future. *Journal of Management, 38,* 1715-1759.
170. Dumais, K., Chernyak, S., Nickerson, L., & Janes, A. (2018). Sex differences in default mode and dorsal attention network engagement. *PLoS ONE 13(6):* e0199049. https://doi.org/10.1371/ journal.pone.0199049
171. Eagly, A., & Wood, W. (2012). Social role theory. In P. van Lange, A. Kruglanski, & E. Higgins (Eds.), *Handbook of theories of social psychology* (pp. 458–476). Thousand Oaks, CA: Sage.
172. Earp, B., & Savulescu, J. (2018). Love drugs: Why scientists should study the effects of pharmaceuticals on human romantic relationships. *Technology in Society, 52,* 10-16.
173. Earp, B., Wudarczyk, O., Foddy, B., & Savulescu, J. (2017). Addicted to love: What is love addiction and when should it be treated? *Philosophy, Psychiatry & Psychology : PPP, 24,* 77-92.
174. Earp, B., Wudarczyk, O., Sandberg, A., & Savulescu, J. (2013). If I could just stop loving you: Anti-love biotechnology and the ethics of a chemical breakup. *The American Journal of Bioethics, 13,* 3-17.
175. Eaton, N., Keyes, K., Krueger, R., Balsis, S., Skodol, A., Markon, K., et al. (2012). An invariant dimensional liability model of gender differences in mental disorder prevalence: Evidence from a national sample. *Journal of Abnormal Psychology, 121,* 282–288.
176. Ehlebracht, D., Stavrova, O., Fetchenhauer, D., & Farrelly, D. (2018). The synergistic effect of prosociality and physical attractiveness on mate desirability. *British Journal of Psychology, 109,* 517-537.
177. Eichstaedt, K., Soble, J., Kamper, J., Bozorg, A., Benbadis, S., Vale, F., & Schoenberg, M. (2015). Sex differences in lateralization of semantic verbal fluency in temporal lobe epilepsy. *Brain & Language, 141,* 11-15.
178. Eid, R., Gobinath, A., & Galea, L. (2019). Sex differences in depression: Insights From clinical and preclinical studies. *Progress in Neurobiology, 176,* 86-102.
179. Eisenegger, C., Haushofer, J., & Fehr, E. (2011). The role of testosterone in social interaction. *Trends in Cognitive Sciences, 15,* 263-271.
180. Ekman, P., & Friesen, W. (1975). *Unmasking the face: A guide to recognizing Emotions from facial expressions.* Eaglewood Cliffs, NJ: Prentice-Hall.

181. Endendijk, J., Spencer, H., Van Baar, A., & Bos, P. (2018). Mothers' neural responses to infant faces are associated with activation of the maternal care system and observed intrusiveness with their own child. *Cognitive, Affective, & Behavioral Neuroscience, 18*, 609-621.
182. Engler-Chiurazzi, E., Brown, C., Povroznik, J., & Simpkins, J. (2017). Estrogens as neuroprotectants: Estrogenic actions in the context of cognitive aging and brain injury. *Progress in Neurobiology, 157*, 188-211.
183. Engman, J., Linnman, C., Van Dijk, K., & Milad, M. (2016). Amygdala subnuclei resting-state functional connectivity sex and estrogen differences. *Psychoneuroendocrinology, 63*, 34-42.
184. Ertugrul, I., Ozay, M., & Vural, F. (2019). Gender classification using mesh networks on multiresolution multitask MRI. *Brain Imaging & Behavior, 1931-7557*: doi:10.1007/s11682-018-0021-z
185. Evans, K., & Hampson, E. (2015). Sex-dependent effects on tasks assessing reinforcement learning and interference inhibition. *Frontiers in Psychology, 6*, 1044.
186. Fabbri, E., An, Y., Gonzalez-Freire, M., Zoli, M., Maggio, M., Studenski, S., Egan, J., Chia, C., & Ferrucci, L. (2016). Bioavailable testosterone linearly declines over a wide age spectrum in men and women from the Baltimore Longitudinal Study of Aging. *J Gerontol A Biol Sci Med Sci, 71*, 1202-1209.
187. Falk, E., Cascio, C., & Coronel, J. (2015). Neural prediction of communication-relevant outcomes. *Communication Methods and Measures, 9*, 30-54.
188. Faure, R., Righetti, F., Seibel, M., & Hofmann, W. (2018). Speech is silver, nonverbal behavior is gold: How implicit partner evaluations affect dyadic interactions in close relationships. *Psychological Science, 29*, 1731-1741.
189. Fawcett, C., Wesevich, V., & Gredebäck, G. (2016). Pupillary contagion in infancy: Evidence for spontaneous transfer of arousal. *Psychological Science, 27(7)*, 997-1003.
190. Federal Bureau of Investigation (2014). Crime in the United States. Retrieved from https://ucr.fbi.gov/crime-in-the-u.s/2014/crime-inthe-u.s.-2014/persons-arrested/main.
191. Feijo, L., Tarman, G., Fontaine, C., Harrison, R., Johnstone, T., & Salomons, T. (2018). Sex-specific effects of gender identification on pain study recruitment. *The Journal of Pain, 19*, 178-185.
192. Feldman, R. (2012). Oxytocin and social affiliation in humans. *Hormones and Behavior, 61*, 380-391.
193. Feldman, R. (2017). The neurobiology of human attachments. *Trends in Cognitive Sciences, 21*, 80-99.
194. Feldman, R., Braun, K., & Champagne, F. (2019). The neural mechanisms and consequences of paternal caregiving. *Nature Reviews Neuroscience, 20*, 205-224.
195. Feldman, R., Gordon, I., Influs, M., Gutbir, T., & Ebstein, R. (2013). Parental oxytocin and early caregiving jointly shape children's oxytocin response and social reciprocity. *Neuropsychopharmacology, 38*, 1154-1162.
196. Feldman, R., Gordon, I., Schneiderman, I., Weisman, O., & Zagoory-Sharon, O. (2010). Natural variations in maternal and paternal care are associated with systematic changes in oxytocin following parent–infant contact. *Psychoneuroendocrinology, 35*, 1133-1141.
197. Feldman, R., Magori-Cohen, R., Galili, G., Singer, M., & Louzoun, Y. (2011). Mother and infant coordinate heart rhythms through episodes of interaction synchrony. *Infant Behavior and Development, 34*, 569-577.
198. Feng, C., Hackett, P., DeMarco, A., Chen, X., Stair, S., Haroon, E., Ditzen, B., Pagnoni, G., & Rilling, J. (2014). Oxytocin and vasopressin effects on the neural response to social cooperation are modulated by sex in humans. *Brain Imaging and Behavior, 9*, 754-764.
199. Fernandez, J., & Tannock, L. (2016). Metabolic effects of hormone therapy in transgender patients. *Endocrine Practice: Official Journal of the American College of Endocrinology and the American Association of Clinical Endocrinologists, 22*, 383-388.
200. Ferrari, C., Ciricugno, A., Urgesi, C., & Cattaneo, Z. (2019). Cerebellar contribution to emotional body language perception: A TMS study. *Social Cognitive and Affective Neuroscience,* doi:10.1093/scan/nsz074
201. Ferreira, K., Guilherme, G., Faria, V., Borges, L., & Uchiyama, A. (2017). Women living together have a higher frequency of menstrual migraine. *Headache: The Journal of Head and Face Pain, 57*, 135-142.

202. Filkowski, M., Olsen, R., Duda, B., Wanger, T., & Sabatinelli, D. (2017). Sex differences in emotional perception: Meta analysis of divergent activation. *NeuroImage, 147*, 925-933.
203. Fisher, H., Brown, L., Aron, A., Strong, G., & Mashek, D. (2010). Reward, addiction, and emotion regulation systems associated with rejection in love. *Journal of Neurophysiology, 104*, 51.
204. Fisher, P., Haahr, M., Jensen, C., Frokjaer, V., Siebner, H., & Knudsen, G. (2015). Fluctuations in [^{11}C]SB207145 PET binding associated with change in threat-related amygdala reactivity in humans. *Neuropsychopharmacology: Official Publication of the American College of Neuropsychopharmacology, 40*, 1510-1518.
205. Fleming, L., Van Riper, M., & Knafl, K. (2017). Management of childhood congenital adrenal hyperplasia-An integrated review of the literature. *Journal of Pediatric Health Care, 31*, 560-577.
206. Flores-Ramos, M., Alcauter, S., Lopez-Titla, M., Bernal-Santamaria, N., Calva-Coraza, E., & Edden, R. (2019). Testosterone is related to GABA+ levels in the posterior-cingulate in unmedicated depressed women during reproductive life. *Journal of Affective Disorders, 242*, 143-149.
207. Floyd, K. (2014). Humans are people, too: Nurturing an appreciation for nature in communication research. *Review of Communication Research, 2*, 1-29.
208. Floyd, K., Boren, J., Hannawa, A., Hesse, C., McEwan, B., & Veksler, A. (2009). Kissing in marital and cohabiting relationships: Effects on blood lipids, stress, and relationship satisfaction. *Western Journal of Communication, 73*, 113–133.
209. Floyd, K., Hesse, C., & Haynes, M. (2007). Human affection exchange: XV. Metabolic and cardiovascular correlates of trait expressed affection. *Communication Quarterly, 55*, 79-94.
210. Floyd, K., Pauley, P., & Hesse, C. (2010). State and trait affectionate communication buffer adults' stress reactions. *Communication Monographs, 77*, 618-636.
211. Floyd, K., Pauley, P., Hesse, C., Eden, J., Veksler, A., & Woo, N. (2018). Supportive communication is associated with markers of immunocompetence. *Southern Communication Journal, 83*, 229-244.
212. Floyd, K., Veksler, A., McEwan, B., Hesse, C., Boren, J., Dinsmore, D., & Pavlich, C. (2017). Social inclusion predicts lower blood glucose and low-density lipoproteins in healthy adults. *Health Communication, 32*, 1039-1042.
213. Foo, Y., Simmons, L., Peters, M., & Rhodes, G. (2018). Perceived physical strength in men is attractive to women but may come at a cost to ejaculate quality. *Animal Behaviour, 142*, 191-197. doi:10.1016/j.anbehav.2018.06.019
214. Forger, N., Strahan, J., & Castillo-Ruiz, A. (2016). Cellular and molecular mechanisms of sexual differentiation in the mammalian nervous system. *Frontiers in Neuroendocrinology, 40*, 67-86.
215. Fox, M., Sandman, C., Davis, E., & Glynn, L. (2018). A longitudinal study of women's depression symptom profiles during and after the postpartum phase. *Depression and Anxiety, 35*, 292-304.
216. Frampton, J., & Fox, J. (2018). Social Media's role in romantic partners' retroactive jealousy: Social comparison, uncertainty, and information seeking. *Social Media + Society, 4*, 205630511880031. doi:10.1177/2056305118800317
217. Franklin, P., Tsujimoto, K., Lewis, M., Tekok-Kilic, A., & Frijters, J. (2018). Sex differences in self-regulatory executive functions are amplified by trait anxiety: The case of students at risk for academic failure. *Personality and Individual Differences, 129*, 131-137.
218. Frankort, A., Roefs, A., Siep, N., Roebroeck, A., Havermans, R., & Jansen, A. (2014). The craving stops before you feel it: Neural correlates of chocolate craving during cue exposure with response prevention. *Cerebral Cortex, 24*, 1589-1600.
219. Fredrickson, B., & Joiner, T. (2018). Reflections on positive emotions and upward spirals. *Perspectives on Psychological Science, 13*, 194-199.
220. Frisén, L., Nordenström, A., Falhammar, H., Filipsson, H., Holmdahl, G., Janson, P., et al. (2009). Gender role behavior, sexuality, and psychosocial adaptation in women with congenital adrenal hyperplasia due to CYP21A2 deficiency. *The Journal of Clinical Endocrinology and Metabolism, 94*, 3432-3439.

221. Frost, D., McClelland, S., & Dettmann, M. (2017). Sexual closeness discrepancies: What they are and why they matter for sexual well-being in romantic relationships. *Archives of Sexual Behavior, 46,* 2353-2364.
222. Fuchs, E., Czeh, B., & Flügge, G. (2004). Examining novel concepts of the pathophysiology of depression in the chronic psychosocial stress paradigm in tree shrews. *Behav Pharmacol, 15,* 315–325.
223. Fujimoto, T., Okumura, E., Kodabashi, A., Takeuchi, K., Otsubo, T., Nakamura, K., Yatsushiro, K., Sekine, M., Kamiya, S., Shimooki, S., & Tamura, T. (2016). Sex differences in gamma band functional connectivity between the frontal lobe and cortical areas during an auditory oddball task, as revealed by imaginary coherence assessment. *The Open Neuroimaging Journal, 10,* 85-101.
224. Fujiwara, K., Kimura, M., & Daibo, I. (2019). Gender differences in synchrony: Females in sync during unstructured dyadic conversation. *European Journal of Social Psychology, 49,* 1042-1054.
225. Ganley, C., Vasilyeva, M., & Dulaney, A. (2014). Spatial ability mediates the gender difference in middle school students' science performance. *Child Development, 85,* 1419-1432.
226. Gao, S., Becker, B., Luo, L., Geng, Y., Zhao, W., Yin, Y., Hu, J., Gao, Z., Gong, Q., Hurlemann, R., Yao, D., & Kendrick, K. (2016). Oxytocin, the peptide that bonds the sexes also divides them. *PNAS, 113,* 7650-7654.
227. Garneau, N., Nuessle, T., Sloan, M., Santorico, S., Coughlin, B., & Hayes, J. (2014). Crowd sourcing taste research: Genetic and phenotypic predictors of bitter taste perception as a model. *Frontiers of Integrative Neuroscience, 8,* 33.
228. Gavin, N., Gaynes, B., Lohr, K., Meltzer-Brody, S., Gartlehner, G., & Swinson, T., (2005). Perinatal depression: A systematic review of prevalence and incidence. *Obstet. Gynecol. 106,* 1071–1083.
229. Gazzola, V., & Keysers, C. (2009). The observation and execution of actions share motor and somatosensory voxels in all tested subjects: Single-subject analyses of unsmoothed fMRI data. *Cereb. Cortex 19,* 1239–1255.
230. Geng, Y., Zhao, W., Zhou, F., Ma, X., Yao, S., Becker, B., & Kendrick, K. (2018). Oxytocin facilitates empathetic- and self- embarrassment ratings by attenuating amygdala and anterior insula responses. *Frontiers in Endocrinology, 9:* 572 doi: 10.3389/fendo.2018.00572
231. Georgiadis, J., & Kringelbach, M. (2012). The human sexual response cycle: Brain imaging evidence linking sex to other pleasures. *Prog. Neurobiol. 98,* 49–81.
232. Gere, J., & Impett, E. (2018). Shifting priorities: Effects of partners' goal conflict on goal adjustment processes and relationship quality in developing romantic relationships. *Journal of Social and Personal Relationships, 35,* 793-810.
233. Gildersleeve, K., Haselton, M., & Fales, M. (2014). Do women's mate preferences change across the ovulatory cycle? A meta-analytic review. *Psychological Bulletin, 140(5),* 1205-1259.
234. Gildersleeve, K., Haselton, M., Larson, C., & Pillsworth, E. (2012). Body odor attractiveness as a cue of impending ovulation in women: Evidence from a study using hormone-confirmed ovulation. *Hormones and Behavior, 61,* 157-166.
235. Gildersleeve, S., Singer, J., Skerrett, K., & Wein, S. (2017). Coding "we-ness" in couple's relationship stories: A method for assessing mutuality in couple therapy. *Psychotherapy Research, 27,* 313-325.
236. Giudice, M., Barrett, E., Belsky, J., Hartman, S., Martel, M., Sangenstedt, S., & Kuzawa, C. (2018). Individual differences in developmental plasticity: A role for early androgens? *Psychoneuroendocrinology, 90,* 165-173.
237. Gleason, C., Dowling, N., Wharton, W., Manson, J., Miller, V., Atwood, C. et al. (2015). Effects of hormone therapy on cognition and mood in recently postmenopausal women: Findings from the randomized, controlled KEEPS-cognitive and affective study. *PLoS Medicine, 12(6),* e1001833; discussion e1001833. doi:10.1371/journal.pmed.1001833
238. Glezerman, M. (2016). Yes, there is a female and a male brain: Morphology versus functionality. *Proc Natl Acad Sci, 113,* E1971.
239. Godard, O., & Fiori, N. (2010). Sex differences in face processing: Are women less lateralized and faster than men? *Brain and Cognition, 73,* 167-175.

240. Goldey, K., & van Anders, S. (2016). Identification with stimuli moderates women's affective and testosterone responses to self-chosen erotica. *Archives of Sexual Behavior, 45,* 2155-2171.
241. Goldstein, J., Seidman, L., Horton, N., Makris, N., Kennedy, D., Caviness, V. Jr, Faraone, S., & Tsuang, M. (2001). Normal sexual dimorphism of the adult human brain assessed by in vivo magnetic resonance imaging. *Cereb Cortex, 11,* 490–497.
242. Goldstein-Piekarski, A., Greer, S., Saletin, J., Harvey, A., Williams, L., & Walker, M. (2017). Sex, sleep deprivation, and the anxious brain. *Journal of Cognitive Neuroscience, 30,* 565-578.
243. Gordon, J., & Girdler, S. (2014). Hormone replacement therapy in the treatment of perimenopausal depression. *Curr Psychiatry Rep, 16,* 517.
244. Gordon, I., Pratt, M., Bergunde, K., Zagoory-Sharon, O., & Feldman, R. (2017). Testosterone, oxytocin, and the development of human parental care. *Hormones and Behavior, 93,* 184-192.
245. Gordon, J., Rubinow, D., Eisenlohr-Moul, T., Xia, K., Schmidt, P., & Girdler, S. (2018). Efficacy of transdermal estradiol and micronized progesterone in the prevention of depressive symptoms in the menopause transition: A randomized clinical trial. *Jama Psychiatry, 75,* 149-157.
246. Gordon, I., Zagoory-Sharon, O., Leckman, J., & Feldman, R. (2010). Prolactin, oxytocin, and the development of paternal behavior across the first six months of fatherhood. *Hormones and Behavior, 58,* 513-518.
247. Gorezyea, A., Sjaarda, L., Mitchell, E., Perkins, N., Schliep, K., Wactawski-Wende, J., & Mumford, S. (2016). Changes in macronutrient, micronutrient, and food group intakes throughout the menstrual cycle in healthy, premenopausal women. *Eur J Nutr, 55,* 1181-1188.
248. Gorges, J., & Kandler, C. (2012). Adults' learning motivation: Expectancy of success, value, and the role of affective memories. *Learning and Individual Differences, 22,* 610-617.
249. Goshvarpour, A., & Goshvarpour, A. (2019). EEG spectral powers and source localization in depressing, sad, and fun music videos focusing on gender differences. *Cognitive Neurodynamics, 13,* 161-173.
250. Grabowska, A. (2017). Sex on the brain: Are gender-dependent structural and functional differences associated with behavior? *Journal of Neuroscience Research, 95,* 200-212.
251. Grafe, L., & Bhatnagar, S. (2018). The contribution of orexins to sex differences in the stress response. *Brain Research*: ttps://doi.org/10.1016/j.brainres.2018.07.026
252. Grattan, D. (2011). A mother's brain knows. *Journal of Neuroendocrinology, 23,* 1188. doi:10.1111/j.1365-2826.2011.02175.x
253. Grebe, N., Sarafin, R., Strenth, C., & Zilioli, S. (2019). Pair-bonding, fatherhood, and the role of testosterone: A meta-analytic review. *Neuroscience and Biobehavioral Reviews, 98,* 221-233.
254. Gressier, F., Calati, R., & Serretti, A. (2016). 5-HTTLPR and gender differences in affective disorders: A systematic review. *Journal of Affective Disorders, 190,* 193-207.
255. Groppe, S., Gossen, A., Rademacher, L., Hahn, A., Westphal, L., Gründer, G., & Spreckelmeyer, K. (2013). Oxytocin influences processing of socially relevant cues in the ventral tegmental area of the human brain. *Biological Psychiatry, 74,* 172-179.
256. Gummadavelli, A., Wang, Y., Guo, X., Pardos, M., Chu, H., Liu, Y., et al. (2013). Spatiotemporal and frequency signatures of word recognition in the developing brain: A magnetoencephalographic study. *Brain Research, 1498,* 20-32.
257. Gur, R., Bockow, T., & Gur, R. (2010). Gender differences in the functional organization of the brain. In: Legato, M.J. (Ed.), *Principles of Gender-Specific Medicine,* 2nd ed. Elsevier, Amsterdam, pp. 75–86.
258. Gur, R., & Gur, R. (2017). Complementarity of sex differences in brain and behavior: From laterality to multimodal neuroimaging. *Journal of Neuroscience Research, 95,* 189-199.
259. Gur, R., Richard, J., Calkins, M., Chiavacci, R., Hansen, J., Bilker, W. et al. (2012). Age group and sex differences in performance on a computerized neurocognitive battery in children age 8-21. *Neuropsychology, 26,* 251-265.
260. Guyer, J., Briñol, P., Petty, R., & Horcajo, J. (2019). Nonverbal behavior of persuasive sources: A multiple process analysis. *Journal of Nonverbal Behavior, 43,* 203-231.
261. Haber, S., & Behrens, T. (2014). The neural network underlying incentive-based learning: Implications for interpreting circuit disruptions in psychiatric disorders. *Neuron, 83,* 1019–1039.

262. Hackney, A., Lane, A., Register-Mihalik, J., & O'leary, C. (2017). Endurance exercise training and male sexual libido. *Medicine and Science in Sports and Exercise, 49,* 1383.
263. Hahn, A., Kranz, G., Sladky, R., Kaufmann, U., Ganger, S., Hummer, A. et al. (2016). Testosterone affects language areas of the adult human brain: Testosterone affects language areas. *Human Brain Mapping, 37,* 1738-1748.
264. Hallam, J., Boswell, R., DeVito, E., & Kober, H. (2016). Gender-related differences in food craving and obesity. *Yale J Biol Med, 89,* 161-173.
265. Hamilton, B., Martin, J., & Osterman, M. (2016). Births: Preliminary data for 2015. National Vital Statistics Reports: From the Centers for Disease Control and Prevention, National Center for Health Statistics, *National Vital Statistics System, 65(3),* 1.
266. Hampson, E. (2018). Regulation of cognitive function by androgens and estrogens. *Current Opinion in Behavioral Sciences, 23,* 49-57.
267. Hampson, E., & Rovet, J. (2015). Spatial function in adolescents and young adults with congenital adrenal hyperplasia: Clinical phenotype and implications for the androgen hypothesis. *Psychoneuroendocrinology, 54,* 60-70.
268. Handa, R., & McGivern, R. (2015). Steroid hormones, receptors, and perceptual and cognitive sex differences in the visual system. *Current Eye Research, 40,* 110-127.
269. Haney, C. (2018). The psychological effects of solitary confinement: A systematic critique. *Crime & Justice, 47,* 365-416.
270. Harlow, H., & Zimmerman, R. (1958). The development of affectionate responses in infant monkeys. *Proceedings, American Philosophical Society, 102,* 501-509.
271. Hausmann, M. (2017). Why sex hormones matter for neuroscience: A very short review on sex, sex hormones, and functional brain asymmetry. *Journal of Neuroscience Research, 95,* 40-49.
272. Helpman, L., Xi, Z., Suarez-Jimenez, B., Lazarov, A., & Neria, Y. (2017). Sex differences in resting state functional connectivity (rs-FC) of limbic circuits in PTSD. *Biological Psychiatry, 81,* S38-S39. doi:10.1016/j.biopsych.2017.02.104.
273. Henningsson, S., Madsen, K., Pinborg, A., Heede, M., Knudsen, G., Siebner, H., & Frokjaer, V. (2015). Role of emotional processing in depressive responses to sex hormone manipulation: A pharmacological fMRI study. *Translational Psychiatry 5 (12),* e688. https://doi.org/10.1038/tp.2015.184
274. Herbenick, D., & Fortenberry, J. (2011). Exercise-induced orgasm and pleasure among women. Sexual and Relationship Therapy: *Special Issue: The Human Orgasm, 26,* 373-388.
275. Hermans, E., Ramsey, N., & van Honk, J. (2008). Exogenous testosterone enhances responsiveness to social threat in the neural circuitry of social aggression in human. *Biological Psychiatry, 63,* 263-270.
276. Herrera, A., & Mather, M. (2015). Actions and interactions of estradiol and glucocorticoids in cognition and the brain: Implications for aging women. *Neuroscience and Biobehavioral Reviews, 55,* 36-52.
277. Herrera, A., Wang, J., & Mather, M. (2018). The gist and details of sex differences in cognition and the brain: How parallels in sex differences across domains are shaped by the locus coeruleus and catecholamine systems. *Progress in Neurobiology,* 10.1016/j.pneurobio.2018.05.005
278. Herting, M., & Sowell, E. (2016). Puberty and structural brain development in humans. *Frontiers in Neuroendocrinology, 44,* 122-137.
279. Hess, C., & Mikkelson, A. (2016). Affection deprivation in romantic relationships. *Communication Quarterly, 65,* 20-38.
280. Hicks, L., & McNulty, J. (2019). The unbearable automaticity of being . . . in a close relationship. *Current Directions in Psychological Science, 28,* 254-259.
281. Hidalgo, V., Pulopulos, M., Puig-Perez, S., Espin, L., Gomez-Amor, J., & Salvador, A. (2015). Acute stress affects free recall and recognition of pictures differently depending on age and sex. *Behav. Brain Res., 292,* 393–402.
282. Hill, A., Cairnduff, V., & McCance, D. (2016). Nutritional and clinical associations of food cravings in pregnancy. *Journal of Human Nutrition and Dietetics, 29,* 281-289.
283. Hines, M., Constantinescu, M., & Spencer, D. (2015). Early androgen exposure and human gender development. *Biology of Sex Differences, 6,* 1-10.

284. Hirnstein, M., Hugdahl, K., & Hausman, M. (2019). Cognitive sex differences and hemispheric asymmetry: A critical review of 40 years of research. *Laterality: Asymetries of body, brain and cognition, 24,* 204-252.
285. Hjelmervik, H., Hausmann, M., Craven, A., Hirnstein, M., Hugdahl, K., & Specht, K. (2018). Sex- and sex hormone-related variations in energy-metabolic frontal brain asymmetries: A magnetic resonance spectroscopy study. *Neuroimage, 172,* 817-825.
286. Hjelmervik, H., Hausmann, M., Osnes, B., Westerhausen, R., & Specht, K. (2014). Resting states are resting traits: An FMRI study of sex differences and menstrual cycle effects in resting state cognitive control networks. *PloS One, 9(7),* e103492.
287. Hodes, G., Walker, D., Labonte, B., Nestler, E., & Russo, S. (2017). Understanding the epigenetic basis of sex differences in depression. *J Neurosci Res, 95,* 692-702.
288. Hoekzema, E., Barba-Muller, E., Pozzobon, C., Picado, M., Lucco, F., Garcia-Garcia, D., Soliva, J., Tobena, A., Desco, M., Crone, E., Ballesteros, A., Carmona, S., & Vilarroya, O. (2017). Pregnancy leads to long-lasting changes in human brain structure. *Nature Neuroscience, 20,* 287-296.
289. Hofer, M., Collins, H., & Whillans, A. (2018). Olfactory cues from romantic partners and strangers influence women's responses to stress. *Journal of Personality and Social Psychology, 114,* 1-9.
290. Hoffmann, H. (2019). The aroma of arousal: Effects of menstrual cycle phase and women's sexual arousal state on men's responsiveness to women's body odor. *Biological Psychology, 142,* 54.
291. Hoffman, M., Doeringer, J., Noreross, M., Johnson, S., & Chappel, P. (2018). Presynaptic inhibition decreases when estrogen levels rise. *Scand J Med Sci Sports, 28,* 2009-2015.
292. Holland, J., Bandelow, S., & Hogervorst, E. (2011). Testosterone levels and cognition in elderly men: A review. *Maturitas, 69,* 322-337.
293. Hollier, L., Mattes, E., Maybery, M., Keelan, J., Hickey, M., & Whitehouse, A. (2013). The association between perinatal testosterone concentration and early vocabulary development: A prospective cohort study. *Biological Psychology, 92,* 212-215.
294. Holm, M., Olsen, A., Kyrø, C., Overvad, K., Kroman, N., & Tjønneland, A. (2018). The influence of menopausal hormone therapy and potential lifestyle interactions in female cancer Development—a population-based prospective study. *Hormones and Cancer, 9,* 254-264.
295. Holt-Lunstad, J., Birmingham, W., & Light, K. (2008). Influence of a "warm touch" support enhancement intervention among married couples on ambulatory blood pressure, oxytocin, alpha amylase, and cortisol. *Psychosomatic Medicine, 70(9),* 976.
296. Homburg, R., Gudi, A., Shah, A., & Layton, A. (2017). A novel method to demonstrate that pregnant women with polycystic ovary syndrome hyper-expose their fetus to androgens as a possible stepping stone for the developmental theory of PCOS. A pilot study. *Reproductive biology and endocrinology, 15,* 61-64.
297. Hu, Y., Hu, Y., Li, X., Pan, Y., & Cheng, X. (2017). Brain-to-brain synchronization Across two persons predicts mutual prosociality. *Social Cognitive and Affective Neuroscience, 12,* 1835-1844. doi:10.1093/scan/nsx118
298. Hu, X., & Lau, C. (2017). Central conduction time in auditory brainstem response and ear advantage in dichotic listening across menstrual cycle. *PloS One, 12(11),* e0187672. doi:10.1371/journal.pone.0187672.
299. Huberman, J., & Chivers, M. (2015). Examining gender specificity of sexual response with concurrent thermography and plethysmography. *Psychophysiology, 52,* 1382-1395.
300. Hughes, S., & Aung, T. (2017). Modern-day female preferences for resources and provisioning by long-term mates. *Evolutionary Behavioral Sciences, 11,* 242-261.
301. Hurley, S. (2008). The shared circuits model (SCM): How control, mirroring, and simulation can enable imitation, deliberation, and mindreading. *Behavioral and Brain Sciences, 31,* 1-58.
302. Hwang, M., Zsido, R., Song, H., Pace-Schott, E., Miller, K., Lebron-Milad, K., Marin, M., & Milad, M. (2015). Contribution of estradiol levels and hormonal contraceptives to sex differences within the fear network during fear conditioning and extinction. *BMC Psychiatry, 15:* 295. DOI 10.1186/s12888-015-0673-9

303. Hyer, M., Phillips, L., & Neigh, G. (2018). Sex differences in synaptic plasticity: Hormones and beyond. *Frontiers in Molecular Neuroscience, 11* doi:10.3389/fnmol.2018.00266
304. Iftikhar, U., & Choudhry, N. (2019). Serum levels of androgens in acne & their role in acne severity. *Pakistan Journal of Medical Sciences, 35,* 146-150. doi:10.12669/pjms.35.1.131
305. lngalhalikar, M., Smith, A., Parker, D., Satterthwaite, T., Elliott, M., Ruparel, K., et al. (2014). Sex differences in the structural connectome of the human brain. *Proceedings of the National Academy of Sciences of the United States of America, 111,* 823-828.
306. Ireland, M., Slatcher, R., Eastwick, P., Scissors, L., Finkel, E., & Pennebaker, J. (2011). Language style matching predicts relationship initiation and stability. *Psychological Science, 22,* 39-44.
307. Irving, S., Schöberl, F., Pradhan, C., Brendel, M., Bartenstein, P., Dieterich, M., Brandt, T., & Zwergal, A. (2018). *J Neurol, 265 (Suppl 1),* S113-S126.https://doi.org/10.1007/s00415-018-8987-4
308. Issler, O., & Nestler, E. (2018). The molecular basis for sex differences in depression susceptibility. *Current Opinion in Behavioral Sciences, 23,* 1-6.
309. Jacobs Bao, K., & Lyubomirsky, S. (2013). Making it last: Combating hedonic adaptation in romantic relationships. *The Journal of Positive Psychology, 8,* 196-206.
310. Jacques, P., Conway, M., & Cabeza, R. (2011). Gender differences in autobiographical memory for everyday events: Retrieval elicited by SenseCam images versus verbal cues. *Memory, 19,* 723-732.
311. Jadva, V., Hines, M., & Golombok, S. (2010). Infants' preferences for toys, colors, and shapes: Sex differences and similarities. *Archives of Sexual Behavior, 39,* 1261-1273.
312. Jakubiak, B., & Feeney, B. (2019). Hand-in-hand combat: Affectionate touch promotes relational well-being and buffers stress during conflict. *Personality and Social Psychology Bulletin, 45,* 431-446.
313. Jakubiak, B., & Feeney, B. (2017). Affectionate touch to promote relational, psychological, and physical well-being in adulthood: A theoretical model and review of the research. *Personality and Social Psychology Review, 21,* 228-252.
314. Jansen, A., Stegerman, S., Roefs A., Nederkoorn, C., Havermans, R. et al. (2010). Decreased salivation to food cues in formerly obese successful dieters. *Psychotherapy & Psychosomatics, 79,* 257–258.
315. Janssen, O., & Van Yperen, N. (2004). Employees' goal orientations, the quality of leader-member exchange, and the outcomes of job performance, and job satisfaction. *Academy of Management Journal, 47,* 368-384.
316. Jaschik, S. (2017). Hoax with multiple targets: Fake article is published, calling for the penis to be seen conceptually, not as a body organ. Debates take off about Gender Studies and Open-Access Journals. *Inside Higher Ed, May 22, 2017,* https://www.insidehighered.com/news/2017/05/22/faux-scholarly-article-sets-criticism-gender-studies-and-open-access-publishing
317. Jentsch, V., Merz, C., & Wolf, O. (2019). Restoring emotional stability: Cortisol effects on the neural network of cognitive emotion regulation. *Behavioral Brain Research*: https://doi.org/10.1016/j.bbr.2019.03.049
318. Jin, B. (2019). Criticism from artificial agents: Prior interaction reduces negative effects. *Communication Research Reports, 36,* 148-157.
319. Joel, D., Berman, Z., Tavor, I., Wexler, N., Gaber, O., Stein, Y., Shefi, N., Pool, J., Urchs, S., Margulies, D., Liem, F., Hanggi, J., Jancke, L., & Assaf, Y. (2015). Sex beyond the genitalia: The human brain mosaic. *Proc Natl Acad Sci, 112,* 15468-15473.
320. Joffe, H., & Hickey, M., (2018). Should hormone therapy be used to prevent depressive symptoms during the menopause transition? *JAMA Psychiatry, 75,* 125-126.
321. Johnson, D., & Johnson, R. (2012). Restorative justice in the classroom: Necessary roles of cooperative context, constructive conflict, and civic values. *Negotiation and Conflict Management Research, 5,* 4-28.
322. Jonsson, E., Bendas, J., Weidner, K., Wessberg, J., Olausson, H., Wasling, H., & Croy, I. (2017). The relation between human hair follicle density and touch perception. *Scientific Reports, 7,* 2499.
323. Jouen, F., Sann, C., & Molina, M. (2012). Haptic processing in newborns of depressed and nondepressed mothers. *Developmental Psychobiology, 54,* 451-459.

324. Juhn, C., & McCue, K. (2017). Specialization then and now: Marriage, children, and the gender earnings gap across cohorts. *Journal of Economic Perspectives, 31,* 183-204.
325. Jung, S., Shin, A., & Kang, D. (2015). Hormone-related factors and post-menopausal onset depression: Results from KNHANES (2010-2012). *Journal of Affective Disorders, 175,* 176-183.
326. Jurek, B., & Neumann, I. (2017). The oxytocin receptor: From intracellular signaling to behavior. *Physiological Reviews, 98,* 1805-1908.
327. Kaldewaij, R., Koch, S., Zhang, W., Hashemi, M., klumpers, F., & Roelofs, K. (2018). F10. Linking emotional control and stress reactivity: Anterior prefrontal cortex activation during emotion control predicts cortisol response after stress induction. *Biological Psychiatry, 83,* S240-S241.
328. Kane, M. (2018). *A Comparison of Micro-Expression Training Methods.* ProQuest Dissertations Publishing.
329. Kang, O., Huffer, K., & Wheatley, T. (2014). Pupil dilation dynamics track attention to high-level information. *PloS One, 9(8),* e102463-e102463. doi:10.1371/journal.pone.0102463
330. Kapoor, T., Banuelos, J., Nippoldt, T., Ciudad, P., Martinez-Jorge, J., & Manrique, O. (2019). Effects of hormone therapy in patients who underwent male-to-female gender confirmation surgery. *European Journal of Plastic Surgery, 42,* 267-272.
331. Karan, A., Rosenthal, R., & Robbins, M. (2019). Meta-analytic evidence that we-talk predicts relationship and personal functioning in romantic couples. *Journal of Social and Personal Relationships, 36,* 2624-2651.
332. Karayiannis, D., Kontogianni, M., Mendorou, C., Mastrominas, M., & Yiannakouris, N. (2018). Adherence to the mediterranean diet and IVF success rate among non-obese women attempting fertility. *Human Reproduction (Oxford, England), 33,* 494-502.
333. Karlamangla, A., Lachman, M., Han, W., Huang, M., & Greendale, G. (2017). Evidence for cognitive aging in midlife women: Study of women's health across the nation. *PLoS ONE, 12:* e0169008.doi:10.1371/journal.pone.0169008
334. Kato, R., & Takeda, Y. (2016). Responses to affective pictures depicting humans: Late positive potential reveals a sex-related effect in processing that is not present in subjective ratings. *Exp Brain Res, 235,* 193-204.
335. Kelly, J., Iannone, N., & McCarty, M. (2016). Emotional contagion of anger is automatic: An evolutionary explanation. *British Journal of Social Psychology, 55,* 182-191.
336. Kendler, K., & Gardner, C. (2014). Sex differences in the pathways to major depression: A study of opposite-sex twin pairs. *Am J Psychiatry, 171,* 426-35.
337. Kendler, K., Gatz, M., Gardner, C., & Pedersen, N. (2006). A Swedish national twin study of lifetime major depression. *American Journal of Psychiatry, 163,* 109-114.
338. Kerschbaum, H., Hofbauer, I., Gfollner, A., Ebner, B., Bresgen, N., & Bauml, K. (2017). Sex, age, and sex hormones affect recall of words in a directed forgetting paradigm. *Journal of Neuroscience Research, 95,* 251-259.
339. Keverne, E. (2015). Genomic imprinting, action, and interaction of maternal and fetal genomes. *Proceedings of the National Academy of Sciences of the United States of America, 112,* 6834-6840.
340. Khajehei M., & Behroozpour E. (2018). Endorphins, oxytocin, sexuality and romantic relationships: An understudied area. *World J Obstet Gynecol, 7,* 17-23.
341. Killgore, W., & Yurgelun-Todd, D. (2010). Sex differences in cerebral responses to images of high versus low-calorie food. *Neuroreport, 21,* 354-358.
342. Kim, P., Feldman, R., Mayes, L. Eicher, V., Thompson, N., Leckman, J. & Swain, J. (2011). Breastfeeding, brain activation to own infant cry, and maternal sensitivity: Breastfeeding, brain, and maternal sensitivity. *Journal of Child Psychology and Psychiatry, 52,* 907-915.
343. Kim, P., Strathearn, L., & Swain, J. (2016). The maternal brain and its plasticity in humans. *Hormones and Behavior, 77,* 113-123.
344. Kingsberg, S., Clayton, A., & Pfaus, J. (2015). The female sexual response: Current models, neurobiological underpinnings and agents currently approved or under investigation for the treatment of hypoactive sexual desire disorder. *CNS Drugs, 29,* 915-933.
345. Kiraly, A., Szabo, N., Toth, E., Csete, G., Farago, P., Koesis, K., Must, A., Vecsei, L., & Kineses, Z. (2016). Male brain ages faster: The age and gender dependence of subcortical volumes. *Brain Imaging and Behavior, 10,* 901-910.

346. Kirchengast, S. (2010). Gender differences in body composition from childhood to old age: An evolutionary point of view. *Journal of Life Sciences, 2,* 1-10.
347. Kogler, L., Muller, V., Seidel, E., Boubela, R., Kalcher, K., Moser, E., Habel, U., Gur, R., Eickhoff, S., & Derntl, B. (2016). Sex differences in the functional connectivity of the amygdala in association with cortisol. *Neuroimage, 134,* 410-423.
348. Kokras, N., & Dalla, C. (2017). Preclinical sex differences in depression and antidepressant response: Implications for clinical research. *Journal of Neuroscience Research, 95,* 731-736.
349. Kolb, B., Mychasiuk, R., Muhammad, A., Li, Y., Frost, D., & Gibb, R. (2012). Experience and the developing prefrontal cortex. *Proceedings of the National Academy of Sciences of the United States of America, 109(Supplement 2),* 17186-17193.
350. Komisaruk, B., & Whipple, B. (2011). Non-genital orgasms. Sexual and Relationship Therapy: *Special Issue: The Human Orgasm, 26,* 356-372.
351. Kong, L., Chen, K., Womer, F., Jiang, W., Luo, X., et al. (2013). Sex differences of gray matter morphology in cortico-limbic-striatal neural system in major depressive disorder. *Journal of Psychiatric Research, 47,* 733-739.
352. Kong, X., Huang, Y., Hao, X., Hu, S., & Liu, J. (2017). Sex-linked association between cortical scene selectivity and navigational ability. *NeuroImage, 158,* 397-405.
353. Kontula, O., & Miettinen, A. (2016). Determinants of female sexual orgasms. *Socioaffective Neuroscience & Psychology, 6,* 31624-21.
354. Kostic, B., & Yadon, C. (2014). Infidelity and kin selection: Does cheating seem as bad when it's "All in the family"? *Evolutionary Psychology, 12(4),* 147470491401200. doi:10.1177/147470491401200402
355. Kramer, K. L. (2010). Cooperative breeding and its significance to the demographic success of humans. *Annual Review of Anthropology, 39,* 417-436.
356. Kranz, G., Wadsak, W., Kaufmann, U., Savli, M., Baldinger, P., Gryglewski, G. et al. (2015). High-dose testosterone treatment increases serotonin transporter binding in transgender people. *Biological Psychiatry, 78,* 525-533.
357. Kraus, C., Castrén, E., Kasper, S., & Lanzenberger, R. (2017). Serotonin and neuroplasticity – links between molecular, functional and structural pathophysiology in depression. *Neuroscience and Biobehavioral Reviews, 77,* 317-326.
358. Kret, M., & De Gelder, B. (2012). A review on sex differences in processing emotional signals. *Neuropsychologia, 50,* 1211-1221.
359. Kreuder, A., Scheele, D., Wassermann, L., Wollseifer, M., Stoffel-Wagner, B., Lee, M. et al. (2017). How the brain codes intimacy: The neurobiological substrates of romantic touch. *Human Brain Mapping, 38,* 4525-4534.
360. Krizman, J., Bonacina, S., & Kraus, N. (2019). Sex differences in subcortical auditory processing emerge across development. *Hearing Research, 380,* 166-174.
361. Kromer, J., Hummel, T., Pietrowski, D., Giani, A., Sauter, J., Ehninger, G., Schmidt, A., & Croy, I. (2016). Influence of HLA on human partnership and sexual satisfaction. *Scientific Reports, 6(1),* 32550-32550. doi:10.1038/srep32550
362. Kudinova, A., Burkhouse, K., Seigle, G., Owens, M., Woody, M., & Gibb, B. (2016). Pupillary reactivity to negative stimuli prospectively predicts recurrence of major depressive disorder in women. *Psychophysiology, 53,* 1836-1842.
363. Kuehner, C. (2017). Why is depression more common among women than men? *The Lancet Psychiatry, 4,* 146-158.
364. Kuhn, C. (2015). Emergence of sex differences in the development of substance use and abuse during adolescence. *Pharmacology and Therapeutics, 153,* 55-78.
365. Kung, K., Browne, W., Constantinescu, M., Noorderhaven, R., & Hines, M. (2016). Early postnatal testosterone predicts sex-related differences in early expressive vocabulary. *Psychoneuroendocrinology, 68,* 111-116.
366. Kuo, P., Carp, J., Light, K., & Grewen, K. (2012). Neural responses to infants linked with behavioral interactions and testosterone in fathers. *Biological Psychology, 91,* 302-306.
367. Kurth, F., Jancke, L., & Luders, E. (2016). Sexual dimorphism of Broca's Region: More gray matter in female brains in Brodmann area 44 and 45. *Journal of Neuroscience Research, 95,* 626-632.

368. Kurth, F., Spencer, D., Hines, M., & Luders, E. (2018). Sex differences in associations between spatial ability and corpus callosum morphology. *J Neuro Res, 96,* 1380-1387.
369. Kurth, F., Zilles, K., Fox, P., Laird, A., & Eickhoff, S. (2010). A link between the systems: Functional differentiation and integration within the human insula revealed by meta-analysis. *Brain Struct Funct., 214,* 519–537.
370. Kwak, J., Willse, A., Preti, G., Yamazaki, K., & Beauchamp, G. (2010). In search of the chemical basis for MHC odourtypes. *Proceedings of the Royal Society B: Biological Sciences, 277,* 2417–2425.
371. Laakkonen, E., Soliymani, R., Karvinen, S., Kaprio, J., Kujala, U., et al. (2017). Estrogenic regulation of skeletal muscle proteome: A study of premenopausal women and postmenopausal MZ cotwins discordant for hormonal therapy. *Aging Cell, 16,* 1276-1287.
372. Lacagnina, S. (2019). Epigenetics. *American Journal of Lifestyle Medicine, 13,* 165-169.
373. Laeng, B., Sirois, S., & Gredebäck, G. (2012). Pupillometry: A window to the preconscious? *Perspectives on Psychological Science, 7,* 18-27.
374. Laguna, E., Barasona, J., Triguero-Ocana, R., Mulero-Pazmany, M., Negro, J., Vicente, J., & Acevedo, P. (2018). The relevance of host overcrowding in wildlife epidemiology: A new spatially explicit aggregation index. *Ecological Indicators, 84,* 695-700.
375. Laier, C., Pawlikowski, M., & Brand, M. (2014). Sexual picture processing interferes with decision-making under ambiguity. *Archives of Sexual Behavior, 43,* 473-482. doi:10.1007/s10508-013-0119-8
376. Lamminmaki, A., Hines, M., Kuiri-Hanninen, T., Kilpelainen, L., Dunkel, L., & Sankilampi, U. (2012). Testosterone measured in infancy predicts subsequent sex-typed behavior in boys and in girls. *Hormones and Behavior, 61,* 611-616.
377. Lane, B., Piercy, C., & Carr, C. (2016). Making it facebook official: The warranting value of online relationship status disclosures on relational characteristics. *Computers in Human Behavior, 56,* 1-8.
378. Lannutti, P., Laliker, M., & Hale, J. (2001). Violations of expectations and social-sexual communication in student-professor interactions. *Communication Education, 50,* 69-82.
379. Lara, L., Scalco, S., Troncon, J., & Lopes, G. (2017). A model for the management of female sexual dysfunctions. *Gynecology and Obstetrics, 39,* 184-194.
380. Lassek, W., & Gaulin, S. (2016). What makes Jessica Rabbit sexy? Contrasting roles of waist and hip size. *Evolutionary Psychology, 14,* 147470491664345.
381. Lassen, A., Lehmann, C., Andersen, E., Werther, M., Thorsen, A., Trolle, E., Gross, G., & Tetens, I. (2015). Gender differences in purchase intentions and reasons for meal selection among fast food customers – Opportunities for healthier and more sustainable food. *Food Quality and Preference, 47,* 123-129.
382. Laurent, H., Powers, S., & Granger, D. (2013). Refining the multisystem view of the stress response: Coordination among cortisol, alpha-amylase, and subjective stress in response to relationship conflict. *Psychology & Behavior, 119,* 52-60.
383. Lawler III, E. (2008). The HR department: Give it more respect. *Wall Street Journal- Eastern Edition, 251,* R8.
384. Leaper, C. (2019). Young adults' conversational strategies during negotiation and self-disclosure in same-gender and mixed-gender friendships. *Sex roles, 81,* 561-575. doi:10.1007/s11199-019-1014-0
385. Leaper, C., & Robnett, R. (2011). Women are more likely than men to use tentative language, aren't they? A meta-analysis testing for gender differences and moderators. *Psychology of Women Quarterly, 35,* 129-142.
386. Leaper, C., & Smith, T. (2004). A meta-analytic review of gender variations in children's language use: Talkativeness, affiliative speech, and assertive speech. *Developmental Psychology, 40,* 993-1027.
387. Lebowitz, S. (2018). 7 common reasons people say they got divorced. *Business Insider, Dec. 17, 2018.* https://www.businessinsider.com/why-people-get-divorced-2017-12.
388. Lee, S., Jeong, B., Choi, J., & Kim, J. (2015). Sex differences in interactions between nucleus accumbens and visual cortex by explicit visual erotic stimuli: An fMRI study. *International Journal of Impotence Research, 27(5),* 161-166.

389. Legger, K., Cornier, M., Bessesen, D., Mohl., B., Thomas, E., & Tregellas, J. (2018). Greater reward-related neuronal response to hedonic foods in women compared with men. *Obesity Biology and Integrated Physiology, 26*, 362-367.
390. Leonti, M., & Casu, L. (2018). Ethnopharmacology of love. *Frontiers in Pharmacology, 9* doi:10.3389/fphar.2018.00567
391. Lerner, T., Ye, L., & Deisseroth, K. (2016). Communication in neural circuits: Tools, opportunities, and challenges. *Cell, 164,* 1136-1150.
392. Levine, S., Foley, A., Lourenco, S., Ehrlich, S., & Ratliff, K. (2016). Sex differences in spatial cognition: Advancing the conversation. *WIREs Cogn Sci, 7,* 127-155.
393. Li, C., Liu, C., Gao, G., Liu, Z., & Wang, Y. (2019). Robust low-rank decomposition of multi-channel feature matrices for fabric defect detection. *Multimedia Tools and Applications, 78,* 7321-7339.
394. Light, K., Grewen, K., & Amico, J. (2005). More frequent partner hugs and higher oxytocin levels are linked lower blood pressure and heart rate in premenopausal women. *Biological Psychology, 69,* 5-21.
395. Likowski, K., Mühlberger, A., Gerdes, A., Wieser, M., Pauli, P., & Weyers, P. (2012). Facial mimicry and the mirror neuron system: Simultaneous acquisition of facial electromyography and functional magnetic resonance imaging. *Frontiers in Human Neuroscience, 6,* 214-224.
396. Lind, A., Richter, S., Craft, C., & Shapiro, A. (2017). Implementation of routine postpartum depression screening and care initiation across a multispecialty health care organization: An 18-month retrospective analysis. *Maternal and Child Health Journal, 21,* 1234-1239.
397. Linden, D., Dunkel, C., & Madison, G. (2017). Sex differences in brain size and general intelligence (g). *Intelligence, 63,* 78-88.
398. Lindsay, J., & Boyle, P. (2017). The conceptual penis as a social construct. *Cogent Social Sciences, 3,* 1-7.
399. Lischke, A., Weippert, M., Mau-Moeller, A., Paschke, S., Jacksteit, R., Hamm, A., & Pahnke, R. (2019). Sex-specific associations between inter-individual differences in heart rate variability and inter-individual differences in emotion regulation. *Frontiers in Neuroscience, 12: 1040.* doi: 10.3389/fnins.2018.01040.
400. Lisofsky, N., Martensson, J., Eckert, A., Lindenberger, U., Gallinat, J., & Kuhn, S. (2015). Hippocampal volume and functional connectivity changes during the female menstrual cycle. *NeuralImage, 118,* 154-162.
401. Little, A., DeBruine, L., & Jones, B. (2014). Sex differences in attraction to familiar and unfamiliar opposite-sex faces: Men prefer novelty and women prefer familiarity. *Archives of Sexual Behavior, 43,* 973-981. doi:10.1007/s10508-013-0120-2
402. Liu, J., Harris, A., & Kanwisher, N. (2010). Perception of face parts and face configurations: an fMRI study. *Journal of Cognitive Neuroscience, 22,* 203–211.
403. Long, M., Steinke, J., Applegate, B., Knight Lapinski, M., Johnson, M., & Ghosh, S. (2010). Portrayals of male and female scientists in television programs popular among middle school-age children. *Science Communication, 3,* 356–382.
404. Losh, S., Wilke, R., & Pop, M. (2008). Some methodological issues with "Draw A Scientist Tests" among young children. *International Journal of Science Education, 30,* 773–792.
405. Lothe, A., Boni, C., Costes, N., Gorwood, P., Bouvard, S., et al. (2009). Association between triallelic polymorphism of the serotonin transporter and [18F]MPPF binding potential at 5-HT1A receptors in healthy subjects. *Neuroimage, 47,* 482-492.
406. Lotze, M., Domin, M., Gerlach, F., Gaser, C., Lueders, E., Schmidt, C., & Neumann, N. (2019). Novel findings from 2,838 adult brains on sex differences in gray matter brain volume. *Scientific Reports, 9:* 1671. https://doi.org/10.1038/s41598-018-38239-2
407. Love, T. (2014). Oxytocin, motivation and the role of dopamine. *Pharmacology, Biochemistry and Behavior, 119,* 49-60.
408. Lübke, K., Hoenen, M., & Pause, B. (2012). Differential processing of social chemosignals obtained from potential partners in regards to gender and sexual orientation. *Behavioural Brain Research, 228,* 375-387.
409. Lubke, K., & Pause, B. (2015). Always follow your nose: The functional significance of social chemosignals in human reproduction and survival. *Hormones and Behavior, 68,* 134-144.

410. Lubkin, I., & Larson, P. (2013). *Chronic Illness: Impact and Intervention (8th ed.).* Jones & Bartlett Learning, Burlington, MA.
411. Lucas, I., Sanchez-Adam, A., Vila, J., & Guerra, P. (2019). Positive emotional reactions to loved names. *Psychophysiology, E13363,* https://doi.org/10.1111/psyp.13363
412. Lum, K., Sundaram, R., Louis, G., & Louis, T. (2016). A Bayesian joint model of menstrual cycle length and fecundity. *Biometrics, 72,* 193-203.
413. Lumsden, J., Miles, L., Richardson, M., Smith, C., & Macrae, C. (2012). Who syncs? Social motives and interpersonal coordination. *Journal of Experimental Social Psychology, 48,* 746-751.
414. Lundström, J., & Jones-Gotman, M. (2009). Romantic love modulates women's identification of men's body odors. *Hormones and Behavior, 55,* 280-284. doi:10.1016/j.yhbeh.2008.11.009
415. Lungu, O., Potvin, S., Tikàsz, A., & Mendrek, A. (2015). Sex differences in effective fronto-limbic connectivity during negative emotion processing. *Psychoneuroendocrinology, 62,* 180-188.
416. Luo, L., Becker, B., Geng, Y., Zhao, Z., Gao, S., Zhao, W., Yao, S., Zheng, X, Ma, X., Gao, Z., Hu, J., & Kendrick, K. (2017). Sex-dependent neural effect of oxytocin during subliminal processing of negative emotion faces. *NeuroImage, 162,* 127-137.
417. Lusk, B., Carr, A., Ranson, V., & Felmingham, K. (2017). Women in the midluteal phase of the menstrual cycle have difficulty suppressing the processing of negative emotional stimuli: An event-related potential study. *Cogn Affect Behav Neurosci, 17,* 886-903.
418. Luster, J., Turner, A., Henry, J., John P., & Gallo, M. (2019). Association between pubic hair grooming and prevalent sexually transmitted infection among female university students. *PloS One, 14(9),* e0221303. doi:10.1371/journal.pone.0221303
419. Ma, X., Zhao, W., Luo, R., Zhou, F., Geng, Y., Xu, L., Gao, Z., Zheng, X., Becker, B., & Kendrick, K. (2018). Sex-and-content dependent effects of oxytocin on social sharing. *NeuroImage, 183,* 62-72.
420. Madison, G. (2017). Presumption and prejudice: Quotas may solve some problems, but create many more. *Mankind Quarterly, 58,* 117-138.
421. Madison, G., & Soderlund, T. (2018). Comparisons of content and scientific quality indicators across peer-reviewed journal articles with more or less gender perspective: Gender studies can do better. *Scientometrics, 115,* 1161-1183.
422. Maeng, L., & Milad, M. (2015). Sex differences in anxiety disorders: Interactions between fear, stress, and gonadal hormones. *Hormones and Behavior, 75,* 106-117.
423. Mahaldar, O., & Aditya, S. (2017). Gender differences in brain activity during exposure to emotional film clips: An EEG study. *Cognition, Brain, Behavior, 21,* 29-53.
424. Mahmoud, R., Wainwright, S., & Galea, L. (2016). Sex hormones and adult hippocampal neurogenesis: Regulation, implications, and potential mechanisms. *Frontiers in Neuroendocrinology, 41,* 129-152.
425. Ma-Kellams, C., Wang, M., & Cardiel, H. (2017). Attractiveness and relationship longevity: Beauty is not what it is cracked up to be: Attractiveness and relationship outcomes. *Personal Relationships, 24,* 146-161.
426. Manippa, V., Padulo, C., van der Laan, L., & Brancucci, A. (2017). Gender differences in food choice: Effects of superior temporal sulcus stimulation. *Frontiers in Human Neuroscience, 11:* 597. doi: 10.3389/fnhum.2017.00597
427. Mankarious, A., Dave, F., Pados, G., Tsolakidis, D., Gidron, Y., & Pang, Y. (2016). The pro-social neurohormone oxytocin reverses the actions of the stress hormone cortisol in human ovarian carcinoma cells in vitro. *International Journal of Oncology, 48,* 1805-1814.
428. Marchewka, A., Jednorog, K., Falkiewicz, M., Szeszkowski, W., Grabowska, A., & Szatkowska, I. (2012). Sex, lies and fMRI--gender differences in neural basis of deception. *PloS One, 7(8),* e43076-e43076. doi:10.1371/journal.pone.0043076
429. Mareckova, K., Holsen, L., Admon, R., Whitfield-Gabrieli, S., Seidman, L., Buka, S., Klibanski, A., & Goldstein, J. (2017). Neural-hormonal responses to negative affective stimuli: Impact of dysphoric mood and sex. *Journal of Affective Disorders, 222,* 88-97.
430. Marrocco, J., & McEwen, B. (2016). Sex in the brain: Hormones and sex differences. *Dialogues Clin Neurosci, 18,* 373-383.
431. Marsland, A., Gianaros, P., Kuan, D., Sheu, L., Krajina, K., & Manuck, S. (2015). Brain morphology links systemic inflammation to cognitive function in midlife adults. *Brain, Behavior, & Immunity, 48,* 195-204.

432. Masihy, M., Monrroy, H., Borghi, G., Pribic, T., Galan, C., Nieto, A., Accarino, A., & Azpiroz, F. (2019). Influence of eating schedule on the postprandial response: Gender differences. *Nutrients, 11*, 401-411. doi:10.3390/nu11020401
433. Mather, M., Cacioppo, J., & Kanwisher, N. (2013). How fMRI can inform cognitive theories. *Perspectives on Psychological Science, 8*, 98-103.
434. Mather, M., Lighthall, N., Nga, L., & Gorlick, M. (2010). Sex differences in how stress affects brain activity during face viewing. *Neuroreport, 21*, 933-937.
435. Matsuda, S., Matsuzawa, D., Ishii, D., Tomizawa, H., Sutoh, C., & Shimizu, E. (2015). Sex differences in fear extinction and involvements of extracellular signal-regulated kinase (ERK). *Neurobiology of Learning & Memory, 123*, 117-124.
436. Mautz, B., Wong, B., Peters, R., & Jennions, M. (2013). Penis size interacts with body shape and height to influence male attractiveness. *Proceedings of the National Academy of Sciences of the United States of America, 110*, 6925-6930. doi:10.1073/pnas.1219361110
437. Mazzuca, S., Kafetsios, K., Livi, S., & Presaghi, F. (2019). Emotion regulation and satisfaction in long-term marital relationships: The role of emotional contagion. *Journal of Social and Personal Relationships, 36*, 2880-2895.
438. McEwen, B. (2018). Redefining neuroendocrinology: Epigenetics of brain-body communication over the life course. *Frontiers in Neuroendocrinology, 49*, 8-30.
439. McEwen, B., & Milner, T. (2016). Understanding the broad influence of sex hormones and sex differences in the brain. *Journal of Neuroscience Research, 95*, 24-39.
440. McEwen, B, Nasca, C., & Gray, J. (2016). Stress effects on neuronal structure: Hippocampus, amygdala, and prefrontal cortex. *Neuropsychopharmacology, 41*, 3-23.
441. McGivern, R., Mosso, M., Freudenberg, A., & Handa, R. (2019). Sex related biases for attending to object color versus object position are reflected in reaction time and accuracy. *PloS One, 14(1)*, e0210272.
442. McHenry, J., Carrier, N., Hull, E., & Kabbaj, M. (2014). Sex differences in anxiety and depression: role of testosterone. *Front Neuroendocrinol, 35*, 42–57.
443. McLaughlin, K., Baran, S., & Conrad, C. (2009). Chronic stress- and sex-specific neuromorphological and functional changes in limbic structures. *Molecular Neurobiology, 40*, 166-182.
444. McNamara, H., Kane, S., Craig, J., Short, R., & Umstad, M. (2015). A review of the mechanisms and evidence for typical and atypical twinning. *American Journal of Obstetrics and Gynecology, 214*, 172-191.
445. McNulty, J., Olson, M., & Joiner, T. (2019). Implicit interpersonal evaluations as a risk factor for suicidality: Automatic spousal attitudes predict changes in the probability of suicidal thoughts. *Journal of Personality and Social Psychology*, doi:10.1037/pspi0000180
446. Melas, P., Wei, Y., Wong, C., Sj€oholm, L., Aberg, E., Mill, J., et al. (2013). Genetic and epigenetic associations of MAOA and NR3C1 with depression and childhood adversities. *Int J Neuropsychopharmacol, 16*, 1513–1528.
447. Melchior, M., Poisbeau, P., Gaumond, I., & Marchand, S. (2016). Insights into the mechanisms and the emergence of sex-differences in pain. *Neuroscience, 338*, 63-80.
448. Menehan, K. (2012). Orphans blossom with massage. *Massage Magazine, 190*, 18.
449. Miller, S., & Maner, J. (2011). Ovulation as a male mating prime: Subtle signs of women's fertility influence men's mating cognition and behavior. *Journal of Personality and Social Psychology, 100*, 295-308.
450. Miller-Ott, A., & Kelly, L. (2015). The presence of cell phones in romantic partner face-to-face interactions: An expectancy violation theory approach. *Southern Communication Journal, 80*, 253-270.
451. Mogan, R., Fischer, R., & Bulbulia, J. (2017). To be in synchrony or not? A meta-analysis of synchrony's effects on behavior, perception, cognition and affect. *Journal of Experimental Social Psychology, 72*, 13-20.
452. Montirosso, R., Casini, E., Borgatti, R., & Urgesi, C. (2016). Relationship between maternal sensitivity during early interaction and maternal ability in perceiving infants' body and face. *Infancy, 21*, 582-602.
453. Morey, A. (2018). Electroencephalography in communication research: A review of the past and a glimpse of future possibilities. *Annals of the International Communication Association, 42*, 243-269.

454. Moses-Kolko, E., Horner, M., Phillips, M., Hipwell, A., & Swain, J. (2014). In search of neural endophenotypes of postpartum psychopathology and disrupted maternal caregiving. *Journal of Neuroendocrinology, 26,* 665-684.
455. Motaqhey, M., Ghanjal, A., Reza, M., Ghabaee, M., Kaka, G., Noroziyan, M., & Fadaee Fathabadi, F. (2015). Sex differences in neuroanatomy of the human mirror neuron system: Impact on functional recovery of ischemic hemiparetic patients. *Iranian Red Crescent Medical Journal, 17,* e28363. doi:10.5812/ircmj.28363
456. Motosko, C., Zakhem, G., Pomeranz, M., & Hazen, A. (2019). A side-effect of masculinizing hormonal therapy. *British Journal of Dermatology, 180(1),* e18-e18. doi:10.1111/bjd.17372.
457. Moulton, C., Pickup, J., & Ismail, K. (2015). The link between depression and diabetes: The search for shared mechanisms. *Lancet Diabetes Endocrinol, 3,* 461–71.
458. Mueller, S., Wierckx, K., Jackson, K., & T'sjoen, G. (2016). Circulating androgens correlate with resting-state MRI in transgender men. *Psychoneuroendocrinology, 73,* 91-98.
459. Muise, A., Impett, E., Kogan, A., & Desmarais, S. (2013). Keeping the spark alive: Being motivated to meet a Partner's sexual needs sustains sexual desire in long-term romantic relationships. *Social Psychological and Personality Science, 4,* 267-273.
460. Mukamel, R., Ekstrom, A., Kaplan, J., Iacoboni, M., & Fried, I. (2010). Single-neuron responses in humans during execution and observation of actions. *Curr. Biol. 20,* 750–756.
461. Mullinax, M., Herbenick, D., Schick, V., Sanders, S., & Reece, M. (2015). In their own words: A qualitative content analysis of women's and men's preferences for women's genitals. *Sex Education, 15,* 421-436. doi:10.1080/14681811.2015.1031884
462. Muram, D., Zhang, X., Cui, Z., & Matsumoto, A. (2015). Use of hormone testing for the diagnosis and evaluation of male hypogonadism and monitoring of testosterone therapy: Application of hormone testing guideline recommendations in clinical practice. *The Journal of Sexual Medicine, 12(9),* 1886.
463. Murdaugh, D., Cox, J., Cook, E., & Seller, R. (2012). fMRI reactivity to high-calorie food pictures predicts short- and long-term outcome in a weight-loss program. *NeuroImage, 59,* 2709–2721.
464. Murray, I., Parry, N., McKeefry, D., & Panorgias, A. (2012). Sex-related differences in peripheral human color vision: A color matching study. *Journal of Vision, 12,* 1-10.
465. Myers, B., Scheimann, J., Franco-Villanueva, A., & Herman, J. (2016). Ascending mechanisms of stress integration: Implications for brainstem regulation of neuroendocrine and behavioral stress responses. *Neuroscience and Behavioral Reviews, 74,* 366-375.
466. Naderi, S. (2016). Testosterone replacement therapy and the cardiovascular system. *Current Atherosclerosis Reports, 18(4),* 1-66. doi: 10.3389/fendo.2018.00066
467. Nakagawa, J., Takahashi, M., Okada, R., Matsushima, E., & Matsuda, T. (2015). Women's preference for a male acquaintance enhances social reward processing of material goods in the anterior cingulate cortex. *PloS One, 10(8),* e0136168-e0136168. doi:10.1371/journal.pone.0136168
468. Nappi, R., & Albani, F. (2016). Recovering sex drive in women - progress and opportunities. *Nature Reviews Urology, 13(2),* 67. doi:10.1035/nrurol.2015.314
469. Nazareth, A., Huang, X., Voyer, D., & Newcombe, N. (2019). A meta-analysis of sex differences in human navigation skills. *Psychonomic Bulletin & Review, 26,* 1503-1528.
470. Necka, E., Kardan, O., Puts, D., Faig, K., Berman, M., & Norman, G. (2019). Visual cues to fertility are in the eye (movements) of the beholder. *Hormones and Behavior, 115,* 104562. doi:10.1016/j.yhbeh.2019.104562
471. Neitz J., & Neitz, M. (2011). The genetics of normal and defective color vision. *Vision Res., 51,* 633–651.
472. Nitschke, J., & Bartz, J. (2020). Lower digit ratio and higher endogenous testosterone are associated with lower empathic accuracy. *Hormones and Behavior, 119,* 104648. doi:10.1016/j.yhbeh.2019.104648
473. Noack, H., Nolte, L., Nieratschker, V., Habel, U., & Derntl, B. (2019). Imaging stress: An overview of stress inductions methods in the MR scanner. *Journal of Neural Transmission.* https://doi.org/10.1007/s00702-018-01965-y

474. Nofal, A., Nicolaou, N., Symeonidou, N., & Shane, S. (2018). Biology and Management: A review, critique, and research agenda. *Journal of Management, 44,* 7-31.
475. Nordin, K., Herlitz, A., Larsson, E., & Söderlund, H. (2017). Overlapping effects of age on associative memory and the anterior hippocampus from middle to older age. *Behavioural Brain Research, 317,* 350-359.
476. Nugent, B., Wright, C., Shetty, A., Hodes, G., Lenz, K., & Mahurkar, A. (2015). Brain feminization requires active repression of masculinization via DNA methylation. *Nature Neuroscience, 18,* 690-700.
477. Núñez, C., Theofanopoulou, C., Senior, C., Cambra, M., Usall, J., Stephan-Otto, C., & Brebion, G. (2018). A large-scale study on the effects of sex on gray matter asymmetry. *Brain Structure and Function, 223,* 183-193.
478. Nuzzi, R., Scalabrin, S., Becco, A., & Panzica, G. (2018). Gonadal hormones and retinal disorders: A review. *Frontiers in Endocrinology, 9,* 66. doi: 10.3389/fendo.2018.00066
479. Oatridge, A., Holdcroft, A., Saeed, N., Hajnal, J., Puri, B., Fusi, L., & Bydder, G. (2002). Change in brain size during and after pregnancy: Study in healthy women and women with pre-eclampsia. *AJNR American Journal of Neuroradiology. 23,* 19-26.
480. Ober, C., Gilad, Y., & Loisel, D. (2008). Sex-specific genetic architecture of human disease. *Nature Reviews Genetics, 9,* 911-922.
481. Ogawa, S., Tsukahara, S., Choleris, E., & Vasudevan, N. (2020). Estrogenic regulation of social behavior and sexually dimorphic brain formation. *Neuroscience and Biobehavioral Reviews, 110,* 46-59.
482. Olderback, S., Wilhelm, O., Hildebrandt, A., & Quoidbach, J. (2019). Sex differences in facial emotion perception ability across the lifespan. *Cognition & Emotion, 33,* 579-588.
483. Oliveira-Pinto, A., Santos, R., Coutinho, R., Oliveira, L., Santos, G., Alho, A., Leite, R., Farfel, J., Suemoto, C., Grinberg, L., Pasqualucci, C., Jacob-Filho, W., & Lent, R. (2014). Sexual dimorphism in the human olfactory bulb: Females have more neurons and glial cells than males. *PLoS ONE 9,* e111733.
484. Oliver, T., Meana, M., & Snyder, J. (2016). Sex differences in concordance rates between auditory event-related potentials and subjective sexual arousal. *Psychophysiology, 53,* 1272-1281. doi:10.1111/psyp.12661
485. Opwis, M., Schmidt, J., Martin, A., & Salewski, C. (2017). Gender differences in eating behavior and eating pathology: The mediating role of rumination. *Appetite, 110,* 103-107.
486. O'Shaughnessy, P., Antignac, J., Le Bizec, B., Morvan, M., Svechnikov, K., & Soder, O., Pavlova, M. (2017). Sex and gender affect the social brain: Beyond simplicity. *Journal of Neuroscience Research, 95,* 235-250.
487. Osterberg, E., Gaither, T., Awad, M., Truesdale, M., Allen, I., Sutcliffe, S., & Breyer, B. (2017). Correlation between pubic hair grooming and STIs: Results from a nationally representative probability sample. *Sexually Transmitted Infections, 93,* 162-166.
488. Oved, O. (2017). Rethinking the place of love needs in Maslow's hierarchy of needs. *Society, 54,* 537-538.
489. Overbeek, G., Nelemans, S., Karremans, J., & Engels, R. (2013). The malleability of mate selection in speed-dating events. *Archives of Sexual Behavior, 42,* 1163-1171. doi:10.1007/s10508-012-0067-8
490. Oyola, M., & Handa, R. (2017). Hypothalamic-pituitary-adrenal and hypothalamic-pituitary-gonadal axes: Sex differences in regulation of stress responsivity. *Stress, 20,* 476-494.
491. Pan, Y., Cheng, X., Zhang, Z., Li, X., & Hu, Y. (2016). Cooperation in lovers: An fNIRS-Based Hyperscanning study. *Human Brain Mapping, 38,* 831-841.
492. Panasevich, E., & Tsitseroshin, M. (2015). The ability to successfully perform different kinds of cognitive activity is reflected in the topological features of intercortical interactions: Sex-related differences between boys and girls aged five to six years. *Human Physiology, 41,* 39-56.
493. Papadakis, G., Hans, D., Gonzalez-Rodriguez, E., Vollenweider, P., Waeber, G., Marques-Vidal, P., & Lamy, O. (2016). The benefit of menopausal hormone therapy on bone density and microarchitecture persists after its withdrawal. *The Journal of Clinical Endocrinology and Metabolism, 101,* 5004-5011.

494. Papadopoulos, V., Aghazadeh, Y., Fan, J., Campioli, E., Zirkin, B., & Midzak, A. (2015). Translocator protein-mediated pharmacology of cholesterol transport and steroidogenesis. *Molecular and Cellular Endocrinology, 408,* 90-98.
495. Parise, M., Pagani, A., Donato, S., & Sedikides, C. (2019). Self-concept clarity and relationship satisfaction at the dyadic level. *Personal Relationships, 26,* 54-72.
496. Park, C. (2010). Making sense of the meaning literature: An integrative review of meaning making and its effects on adjustment to stressful life effects. *Psychological Bulletin, 136,* 257-301.
497. Park, J., Carter, E., & Larson, A. (2019). Risk factors for acne development in the first 2 years after initiating masculinizing testosterone therapy among transgender men. *Journal of the American Academy of Dermatology, 81,* 617-618.
498. Parma, V., Tirindelli, R., Bisazza, A., Massaccesi, S., & Castiello, U. (2012). Subliminally perceived odours modulate female intrasexual competition: An eye movement study. *PloS One, 7(2),* e30645. doi:10.1371/journal.pone.0030645
499. Parsons, C., Young, K., Jegindoe Elmholdt, E., Stein, A., & Kringelbach, M. (2017). Interpreting infant emotional expressions: Parenthood has differential effects on men and women. *The Quarterly Journal of Experimental Psychology, 70,* 554-564.
500. Pasterski, V., Acerini, C., Dunger, D., Ong, K., Hughes, I., Thankamony, A., & Hines, M. (2015). Postnatal penile growth concurrent with mini-puberty predicts later sex-typed play behavior: Evidence for neurobehavioral effects of the postnatal androgen surge in typically developing boys. *Hormones and Behavior, 69,* 98-105.
501. Paterson, L., Jin, E., Amsel, R., & Binik, Y. (2014). Gender similarities and differences in sexual arousal, desire, and orgasmic pleasure in the laboratory. *The Journal of Sex Research, 51,* 801-813.
502. Pauley, P., Floyd, K., & Hess, C. (2014). The stress-buffering effects of a brief dyadic interaction before an accurate stressor. *Health Communication, 30,* 646-659.
503. Pavlicev, M., & Wagner, G. (2016). The evolutionary origin of female orgasm. *J. Exp. Zool. (Mol. Dev. Evol.) 326B:* 326-337.
504. Pavlova, M. (2017). Sex and gender affect the social brain: Beyond simplicity. *Journal of Neuroscience Research, 95,* 235-250.
505. Pazzaglia, M. (2015). Body and odors: Not just molecules, after all. *Current Directions in Psychological Science, 24,* 329-333. doi:10.1177/0963721415575329
506. Pecho, O., Ghinea, R., Perez, M., & Bona, A. (2017). Influence of gender on visual shade matching in dentistry. *Journal of Esthetic and Restorative Dentistry, 29,* E15-E23.
507. Pedrazzini, E., & Ptak, R. (2019). Damage to the right temporoparietal junction, but not the lateral prefrontal or insular cortex, amplifies the role of goal-directed attention. *Scientific Reports, 9,* 1-12.
508. Peltola, M., Strathearn, L., & Puura, K. (2018). Oxytocin promotes face-sensitive neural responses to infant and adult faces in mothers. *Psychoneuroendocrinology, 91,* 261-270.
509. Perani, C., & Slattery, D. (2014). Using animal models to study post-partum psychiatric disorders. *British Journal of Pharmacology, 171,* 4539–4555.
510. Perfalk, E., Cunha-Bang, S., Holst, K., Keller, S., Svarer, C., Knudsen, G., & Frokjaer, V. (2017). Testosterone levels in healthy men correlate negatively with serotonin 4 receptor binding. *Psychoneuroendocrinology, 81,* 22-28.
511. Perri, R., Berchicci, M., Bianco, V., Quinzi, F., Spinelli, D., & Russo, F. (2018). Awareness of perception and sensory-motor integration: ERPs from the anterior insula. *Brain Structure and Function, 223,* 3577-3592.
512. Perry, L., Goldstein-Piekarski, A., & Williams, L. (2017). Sex differences modulating serotonergic polymorphisms implicated in the mechanistic pathways of risk for depression and related disorders. *Journal of Neuroscience Research, 95,* 737-762.
513. Petering, R., & Brooks, N. (2017). Testosterone therapy: Review of clinical applications. *American Family Physician, 96,* 441-449.
514. Petersen, J. (2018). Gender differences in verbal performance: a meta-analysis of United States state performance assessments. *Educational Psychology Review, 30,* 1269-1281.
515. Petherick, A. (2017). Sexual arousal: Sex matters. *Nature, 550(7674),* S2-S3. doi:10.1038/550S2a
516. Pfaus, J. G. (2009). Pathways of sexual desire. *The Journal of Sexual Medicine, 6,* 1506-1533.

517. Pienta, R. & Smith, M. (2012). Women on the margins: The politics of gender in the language and content of science textbooks. In H. Hickman & B. J. Porfilio (Eds.), *The new politics of the textbook: Problematizing the portrayal of marginalized groups in textbooks (pp. 49–68)*. Rotterdam, The Netherlands: Sense.
518. Pierse, N., Carter, K., Bierre, S., Law, D., & Howden-Chapman, P. (2016). Housing, neighborhoods, & health: Examining the role of tenure, household crowding and housing affordability on psychological distress, using longitudinal data. *Epidemioology & Community Health, 70,* 961-966.
519. Pietromonaco, P., & Collins, N. (2017). Interpersonal mechanisms linking close relationships to health. *American Psychologist, 72,* 531-542.
520. Pineau, J., Montemerlo, M., Pollack, M., Roy, N., & Thrun, S. (2003). Towards robotic assistants in nursing homes: Challenges and results. *Robotics and Autonomous Systems, 42,* 271-281.
521. Pintzka, C., Evensmoen, H., Lehn, H., & Håberg, A. (2016). Changes in spatial cognition and brain activity after a single dose of testosterone in healthy women. *Behavioural Brain Research, 298,* 78-90.
522. Pletzer, B. (2016). Sex differences in numbers processing: Differential systems for subtraction and multiplication were confirmed in men, but not in women. *Scientific Reports, 6,* 39064 http://dx.doi.org/10.1038/srep39064.
523. Pletzer, B., Harris, T., & Ortner, T. (2017). Sex and menstrual cycle influences on three aspects of attention. *Psychology & Behaviors, 179,* 384-390.
524. Pletzer, B., Petasis, O., & Cahill, L. (2014). Switching between forest and trees: Opposite relationship of progesterone and testosterone to global–local processing. *Horm. Behav. 66,* 257–266.
525. Poels, S., Bloemers, J., Rooij, K., Koppeschaar, H., Olivier, B., & Tuiten, A. (2014). Two novel combined drug treatments for women with hypoactive sexual desire disorder. *Pharmacology, Biochemistry, and Behavior, 121,* 71-79.
526. Poeppl, T., Langguth, B., Rupprecht, R., Safron, A., Bzdok, D., Laird, A., & Eickhoff, S. B. (2016). The neural basis of sex differences in sexual behavior: A quantitative meta-analysis. *Frontiers in Neuroendocrinology, 43,* 28-43.
527. Polo, P., Muñoz-Reyes, J., Pita, M., Shackelford, T., & Fink, B. (2019). Testosterone-dependent facial and body traits predict men's sociosexual attitudes and behaviors. *American Journal of Human Biology, 31,* e23235-n/a. doi:10.1002/ajhb.23235
528. Porter, A., Leckie, R., & Verstynen, T. (2018). White matter pathways of both a target and mediator of health behaviors. *Ann. NY. Acad. Sci, 148,* 71-88.
529. Potter, R. & Bolls, P. (2011). *Psychophysiological measurement and meaning: Cognitive and emotional processing of media.* New York, NY: Routledge.
530. Pozzato, L. (2010). Interpreting nonverbal communication for use in detecting deception. *Forensic Examiner, 19,* 86-97.
531. Prause, N., Park, J., Leung, S., & Miller, G. (2015). Women's preferences for penis size: A new research method using selection among 3D models. *PLoS ONE 10(9):* e0133079. doi:10.1371/journal.pone.0133079
532. Pressman, S. & Sheldon, S. (2005). Does positive affect influence health? *Psychological Bulletin, 131,* 925-971.
533. Previs, K. (2016). Gender and race representations of scientists in Highlights for Children: A content analysis. *Science Communication, 38,* 303–327.
534. Prochazkova, E., & Kret, M. (2017). Connecting minds and sharing emotions through mimicry: A neurocognitive model of emotional contagion. *Neuroscience and Biobehavioral Reviews, 80,* 99-114.
535. Prokop, P. (2016). Male preference for female pubic hair: An evolutionary view. *Anthropologischer Anzeiger, 73,* 169-175.
536. Proverbio, A. (2017). Sex differences in social cognition: The case of face processing. *Journal of neuroscience Research, 95,* 222-234.
537. Proverbio, A., Galli, J. (2016). Women are better at seeing faces where there are none: An ERP study of face pareidolia. *Soc Cogn Affect Neurosci, 11,* 1501–1512.
538. Proverbio, A., Ornaghi, L., & Gabaro, V. (2018). How face blurring affects body language processing of static gestures in women and men. *Social Cognition & Affective Neuroscience, 13,* 590-603.

539. Przybyszewski, A., & Polkowski, L. (2017). Theory of mind and empathy: Part I – Model of social emotional thinking. *Fundamenta Informaticae, 150,* 221-230.
540. Public Law 103-66. Omnibus Reconciliation Act of 1993.
541. Public Law 104-193. Personal Responsibility and Work Opportunity Reconciliation Act of 1996.
542. Quast, A., Hesse, V., Hain, J., Wermke, P., & Wermke, K. (2016). Baby babbling at five months linked to sex hormone levels in early infancy. *Infant Behavior and Development, 44,* 1-10.
543. Rahman, U., Hamid, N., Ubaidullah, Ahmad, N., Safeer, M., Tariq, M., & Rehman, J. (2012). The age at which testosterone starts decreasing in men now-a-days. *KMUJ-Khyber Medical University Journal, 4,* 174-178.
544. Raj, R., Korja, M., Koroknay-Pál, P., & Niemelä, M. (2018). Multiple meningiomas in two male-to-female transsexual patients with hormone replacement therapy: A report of two cases and a brief literature review. *Surgical Neurology International, 9,* 109-109.
545. Rajhans, P., Goin-Kochel, R., Strathearn, L., & Kim, S. (2019). It takes two! Exploring sex differences in parenting neurobiology and behaviour. *Journal of Neuroendocrinology, 31(9),* e12721-n/a. doi:10.1111/jne.12721
546. Rawson, C., & McCool, M. (2014). Just like all the other humans? Analyzing images of scientists in children's trade books. *School Science and Mathematics, 114,* 10-18.
547. Reber, J., & Tranel, D. (2017). Sex differences in the functional lateralization of emotion and decision making in the human brain. *Journal of Neuroscience Research, 95,* 270-278.
548. Rebman, P., Caines, M., & Harrison, P. (2018). In-hospital paternity establishment: Experiences and meaning perceived by unmarried parents. *Journal of Healthcare for the Poor and Underserved, 29,* 497-508.
549. Reid, V., Dunn, K., Young, R., Amu, J., Donovan, T., & Reissland, N. (2017). The human fetus preferentially engages with face-like visual stimuli. *Current Biology 27,* 1825–1828.
550. Reilly, D., Neumann, D., & Andrews, G. (2019). Gender differences in reading and writing achievement: Evidence from the national assessment of educational progress (NAEP). *American Psychologist, 74,* 445-458.
551. Renfro, K., & Hoffmann, H. (2013). The relationship between oral contraceptive use and sensitivity to olfactory stimuli. *Hormones and Behavior, 63,* 491-496.
552. Rentscher, K., Rohrbaugh, M., Shoham, V., & Mehl, M. (2013). Asymmetric partner pronoun use and demand-withdraw interaction in couples coping with health problems. *Journal of Family Psychology, 27,* 691-701.
553. Rezzani, R., Franco, C., & Rodella, L. (2019). Sex differences of brain and their implications for personalized therapy. *Pharmacological Research, 141,* 429-442.
554. Rice, W., Friberg, U., & Gavrilets, S. (2016). Epigenetic studies in ecology and evolution: Sexually antagonistic epigenetic marks that canalize sexually dimorphic development. *Molecular Ecology, 25,* 1812-1822.
555. Rieger, G., Chivers, M., & Bailey, J. (2005). Sexual arousal patterns of bisexual men. *Psychological Science, 16,* 579–584.
556. Rieger, G., & Savin-Williams, R. (2012). The eyes have it: Sex and sexual orientation differences in pupil dilation patterns. *PloS One, 7(8),* e40256-e40256. doi:10.1371/journal.pone.0040256
557. Righetti, F., Gere, J., Hofmann, W., Visserman, M., & Van Lange, P. (2016). The burden of empathy: Partners' responses to divergence of interests in daily life. *Emotion (Washington, D.C.), 16,* 684-690.
558. Rigo, P., Kim, P., Esposito, G., Putnick, D., Venuti, P., & Bornstein, M. (2019). Specific maternal brain responses to their own child's face: An fMRI meta-analysis. *Developmental Review, 51,* 58-69.
559. Rilling, J., & Young, L. (2014). The biology of mammalian parenting and its effect on offspring social development. *Science (New York, N.Y.), 345(6198),* 771.
560. Rincón-Cortés, M., & Grace, A. (2017). Sex-dependent effects of stress on immobility behavior and VTA dopamine neuron activity: Modulation by ketamine. *The International Journal of Neuropsychopharmacology, 20,* 823-832.

561. Rinn, J., Rozowsky, J., Laurenzi, I., Petersen, P., Zou, K., Zhong, W. et al. (2004). Major molecular differences between mammalian sexes are involved in drug metabolism and renal function. *Developmental Cell, 6,* 791-800.
562. Ritchie, S., Cox, S., Shen, X., Lombardo, M., Rein, L., Alloza, C., Harris, M., Alderson, H., Hunter, S., Neilson, E., Liewald, D., Auyeung, B., Whalley, H., Lawrie, S., Gale, C., Bastin, M., McIntosh, A., & Deary, I. (2018). Sex differences in the adult human brain: Evidence from 5216 UK Biobank participants. *Cerebral Cortex, 28,* 2959-2975.
563. Robbins, W., Xun, L., FitzGerald, L., Esguerra, S., Henning, S., & Carpenter, C. (2012). Walnuts improve semen quality in men consuming a western-style diet: Randomized control dietary intervention trial. *Biology of Reproduction, 87,* 101-108.
564. Roberts, A, &, Lopez-Duran, N. (2019). Developmental influences on stress response systems: Implications for psychopathology vulnerability in adolescence. *Comprehensive Psychiatry, 88,* 9-21.
565. Rodman, A. (2019). The real reason for divorce at midlife. Betterafter50.com https://betterafter50.com/the-real-reason-for-divorce-at-midlife/
566. Rodrigues, D., & Lopes, D. (2015). Development and validation of the measure of initial attraction- short interest scale (MIA-I). *Psicologia: Reflexão e Crítica, 28,* 261-269. doi:10.1590/1678-7153.201528206
567. Rodrigues, D., Lopes, D., Alexopoulos, T., & Goldenberg, L. (2017). A new look at online attraction: Unilateral initial attraction and the pivotal role of perceived similarity. *Computers in Human Behavior, 74,* 16-25. doi:10.1016/j.chb.2017.04.009
568. Rodriguez, L., Fillo, J., Hadden, B., Øverup, C., Baker, Z., & DiBello, A. (2019). Do you see what I see? Actor and partner attachment shape biased perceptions of partners. *Personality and Social Psychology Bulletin, 45,* 587-602.
569. Romero-Silva, R., Santos J., & Hurtado, M. (2018). A note on defining organisational systems for contingency theory in OM, *Production Planning & Control, 29,* 1343-1348, DOI: 10.1080/09537287.2018.1535146
570. Roney, J., & Simmons, Z. (2013). Hormonal predictors of sexual motivation in natural menstrual cycles. *Hormones and Behavior, 63,* 636-645.
571. Roney, J., & Simmons, Z. (2017). Ovarian hormone fluctuations predict within cycle shifts in women's food intake. *Hormones and Behavior, 90,* 8-14.
572. Roozendaal, B., & Hermans, E. (2017). Norepinephrine effects on the encoding and consolidation of emotional memory: Improving synergy between animal and human studies. *Curr. Opin. Behav. Sci., 14,* 115–122.
573. Roper, W. (2016). Architectonics of male amygdala. *Medical Hypotheses, 96,* 73-74.
574. Ross, J., Karney, B., Nguyen, T., & Bradbury, T. (2019). Communication that is maladaptive for middle-class couples is adaptive for socioeconomically disadvantaged couples. *Journal of Personality and Social Psychology, 116,* 582-597.
575. Ross, E., & Pulusu, V. (2013). Posed versus spontaneous facial expressions are modulated by opposite cerebral hemispheres. *Cortex, 49,* 1280-1291. doi:10.1016/j.cortex.2012.05.002
576. Routasalo, P. (1999). Physical touch in nursing studies: A literature review. *Journal of Advanced Nursing, 30,* 843-850.
577. Rubin, L., Yao, L., Keedy, S., Reilly, J., Bishop, J., Carter, C., Pournajafi-Nazarloo, H., Drogos, L., Tamminga, C., Pearlson, G., Keshavan, M., Clementz, B., Hill, S., Liao, W., Ji, G., Lui, S., & Sweeney, J. (2017). Sex differences in associations of arginine vasopressin and oxytocin with resting-state functional brain connectivity. *Journal of Neuroscience Research, 95,* 576-586.
578. Ruigrok, A., Salimi-Khorshidi, G., Lai, M., Baron-Cohen, S., Lombardo, M., Tait, R., & Suckling, J. (2014). A meta-analysis of sex differences in human brain structure. *Neuroscience and Biobehavioral Reviews, 39,* 34-50.
579. Rus, H., & Tiemensma, J. (2017). "It's Complicated." A systematic review of associations between social network site use and romantic relationships. *Computers in Human Behavior, 75,* 684-703.
580. Sachs, M., Habibi, A., Damasio, A., & Kaplan, J. (2018). Decoding the neural signatures of emotions expressed through sound. *NeuroImage, 174,* 1-10.
581. Salonia, A., Nappi, R., Pontillo, M., Daverio, R., Smeraldi, A., Briganti, A., et al. (2005). Menstrual cycle-related changes in plasma oxytocin are relevant to normal sexual function in healthy women. *Hormones and Behavior, 47,* 164-169.

582. Sandman, C., Glynn, L., & Davis, E. (2013). Is there a viability-vulnerability tradeoff? Sex differences in fetal programming. *Journal of Psychosomatic Research, 75,* 327-335.
583. Saunders, D., White, N., Dawson, R., & Mawson, P. (2018). Breeding site infidelity, and breeding pair infidelity in the endangered Carnaby's Cockatoo Calyptorhynchus latirostris. *Nature Conservation, 27,* 59-74.
584. Saxbe, D., Edelstein, R., Lyden, H., Wardecker, B., Chopik, W., & Moors, A. (2017). Fathers' decline in testosterone and synchrony with partner testosterone during pregnancy predicts greater postpartum relationship investment. *Hormones and Behavior, 90,* 39-47.
585. Saxton, T., Steel, C., Rowley, K., Newman, A., & Baguley, T. (2017). Facial resemblance between women's partners and brothers. *Evolution and Human Behavior, 38,* 429-433. doi:10.1016/j.evolhumbehav.2017.04.006
586. Schaadt, G., Hesse, V., & Friederici, A. (2015). Sex hormones in early infancy seem to predict aspects of later language development. *Brain & Language, 141,* 70-76.
587. Scheele, D., Plota, J., Stoffel-Wagner, B., Maier, W., & Hurlemann, R. (2016). Hormonal contraceptives suppress oxytocin-induced brain reward responses to the partner's face. *Social Cognitive and Affective Neuroscience, 11,* 767-774.
588. Scheibel, W. (2013). Marilyn monroe, 'sex symbol': Film performance, gender politics and 1950s hollywood celebrity. *Celebrity Studies, 4,* 4-13. doi:10.1080/19392397.2012.750095
589. Scheuringer, A., & Pletzer, B. (2017). Sex differences and menstrual cycle dependent changes in cognitive strategies during spatial navigation and verbal fluency. *Frontiers in Psychology, 8,* 1-12.
590. Schild-Suhren, M., Soliman, A., & Malik, E. (2017). Pubic hair shaving is correlated to vulvar dysplasia and inflammation: A case-control study. *Infectious Diseases in Obstetrics and Gynecology, 2017,* 9350307-5. doi:10.1155/2017/9350307
591. Schindler, S., Schmidt, L., Stroske, M., Storch, M., Anwander, A., Trampel,R., Strauß, M., Hegerl, U., Geyer, S., & Schonknecht, P. (2019). Hypothalamus enlargement in mood disorders. *Acta Psychiatricia Scandinavica, 139,* 56-67.
592. Schirmer, A., & Gunter, T. (2017). Temporal signatures of processing voiceness and emotion in sound. *Social Cognitive and Affective Neuroscience, 2017,* 902-909.
593. Schmidt, P., Ben, D., Martinez, P., Guerrieri, G., Harsh, V., Thompson, K., Koziol, D., Nieman, L., & Rubinow, D. (2015). Effects of estradiol withdrawal on mood in women with past perimenopausal depression: A randomized clinical trial. *JAMA Psychiatry, 72,* 714-726.
594. Schneider, F., Kliesch, S., Schlatt, S., & Neuhaus, N. (2017). Andrology of male-to-female transsexuals: Influence of cross-sex hormone therapy on testicular function. *Andrology, 5,* 873-880.
595. Schneiderman, I., Kanat-Maymon, Y., Zagoory-Sharon, O., & Feldman, R. (2014). Mutual influences between partners' hormones shape conflict dialog and relationship duration at the initiation of romantic love. *Social Neuroscience, 9,* 337-351.
596. Schwitzer, A., & Choate, L. (2015). College women eating disorder diagnostic profile and DSM-5. *Journal of American College Health, 63,* 73-78.
597. Segerdahl, A., Mezue, M., Okell, T., Farrar, J., & Tracey, I. (2015). The dorsal posterior insula subserves a fundamental role in human pain. *Nat Neurosci., 18,* 499–500.
598. Seider, B., Hirschberger, G., Nelson, K., & Levenson, R. (2009). We can work it out: Age differences in relational pronouns, physiology, and behavior in marital conflict. *Psychology and Aging, 24,* 604-613.
599. Seiffge-Krenke, I. (2011). Coping with relationship stressors: A decade review. *Journal of Research on Adolescence, 21,* 196-210.
600. Sels, L., Ceulemans, E., & Kuppens, P. (2017). Partner-expected affect: How you feel now is predicted by how your partner thought you felt before. *Emotion (Washington, D.C.), 17,* 1066-1077.
601. Senderovich, H., Ip, M., Berall, A., Karuza, J., Gordon, M., Binns, M., Wignarajah, S., Grossman, D., & Dunal, L. (2016). Therapeutic touch in a geriatric palliative care unit A retrospective review. *Complementary Therapies in Clinical Practice, 24,* 134-138.
602. Seo, D., Ahluwalia, A., Potenza, M., & Sinha, R. (2017). Gender differences in neural correlates of stress-induced anxiety. *Journal of Neuroscience Research, 95(1-2),* 115-125.

603. Seok, J., Sohn, J., & Cheong, C. (2016). Neural substrates of sexual arousal in heterosexual males: Event-related fMRI investigation. *Journal of Physiological Anthropology, 35*: 8. doi:10.1186/s40101-016-0089-3
604. Sethna, V., Perry, E., Domoney, J., Iles, J., Psychogiou, L., Rowbotham, N., Stein, A., Murray, L., & Ramchandani, P. (2017). Father–child interactions at 3 months and 24 months: Contributions to children's cognitive development at 24 months. *Infant Mental Health Journal, 38*, 378-390. doi:10.1002/imhj.21642
605. Shah, S. (2018). Systemic non-reproductive effects of sex steroids in adult males and females. *Human Physiology, 44*, 83-87.
606. Shamay-Tsoory, S., & Abu-Akel, A. (2016). The social salience hypothesis of oxytocin. *Biological Psychiatry, 79*, 194-202.
607. Shansky, R., & Woolley, C. (2016). Considering sex as a biological variable will be valuable for neuroscience research. *The Journal of Neuroscience: The Official Journal of the Society for Neuroscience, 36*, 11817-11822.
608. Shaqiri, A., Roinishvili, M., Grzeczkowski, L., Chkonia, E., Pilz, K., Mohr, C. et al. (2018). Sex-related differences in vision are heterogeneous. *Scientific Reports, 8*, 7521-10. doi:10.1038/s41598-018-25298-8
609. Shen, X., Wu, Y., Qian, M., Wang, X., Hou, Z., Liu, Y., et al. (2011). Tryptophan hydroxylase 2 gene is associated with major depressive disorder in a female Chinese population. *J Affect Disord, 133*, 619–624.
610. Sherry, J. (2015). Neuroscience and communication. *Communication Methods and Measures, 9*, 117-122.
611. Sherwin, B. (2012). Estrogen and cognitive functioning in women: Lessons we have learned. *Behavioral Neuroscience, 126*, 123-127.
612. Shi, L., Lou, W., Wong, A., Zhang, F., Abrigo, J., Chu, W. et al. (2019). Neural evidence for long-term marriage shaping the functional brain network organization between couples. *Neuroimage, 199*, 87-92.
613. Shuster, B., Depireux, D., Mong, J., & Hertzano, R. (2019). Sex differences in hearing: Probing the role of estrogen signaling. *The Journal of Acoustical Society of America, 145*, 3656. doi: 10.1121/1.5111870
614. Simaki, V., Aravantinou, C., Mporas, I., Kondyli, M., & Megalooikonomou, V. (2017). Sociolinguistic features for author gender identification: From qualitative evidence to quantitative analysis. *Journal of Quantitative Linguistics, 24*, 65-84.
615. Siman-Tov, T., Granot, R., Shany, O., Singer, N., Hendler, T., & Gordon, C. (2019). Is there a prediction network? Meta-analytic evidence for a cortical-subcortical network likely subserving prediction. *Neuroscience and Biobehavioral Reviews, 105*, 262-275.
616. Simpson, E., Maylott, S., Lazo, R., Leonard, K., Kaburu, S., Suomi, S., Paukner, A., & Ferrari, P. (2019). Social touch alters newborn monkey behavior. *Infant Behavior and Development, 57*, 101368. doi:10.1016/j.infbeh.2019.101368
617. Simson, V., Brewer, G., & Hendrie, C. (2014). Evidence to suggest that women's sexual behaviors is influenced by hip width rather than waist-to-hip ratio. *Arch Sex Behav, 43*,1367-1371.
618. Sletten, J., Cornelissen, G., Assmus, J., Kiserud, T., Albrechtsen, S., & Kessler, J. (2018). Maternal exercise, season and sex modify the daily fetal heart rate rythym. *Acta Physiologica, 224*, 1-15.
619. Smith, P., & Koehoorn, M. (2016). Measuring gender when you don't have a gender measure: Constructing a gender index using survey data. *International Journal for Equity in Health, 15*, 82-92.
620. Smy, L., & Straseski, J. (2018). Measuring estrogens in women, men, and children: Recent advances 2012-2017. *Clinical Biochemistry, 62*, 11-23.
621. Snowden, R., & Gray, N. (2013). Implicit sexual associations in heterosexual and homosexual women and men. *Archives of Sexual Behavior, 42*, 475-485. doi:10.1007/s10508-012-9920-z
622. Snyder, P., Bhasin, S., Cunningham, G., Matsumoto, A., Stephens-Shields, A., et al. (2016). Effects of testosterone treatment in older men. *The New England Journal of Medicine, 374*, 611-624.

623. Sodavari, M., Shahidi, M., Almadani, S, Moazedian, A., & Imani, M. (2014). The role of pleasant and unpleasant odors in the individual and social attractiveness. *Journal of Educational and Management Studies, 4(2),* 311–315.
624. Soderkvist, S., Ohlen, K., & Dimberg, U. (2018). How the experience of emotion is modulated by facial feedback. *Journal of Nonverbal Behavior, 42,* 129-151.
625. Soderlund, T., & Madison, G. (2017). Objectivity and realms of explanation in academic journal articles concerning sex/ gender: a comparison of Gender studies and the other social sciences. *Scientometrics, 112,* 1093-1109.
626. Solomon, D., & Brisini, K. (2019). Relational uncertainty and interdependence processes in marriage: A test of relational turbulence theory. *Journal of Social and Personal Relationships, 36,* 2416-2436.
627. Sorokowski, P., Karwowski, M., Misiak, M., Marczak, M., Dziekan, M., Hummel, T., & Sorokowska, A. (2019). Sex differences in human olfaction: A meta-analysis. *Front. Psychol.* 10: 242. doi: 10.3389/fpsyg.2019.00242
628. Sorokowski, P., Sorokowski, A., & Witzel, C. (2014). Sex differences in color preferences transcend extreme differences in culture and ecology. *Psychon Bull Rev, 21,* 1195-1201.
629. Spence, C. (2015). Just how much of what we taste derives from the sense of smell? *Flavour,* 4: 30. DOI 10.1186/s13411-015-0040-2.
630. Spence, C. (2019). Do men and women really live in different taste worlds? *Food Quality and Preference, 73,* 38-45.
631. Spence, C., Velasco, C., & Knoeferle, K. (2014). A large sample study on the influence of the multisensory environment on the wine drinking experience. *Flavour,* 3: 8. https://flavourjournal.biomedcentral.com/articles/10.1186/2044-7248-3-8
632. Staley, J., Sanacora, G., Tamagnan, G., Maciejewski, P., Malison, R., Berman, R., et al. (2006). Sex differences in diencephalon serotonin transporter availability in major depression. *Biol Psychiatry, 59,* 40–47.
633. Steinke, J. (2013). Portrayals of female scientists in the mass media. In A. Valdivia & S. R. Mazzarella (Eds.), *The international encyclopedia of media studies (pp. 1–18).* Oxford, UK: Blackwell.
634. Stenstrom, E., Saad, G., & Hingston, S. (2018). Menstrual cycle effects on prosocial orientation, gift giving, and charitable giving. *Journal of Business Research, 84,* 82-88.
635. Stevens, J., & Hamann, S. (2012). Sex differences in brain activation to emotional stimuli: A meta-analysis of neuroimaging studies. *Neuropsychologia, 50,* 1578-1593.
636. Stevenson, M., Sineath, R., Goodman, M., & Tangpricha, V. (2019). Breast cancer screening in transgender females on hormone therapy. *Endocrine Practice, 25,* 201-202.
637. Stoet, G. (2017). Sex differences in the simon task help to interpret sex differences in selective attention. *Psychological Research, 81,* 571-581.
638. Stone, N., Graham, C., & Baysal, I. (2017). Women's engagement in pubic hair removal: Motivations and associated factors. *International Journal of Sexual Health, 29,* 89-96.
639. Strahler, J., Kruse, O., Wehrum-Osinsky, S., Klucken, T., & Stark, R. (2018). Neural correlates of gender differences in distractibility by sexual stimuli. *Neuroimage, 176,* 499-509.
640. Strandqvist, A., Herlitz, A., Nordenskjöld, A., Örtqvist, L., Frisén, L., Hirschberg, A. L., & Nordenström, A. (2018). Cognitive abilities in women with complete androgen insensitivity syndrome and women with gonadal dysgenesis. *Psychoneuroendocrinology, 98,* 233-241.
641. Strathearn, L., Fonagy, P., Amico, J., & Montague, P. (2009). Adult attachment predicts maternal brain and oxytocin response to infant cues. *Neuropsychopharmacology, 34,* 2655-2666.
642. Striegel-Moore, R., Rosselli, F., Perrin, N., DeBar, L., Wilson, G., May, A., & Kraemer, H. (2009). Gender difference in the prevalence of eating disorder symptoms. *Int J Eat Disord, 42,* 471-474.
643. Sullivan, R. (2017). Attachment figure's regulation of infant brain and behavior. *Psychodynamic Psychiatry, 45,* 475-498.
644. Sunahara, C., Zelkowitz, P., Bolger, N., Sadikaj, G., Samuel, S., Gold, I., Hayton, B., Feeley, N., Carter, S., & Bartz, J. (2019). Maternal oxytocin predicts relationship survival during the perinatal transition period: Preliminary evidence. *International Journal of Psychophysiology, 136,* 33-38.

645. Sunwoo, H., Colognori, D., Froberg, J., Jeon, Y., & Lee, J. (2017). Repeat E anchors Xist RNA to the inactive X chromosomal compartment through CDKN1A-interacting protein (CIZ1). *PNAS, 114,* 10654-10659.
646. Sussman, D., Leung, R., Chakravarty, M., Lerch, J., & Taylor, M. (2016). The developing human brain: Age-related changes in cortical, subcortical, and cerebellar anatomy. *Brain and Behavior, 6(4),* e00457-n/a. doi:10.1002/brb3.457
647. Svedholm-Hakkinen, A. & Lindeman, M. (2016). Testing the empathizing-sympathizing theory in the general population: Occupations, vocational interests, grades, hobbies, friendship quality, social intelligence, and sex role identity. *Personality and Individual Differences, 90,* 365-370.
648. Swami, V. (2015). Cultural influences on body size ideals: Unpacking the impact of westernization and modernization. *European Psychologist, 20,* 44-51. doi:10.1027/1016-9040/a000150
649. Takeuchi, H., Taki, Y., Nouchi, R., Yokoyama, R., Kotozaki, Y., Nakagawa, S., Sekiguchi, A., Iizuka, K., Yamamoto, Y., Hanawa, S., Araki, T., Makoto Miyauchi, C., Shinada, T., Sakaki, K., Sassa, Y., Nozawa, T., Ikeda, S., Yokota, S., Daniele, M., & Kawashima, R. (2017). Creative females have larger white matter structures: Evidence from a large sample study. *Hum. Brain Mapp., 38:* 414-430.
650. Tang, D., Fellows, L., Small, D., & Dagher, A. (2012). Food and drug cues activate similar brain regions: A meta-analysis of functional MRI studies. *Physiol Behav., 106,* 317–324.
651. Tannen, D. (1990). *You just don't understand: Women and men in conversation.* New York: Morrow.
652. Tayah, T., Savard, M., Desbiens, R., & Nguyen, D. (2013). Ictal bradycardia and asystole in an adult with a focal left insular lesion. *Clin Neurol Neurosurg, 115,* 1885–1887.
653. Timmons, A., Arbel, R., & Margolin, G. (2017). Daily patterns of stress and conflict in couples: Associations with marital aggression and family-of-origin aggression. *Journal of family Psychology, 31,* 93-104.
654. Todd, B., Barry, J., & Thommessen, S. (2017). Preferences for 'Gender-typed' toys in boys and girls aged 9 to 32 months: Young children's 'Gender-typed' toy preferences. *Infant and Child Development, 26(3),* e1986. doi:10.1002/icd.1986
655. Traish, A., Botchevar, E., & Kim, N. (2010). Biochemical factors modulating female genital sexual arousal physiology. *The Journal of Sexual Medicine, 7,* 2925-2946.
656. Tran, M., Kuhn, J., Braz, J., & Basbaum, A. (2017). Neuronal aromatase expression in pain processing regions of the modullary and spinal cord dorsal horn. *The Journal of Comparative Neurology, 525,* 3414-3428.
657. Traustadóttir, T., Harman, S., Tsitouras, P., Pencina, K., Li, Z., Travison, T., et al. (2018). Long-term testosterone supplementation in older men attenuates age-related decline in aerobic capacity. *The Journal of Clinical Endocrinology & Metabolism, 103,* 2861-2869.
658. Triscoli, C., Croy, I., Olausson, H., & Sailer, U. (2014). Liking and wanting pleasant odors: Different effects of repetitive exposure in men and women. *Frontiers in Psychology, 5,* 526.
659. Tschernegg, M., Neuper, C., Schmidt, R., Wood, G., Kronbichler, M., Fazekas, F., Enzinger, C., & Koini, M. (2017). FMRI to probe sex-related differences in brain function with multitasking. *PloS One, 12(7),* e0181554. doi:10.1371/journal.pone.0181554
660. Tuominen, L., Miettunen, J., Cannon, D., Drevets, W., Frokjaer, V., & Hirvonen, J. (2017). Neuroticism associates with cerebral in vivo serotonin transporter binding differently in males and females. *The International Journal of Neuropsychopharmacology, 20,* 963-970.
661. Turner, B., Huskey, R., & Weber, R. (2018). Charting a future for fMRI in Communication Science. *Communication Methods and Measures.* DOI: 10.1080/19312458.2018.1520823.
662. Twyman, N., Elkins, A., Burgoon, J., & Nunamaker, J. (2014). A rigidity detection system for automated credibility assessment. *Journal of Management Information Systems, 31,* 173-202.
663. Uddin, L., Nomi, J., Hebert-Seropian, B., Ghaziri, J., & Bouchar, O. (2017). Structure and function of the human insula. *J Clin Neurophysiol, 34,* 300-306.

664. Ulmer-Yaniv, A., Avitsur, R., Kanat-Maymon, Y., Schneiderman, I., Zagoory-Sharon, O., & Feldman, R. (2016). Affiliation, reward, and immune biomarkers coalesce to support social synchrony during periods of bond formation in humans. *Brain, Behavior, and Immunity, 56,* 130-139.
665. Ulubay, M., Keskin, U., Fidan, U., Ozturk, M., Bodur, S., Yılmaz, A., Kinci, M., & Yenen, M. (2016). Safety, efficiency, and outcomes of perineoplasty: Treatment of the sensation of a wide vagina. *BioMed Research International, 2016,* 2495105-5. doi:10.1155/2016/2495105
666. U.S. Department of Commerce, Economics and Statistics Administration (2010). Women-owned businesses in the 21st century. Retrieved from: http://www.esa.doc.gov/sites/default/files/reports/documents/women-owned-businesses.pdf
667. U.S. Department of Education, National Center for Education Statistics (2012). The condition of education 2012 (NCES 2012-045), Indicator 47. Retrieved from: nces.ed.gov/pubs2012/2012045_4.pdf
668. Valdesolo, P., Ouyang, J., & DeSteno, D. (2010). The rhythm of joint action: Synchrony promotes cooperative ability. *Journal of Experimental Social Psychology, 46,* 693-695.
669. Valentova, J., Tureček, P., Varella, M., Šebesta, P., Mendes, F., Pereira, K. et al. (2019). Vocal parameters of speech and singing covary and are related to vocal attractiveness, body measures, and sociosexuality: A cross-cultural study. *Frontiers in Psychology, 10* doi:10.3389/fpsyg.2019.02029
670. Van Caenegem, E., Wierckx, K., Taes, Y., Schreiner, T., Vandewalle, S., et al. (2015). Body composition, bone turnover, and bone mass in trans men during testosterone treatment: 1-year follow-up data from a prospective case-controlled study (ENIGI). *European Journal of Endocrinology, 172,* 163-171. doi:10.1530/EJE-14-0586
671. Van den Bos, R., Homberg, J., & De Visser, L. (2013). A critical review of sex differences in decision-making tasks: Focus on the Iowa gambling task. *Behavioural Brain Research, 238,* 95-108.
672. Van der Hoort, B., & Ehrsson, H. (2014). Body ownership affects visual perception of object size by rescaling the visual representation of external space. *Atten Percept Psychophys 76,* 1414–1428.
673. Van Der Laan, L., De Ridder, D., Charbonnier, L., Viergever, M., & Smeets, P. (2014). Sweetlies: neural, visual, and behavioral measures reveal a lack of self-control conflict during food choice in weight-concerned women. Front.Behav.Neurosci.8:184.doi:10.3389/fnbeh.2014.00184
674. Van der Linden, D., Dunkel, C., & Madison, G. (2017). Sex differences in brain size and general intelligence (g). *Intelligence, 63,* 78-88.675. Vanston, J., & Strother, L. (2017). Sex differences in the human visual system. *Journal of Neuroscience Research, 95,* 617-625.
676. Van Straalen, N. (2018). The naked ape as an evolutionary model, 50 years later. *Animal Biology, 68,* 227-246.
677. Varlamov, O., Bethea, C., & Roberts, J., & Charles T. (2014). Sex-specific differences in lipid and glucose metabolism. *Frontiers in Endocrinology, 5,* 241. doi:10.3389/fendo.2014.00241
678. Velten, J., Margraf, J., Chivers, M., & Brotto, L. (2018). Effects of a mindfulness task on women's sexual response. *The Journal of Sex Research, 55,* 747-757.
679. Verbeek, T., Bockting, C., Van Pampus, M., Ormel, J., Meijer, J., Hartman, C., & Burger, H. (2012). Postpartum depression predicts offspring mental health problems in adolescence independently of parental lifetime psychopathology. *Journal of Affective Disorders, 136,* 948–954.
680. Verriotis, M., Jones, L., Whitehead, K., Laudiano-Dray, M., Panayotidis, I., Patel, H., Meek, J., Fabrizi, L., & Fitzgerald, M. (2018). The distribution of pain activity across the human neonatal brain is sex dependent. *NeuroImage, 178,* 69-77.
681. Vetvik, K., & MacGregor, E., (2017). Sex differences in the epidemiology, clinical features, and pathophysiology of migraine. *Lancet Neurol, 16,* 76–87.
682. Vicaria, I., & Dickens, L. (2016). Meta-analyses of the intra- and interpersonal outcomes of interpersonal coordination. *Journal of Nonverbal Behavior, 40,* 335-361.
683. Victor, T., Drevets, W., Misaki, M., Bodurka, J., & Savitz, J. (2017). Sex differences in neural responses to subliminal sad and happy faces in healthy individuals: Implications for depression. *Journal of Neuroscience Research, 95,* 703-710.

684. Voyer, D., Voyer, S., & Saint-Aubin, J. (2017). Sex differences in visual-spatial working memory: A meta-analysis. *Psychon Bull Rev, 24,* 307-334.
685. Wade, T., & Feldman, A. (2016). Sex and the perceived effectiveness of flirtation techniques. *Human Ethology Bulletin, 31,* 30-44.
686. Wallen, K. (2001). Sex and context: Hormones and primate sexual motivation. *Hormones and Behavior, 40,* 339-357.
687. Wang, G., Cao, M., Sauciuvenaite, J., Bissland, R., Hacker, M., Hambly, C., Vaanholt, L., Niu, C., Faries, M., & Speakman, J. (2018). Different impacts of resources on opposite sex ratings of physical attractiveness by males and females. *Evolution and Human Behavior, 39,* 220-225. doi:10.1016/j.evolhumbehav.2017.12.008
688. Wang, Y., Zheng, D., Chen, J., Rao, L., Li, S., & Zhou, Y. (2019). Born for fairness: evidence of genetic contribution to a neural basis of fairness intuition. *Social Cognition and Affective Neuroscience, 14,* 539-548.
689. Warrier, V., Grasby, K., Uzefovsky, F., Toro, R., Smith, P., Chakrabarti, B., Khadake, J., Mawbey-Adamson, E., Litterman, N., Hottenga, J., Luke, G., Boomsa, D., Martin, N., Hatemi, P., Medland, S., Hinds, D., Bourgeron, T., & Baron-Cohen, S. (2018). Genome-wide meta-analysis of cognitive empathy: Heritability, and correlates with sex, neuropsychiatric conditions and cognition. *Molecular Psychiatry, 23,* 1402-1409.
690. Waters, S., West, T., Karnilowicz, H., & Mendes, W. (2017). Affect contagion between mothers and infants: Examining valence and touch. *Journal of Experimental Psychology. General, 146,* 1043-1051.
691. Watt, S., Tskhay, K., & Rule, N. (2018). Masculine voices predict well-being in female-to-male transgender individuals. *Archives of Sexual Behavior, 47,* 963-972.
692. Watts, T., Holmes, L., Savin-Williams, R., & Rieger, G. (2017). Pupil dilation to explicit and non-explicit sexual stimuli. *Archives of Sexual Behavior, 46,* 155-165. doi:10.1007/s10508-016-0801-8
693. Weber, R. (2015). Biology and brains - methodological innovations in communication science: Introduction to the special issue. *Communication Methods and Measures, 9,* 1-4.
694. Weber, R., Fisher, J., Hopp, F., & Lonergan, C. (2018). Taking messages into the magnet: Method-theory synergy in communication neuroscience. *Communication Monographs, 85,* 81-102.
695. Weber, R., Mangus, M., & Huskey, R. (2015). Brain imaging in communication research: A practical guide to understanding and evaluating fMRI studies. *Communication Methods and Measures, 9,* 5-29.
696. Weinand, J. & Safer, J. (2015). Hormone therapy in transgender adults is safe with provider supervision: A review of hormone therapy sequelae for transgender individuals. *Journal of Clinical & Translational Endocrinology, 2(2),* 55-60.
697. Weisman, O., Granat, A., Gilboa-Schechtman, E., Singer, M., Gordon, I., Azulay, H., Kuint, J., & Feldman, R., (2010). The experience of labor, maternal perception of the infant, and the mother's postpartum mood in a low-risk community cohort. *Arch. Womens Ment. Health 13,* 505–513.
698. Weng, D., Wang, Y., Gong, M., Tao, D., Wei, H., & Huang, D. (2015). "DERF: Distinctive efficient robust features from the biological modeling of the P ganglion cells," *IEEE Trans. Image Process., vol. 24,* 2287–2302.
699. West, E. (2009) Doing gender difference through greeting cards. *Feminist Media Studies, 9,* 285-299.
700. Wiesman, A., & Wilson, T. (2019). The impact of age and sex on the oscillatory dynamics of visuospatial processing. *Neuroimage, 185,* 513-520.
701. Wilcox, T., Alexander, G., Wheeler, L., & Norvell, J. (2012). Sex differences during visual scanning of occlusion events in infants. *Developmental Psychology, 48,* 1091-1105.
702. Williams, L. (2016). Precision psychiatry: a neural circuit taxonomy for depression and anxiety. *Lancet Psychiatry, 3,* 472–480.
703. Williams, D., Tracy, L., Gerardo, G., Rahman, T., Spangler, D., Koening, J., & Thayer, J. (2018). Sex moderates the relationship between resting heart rate variability and self-reported difficulties in emotion regulation. *Emotion.* Advance online publication. http://dx.doi.org/10.1037/emo0000500

704. Williamson, H. (2015). Social pressures and health consequences associated with body hair removal. *Journal of Aesthetic Nursing, 4,* 131-133. doi:10.12968/joan.2015.4.3.131
705. Wilson, S., Bailey, B., Jaremka, L., Fagundes, C., Andridge, R., Malarkey, W., Gates, K., & Kiecolt-Glaser, J. (2018). When couples' hearts beat together: Synchrony in heart rate variability during conflict predicts heightened inflammation throughout the day. *Psychoneuroendocrinology, 93,* 107-116.
706. Winternitz, J., Abbate, J., Huchard, E., Havlíček, J., & Garamszegi, L. (2016). Patterns of MHC-dependent mate selection in humans and nonhuman primates: A meta-analysis. *Molecular Ecology, 26,* 668-688. doi:10.1111/mec.13920
707. Wisman, A., & Shrira, I. (2020). Sexual chemosignals: Evidence that men process olfactory signals of women's sexual arousal. *Archives of Sexual Behavior.* https://doi.org/10.1007/s10508-019-01588-8
708. Wojciechowski, J., Stolarski, M., & Matthews, G. (2014). Emotional intelligence and mismatching expressive and verbal messages: A contribution to detection of deception. *PloS One, 9,* e92570-e92570. doi:10.1371/journal.pone.0092570
709. Wright, R., Riedel, R., Sechrest, L., Lane, R., & Smith, R. (2018). Sex differences in emotion recognition ability: The mediating role of trait emotional awareness. *Motiv Emot, 42,* 149-160.
710. Wu, Y., Li, H., Zhou, Y., Yu, J., Zhang, Y., Song, M., Qin, W., Yu, C., & Jiang, T. (2016). Sex-specific neural circuits of emotion regulation in the centromedial amygdala. *Scientific Reports, 6:* 23112. DOI: 10.1038/srep23112
711. Wu, K., Taki, Y., Sato, K., Hashizume, H., Sassa, Y., Takeuchi, H., Thryeau, B., He, Y., Evans, A., Li, X., Kawashima, R., & Fukuda, H. (2013). Topological organization of functional brain networks in healthy children: Differences in relation to age, sex, and intelligence. *PLOS One, 8:* e55347. doi: 10.1371/journal.pone.0055347
712. Xin, J., Zhang, Y., Tang, Y., & Yang, Y. (2019). Brain differences between men and women: Evidence from deep learning. *Frontiers in Neuroscience, 13,* 185-195. doi:10.3389/fnins.2019.00185
713. Xu, Y. (2017). Attrition of women in STEM: Examining job/major congruence in the career choices of college graduates. *Journal of Career Development, 44,* 3-19.
714. Yeung, A., Goto, T., & Leung, W. (2018). Affective value, intensity and quality of liquid tastants/food discernment in the human brain: An activation likelihood estimation meta-analysis. *NeuroImage, 169,* 189-199.
715. Yih, J., Beam, D., Fox, K., & Parvizi, J. (2019). Intensity of affective experience is modulated by magnitude of intracranial electrical stimulation in human orbitofrontal, cingulate and insular cortices. *Social Cognition and Affective Neuroscience, 14,* 339-351.
716. Yin, J., Zou, Z., Song, H., Zhang, Z., Yang, B., & Huang, X. (2018). Cognition, emotion and reward networks associated with sex differences for romantic appraisals. *Scientific Reports, 8:* 2835. DOI:10.1038/s41598-018-21079-5
717. Young, K., Bodurka, J., & Drevets, W. (2017). Functional neuroimaging of sex differences in autobiographical memory recall in depression. *Psychological Medicine, 47,* 2640-2652.
718. Youyou, W., Stillwell, D., Schwartz, H., & Kosinski, M. (2017). Birds of a feather do flock together: Behavior-based personality-assessment method reveals personality similarity among couples and friends. *Psychological Science, 28,* 276-284.
719. Yrttiaho, S., Niehaus, D., Thomas, E., & Leppänen, J. (2017). Mothers' pupillary responses to infant facial expressions. *Behavioral and Brain Functions: BBF, 13:* 2. doi:10.1186/s12993-017-0120-9
720. Yu, V., MacDonald, M., Oh, A., Hua, G., De Nil, L., & Pang, E. (2014). Age-related sex differences in language lateralization: A magnetoencephalography study in children. *Developmental Psychology, 50,* 2276-2284.
721. Yuan, F., & Woodman, R. (2010). Innovative behavior in the workplace: The role of performance and image outcome expectations. *Academy of management Journal, 53,* 323-342.
722. Zanatta, A., Pereira, R., Rocha, A., Cogliati, B., Baracat, E., Taylor, H., Motta, E., & Serafini, P. (2015). The relationship among HOXA10, estrogen receptor α, progesterone receptor, and progesterone receptor B proteins in rectosigmoid endometriosis: A tissue microarray study. *Reproductive Sciences, 22,* 31-37. doi:10.1177/1933719114549846

723. Zancada-Menendez, C., Sampedro-Piquero, P., Lopez, L., & McNamara, T. (2016). Age and gender differences in spatial perspective taking. *Aging Clinical and Experimental Research, 28,* 289-296.
724. Zekveld, A., Heslenfeld, D., Johnsrude, I., Versfeld, N., & Kramer, S. (2014). The eye as a window to the listening brain: Neural correlates of pupil size as a measure of cognitive listening load. *NeuroImage, 101,* 76-86.
725. Żelaźniewicz, A., & Pawłowski, B. (2018). Maternal hand grip strength in pregnancy, newborn sex and birth weight. *Early Human Development, 119,* 51-55.
726. Zelazniewicz, A., & Pawlowski, B. (2014). Disgust in pregnancy and fetus sex- longitudinal study. *Psychology & Behavior, 139,* 177-181.
727. Zhang, M., Liu, T., Pelowski, M., & Yu, D. (2017). Gender difference in spontaneous deception: A hyperscanning study using functional near-infrared spectroscopy. *Scientific Reports, 7:* 7508. DOI:10.1038/s41598-017-06764-1
728. Zhao, Y., Liu, X., Qu, Y., Wang, L., Geng, D., Chen, W., Li, L., Tian, Y., Chang, S., Zhao, C., Zhano, X., & Lv, P. (2019). The roles of p38 MAPK→COX2 and NF-κB→COX2 signal pathways in age-related testosterone reduction. *Scientific Reports, 9(1),* 10556-11. doi:10.1038/s41598-019-46794-5.
729. Zhilgeldina, N. (2017). Options of hormone replacement therapy effect on female's self-rating at perimenopause. *Maturitas, 100,* 188-188.
730. Zhou, W., & Chen, D. (2008). Encoding human sexual chemosensory cues in the orbitofrontal and fusiform cortices. *Journal of Neuroscience, 28,* 14416-14421
731. Ziabari, S., & Treur, J. (2018). Computational analysis of gender differences in coping with extreme stressful emotions. *Procedia Computer Science, 145,* 376-385.

INDEX

affection, 152, 162
    See also love; love physiology
affectionate communication, 93, 97, 100
affiliative language, female, 61, 62, 209
aggression levels, sex differences and, 91
aging, gender and, 172, 200–201, 217
    depression, 201
    gray matter of brain, 200
    hearing, 200
    language ability gap, 200
    memory capabilities, 200
    sex hormones, 200
    testosterone levels 228
amygdala, 32, 43–44, 85
    cortisol and, 43, 191
    emotion and, 37, 38, 39–40, 42–43, 85–86
    female resting state functional connectivity, 114
    memory and, 42
    mother-infant bonding and, 188–189
    sex differences, 85–86, 97
    stress and impairment of, 98–99, 154–155
    stress-processing and, 37, 39–40, 42, 85, 95, 97
androgen, 34
    aggressive behavior and, 35
    career choice and, 35
    fetal exposure to and spatial ability, 41, 64, 122
    fetal exposure to and substance control problems, 84
    mental object rotation and, 123
    mini-puberty and, 207
    prenatal exposure in males, 194
    spatial ability and, 208–209
    toy choice and, 35
    width-to-height face ratio and, 133
    See also congenital adrenal hyperplasia, females with
androstadienone, 149
androsterone, 34
anterior cingulate cortex, 86, 87, 94, 98, 155, 160, 191
anterior cingulate gyrus, 32, 99, 152
antidepressants
    for love addiction, 159
    postpartum depression and, 192
    sexual desire and, 153
anxiety, 33, 36, 157
    demand and withdrawal communication pattern and, 167
    females, 37, 44, 84, 86–87, 88–89, 96, 114, 202
    sexual arousal and motivation, 138
attention span, male versus female, 40
attractiveness, 143–151
    body odor, 148–151
    evolutionary, 146–147, 150
    See also attractiveness to females, male; attractiveness to males, female
attractiveness to females, male, 143–144
    appearance, 143–144, 146, 147–148, 150
    health, 146
    odor, 148–149, 150–151
    provider ability, 143, 146, 150
    sense of humor, 144

strength and physical ability, 143–144, 186
voice, 144
youthfulness, 146
attractiveness to males, female, 144–145, 146, 150, 186
    appearance, 144–145, 146, 186
    fertility, 144–145, 150–151
    health, 144, 145
    odor, 150
    youthfulness, 146, 150
autobiographical memory, female, 125
babies. *See* infants
basil ganglia, 32
Bezos, Jeff, 157
bilateral amygdala, female brain activation in, 114
biobehavioral synchrony, 156, 188–189
    marriage and, 156
    mother and newborn child, 188–189
    relationship bonding, 156
biological science research, 12
    communication and, 19–20, 25–26
births, nonmarital, 132
body hair, male attractiveness and, 147
body odor
    attractiveness and, 148–150, 151, 154
    as communication, 149, 150–151
    mother-infant bonding and, 187–188
    sexual attention and, 134
    See also chemosignals
boys. *See* children, male
brain
    blood flow, 58–59
    communication and, 15, 16–18, 20, 220
    detecting energy activity, 30
    endocrine system and, 18
    human communication and, 11
    immune system and, 18
    peripheral nervous system and, 18
    sex hormones and development of, 31, 34–35, 39–40
    sexually dimorphic, 31
    structural sex differences, 220
    See also specific parts and areas of the brain; brain sex differences
brain sex differences, 30–31, 35, 39–45, 93–95
    chromosomal, 31
    controversies, 32–33
    emotions, 39
    general intelligence, 40–41
    hemispheric, 33, 45
    language, 39
    learning, 39
    memory, 39, 40–41
    perception, 40
    predicting, 32
    size of brain, 31, 39
    social skills, 39
    spatial ability, 34, 35, 40–42
    stress, 93–98
    structural, 42–45
    See also specific parts and areas of the brain; children, female; children, male; females; males
breastfeeding, 5, 187–188, 197198
Broca's region, brain, 57
Brodmann areas, brain, 45, 55, 76, 104
Buds to Blossom organization, 5
bupropion, 203
canonical androgenic pathway, 34
career
    choice, 207, 208
    language skills and, 210
    prenatal sex hormones and choice of, 207
    spatial abilities and, 209
    sports industry gender differences, 209
caudate, 32, 94
central nervous system, 20, 30, 31
    See also neural messages; neurons; synapsis
cerebellum, 32, 45, 53, 64, 104
cerebral cortex, 45, 64
chemosignals, 134–135, 150–151, 154, 163
    females and, 134–135
    finding a mate and, 150–151, 154
    sexual arousal and, 135–136, 155
    See also body odor; scent communication
children, female, 196–197, 201
    appearance and social status, 197
    attention to detail and semantic aspects of objects, 196
    face processing, 196
    language abilities, 196, 197
    nonverbal communication skills, 197
    social abilities, 196–197
    See also congenital adrenal hyperplasia, females with; estrogen; females
children, gender and, 194–197
    females, 196–197
    males, 194196
    See also children, female; children male; infants
children, male, 194–196, 201
    activity engagement and self-

disclosure, 195–196
adolescence, 195
androgen surge, 207
attention to spatial aspects of objects, 194
communication style, 195
language skills, 195
male siblings, 195
mini-puberty, 53, 180, 194, 207
prenatal androgen exposure, 194
spatial skills, 197, 207
testosterone levels, 194–195
toddler language skills and fetal testosterone levels, 52, 57, 71, 126, 164, 181, 195
toddler language skills and infant testosterone levels, 57, 71, 73, 126, 210
See also androgen; males; testosterone
clothing, 199
cognitive empathy, 33, 104
color, female perception and preference, 70, 77, 110, 111–112, 124, 125
color blindness, 111
communibiology, 16, 17, 19–20, 206
communication, 3–4
affectionate, 93, 97, 100
biological research and, 19–20
biology and, 15, 16–18, 26
brain and, 15, 20, 220
nonverbal, 76, 105, 108, 124, 125, 197, 213
predicting, 20
relationships and, 4
scent as, 134–135, 149, 154
styles, 53, 212–213
survival and, 3–4
See also communication, female; communication, male; gender communication differences
communication, female
empathy and, 57–58, 62, 68, 104–108, 111, 124, 126
indirect, 67, 70
nonverbal, 105, 108, 124, 125, 213
people-oriented, 61
style, 53
tips for talking to males, 70, 76
See also language, females and
communication, male
assertive, 62, 195
compartmentalized, 63, 71
literal, 69, 70
style, 53, 212, 213
task-oriented, 61
See also language, males and

communication anxiety/apprehension, neurology and, 16–17
conflict, 165, 166
See also conflict management styles
conflict management styles, 165–167
female, 165, 166
male, 165, 166–167
See also demand and withdraw communication
congenital adrenal hyperplasia, females with, 179–180, 207, 209
spatial ability, 122, 179, 181, 207, 209
conversation, 61, 75–79
female behaviors, 61
female recall, 75–76, 77–79
male recall, 76, 77–79
See also conversations about problems, relationship
conversations about problems, relationship, 169–176
communicating empathy, 174
couple-inclusive language, 172
criticizing correctly, 172, 173–174
detecting deception, 174–176
menopause and, 172–173
relationship perception and, 173–174
scheduling, 171–172
timing, 176
uncertainty reductions theory and, 169–171
corpus callosum, 45, 47, 55–56, 66, 76
cortical circuits, 32
cortisol, 37, 100, 165–166
amygdala and, 39–40, 43–44
female reactivity to, 98, 99, 191
rest and relaxation and, 114, 182
smell and, 108–109
stress and release of, 36, 155
criminal behavior, male, 96, 121
testosterone and, 63, 91, 121
Darwin, Charles, 16
deception, relationship conversation, 174–176
decision-making, 56, 125, 212
female, 56, 125, 212
male, 56, 212, 213
demand and withdraw communication pattern, 163–168, 169
anxiety in women and, 167
communication adjustment tips, 167–168
conflict management styles and, 165–167
emotionally focused couple therapy

(EFT) and, 168
reasons for, 164
substance abuse in men and, 167
depression
   aging and, 200–201
   anxiety and, 84, 96
   exogenous hormone use and, 201
   females and, 44, 83, 84, 86, 87, 88–89, 94, 95, 98, 99–100, 191, 201
   gray matter reduction and, 84, 96
   heritability, 88
   hormone therapy and, 91, 218, 219
   lower estrogen and, 90, 91
   male reduced impulse control and, 96
   males and, 84, 87, 88, 94, 95
   menopause and, 201
   more pregnancies and, 201
   neurobiobehavioral disorder, 87
   perimenopause and, 90
   postmenopausal, 90
   puberty and, 90
   risks for, 87
   sex differences, 84, 87–88
   sexual problems and, 138, 218
   stress and, 99–100, 219
   substance control problems and, 84
   susceptibility, 87–88, 94
   treatments, 89, 90, 91
   X-linked genes and, 88–89
   See also depression, postpartum
depression, postpartum, 90, 191–192
   causes, 191
   estrogen and, 192
   mother insensitivity and, 192
   treatments, 192
desensitization, weight loss and systematic, 203
divorce, 6, 133, 153
dopamine
   attention and physiological desire functioning and, 137
   love addiction and, 158
   love and, 157–158
   medications that reduce, 159
dorsal attention network, 208
dorsal midbrain, 86
dorsomedial prefrontal cortex, 94
eating disorders, 204
EEG, 19, 23–24
electroencephalography. *See* EEG
emotional memory, 95
emotional reappraisal, orgasm and, 139
emotionally focused couple therapy (EFT), 168

emotions, 83, 85–91, 204
   eating disorders and, 204
   genes on sex chromosomes and, 83
   negative, 86–87
   serotonin and, 87–89
   sex hormones and, 83, 91
   stress and, 89–91
   structural brain differences and, 83, 85–86
   See also emotions, females and; emotions, males and
emotions, females and, 72, 85–87
   approach to and processing of negative, 85–86, 96
   distinguishing from others' tone of voice, 67–68, 104, 109
   personal memories link, 54, 73, 74, 94, 166
   processing, 85–86, 95–96, 106, 126
   susceptibility to negative, 86–87, 97
emotions, males and, 84
   approach to negative, 85–86, 96
   fluctuations, 84
   processing, 56, 58, 66–67, 86
   regulation, 43, 44, 45, 84
empathy
   cognitive, 33, 104
   communicating in relationship problem conversations, 174
   definition, 67
   female communication and, 57–58, 62, 68, 104–105, 111, 124, 126
   insula and, 106–107
   oxytocin and, 107
   stress and, 95
   trait, 104
endocannabinoids, lack of sexual desire and, 136
endocrine system, brain and, 18
epigenetics, 120, 186–187
episodic memory, female, 125
estradiol, 34
   female child language development and, 196
   language performance and, 57
   testosterone transformation into, 198
   See also estrogen
estrogen
   aging and, 200, 201
   cardiovascular regulation and, 36
   cerebellum and, 104
   cognitive functioning and, 40
   conditions related to low levels, 99–100

depression and, 36, 90, 91, 99–100
dimorphic female brain and, 35–36
emotions and, 86, 87
female brain and, 31, 35, 122
female versus male amount, 35, 54–55, 125, 181, 190, 210, 216
fetal levels and later language performance, 56–57
food intake and cravings, 203–204
headaches and, 99–100
hearing and, 110, 126, 190–191, 200
hippocampus and, 41, 54, 68, 72, 73, 83, 86, 96
language performance and, 54, 57, 68, 72, 73, 181, 210
listening abilities and, 216
memory and, 68, 125–126
menopause and, 84, 85, 90, 153, 200–201, 216
menstrual cycle levels, 139
migraines and, 36
muscle control and, 109
oxytocin and, 68, 76, 107, 126, 182, 192, 197–198, 210
pain sensitivity and, 36, 68, 84, 125–126
perimenopause and, 99
postpartum levels, 99, 192
prefrontal cortex and, 41
puberty and, 31, 90, 99
recognition and, 68, 125–126
rest and relaxation and, 114
sexual arousal and, 136
sexual desire and, 204
social awareness and, 210
social skills and strengths and, 31, 68, 72–73, 83, 125, 126, 182, 192, 197–198, 210
spatial abilities and navigation and, 42, 64, 122
stress and, 90–91
touch and, 109
See also estradiol; menstrual cycle; sex hormones
evolution, gender differences and
attractiveness, 146, 150
brain, 121–123
distinct roles, 120, 121, 123–127
female biological traits, 124–127
female role, 53, 124–127
female socializing skills, 68–69, 196–197
female superior empathy, 107–108, 112
functional brain, 52
infants and mothers, 184–185, 192
male biological traits, 121–124
male hunting and, 121, 123–124
male role, 48, 121, 123–124
male size and muscle mass, 121
male spatial abilities and performance, 64, 123
male strength, 123
mate selection, 142–143, 150–151
sex hormones, 52
structural brain, 52, 119
survival tactics, 65
See also epigenetics
excitation transfer theory, 161
expectancy violations theory, conversation recall and, 77–79
conversational tips, 79
emotional experiences and, 78–79
eye contact, 6, 141
females and oxytocin and, 61
first meetings and, 142
males and testosterone and, 62
as synchronous behavior, 156
face processing, female, 42, 43, 56, 67, 77, 103, 104, 125, 149, 190, 196
face ratio, width-to-height, 133
family unit, 197–199
empathy among members, 199
extended family and, 199
fathers and infants, 198–199
hormonal changes in mothers and fathers, 197–198
mothers and infants, 198
mother and father parenting differences, 198–199
norm compliance, 199
protection against threats, 199
trust and cooperation, 199
two parents versus one, 197
See also children, female; children, male; infants
fear, female, 42–43, 44
females
adapting to partner's behavior, 105
anxiety, 44, 84, 87, 88, 96, 167
brain blood flow, 58–59
as caregivers, 186
color and, 70, 77, 110, 111–112, 124, 210
conflict management style, 165, 166
conversation behaviors, 61
conversation recall, 75–79
creativity, 46
decision-making, 56, 125, 212
detail focus and recognition, 47, 64,

70, 74, 125, 190, 210, 213
emotional processing, 85–86, 95, 106, 126, 159
emotions-personal memories link, 54, 73, 74, 94, 166
estrogen amount versus males, 35, 54, 125, 181, 190, 210, 216
exploratory face scanning, 190
face processing, 42, 43, 56, 67, 77, 103–104, 125, 149, 190, 196
fear, 42, 44
food and, 202–204
gift preferences, 160–161
harm avoidance, 86
hearing sensitivity, 109–110, 125, 126, 190–191, 200
indirect communication, 67, 70
information processing, 56
inner speech, 42
integrated brain, 95
interhemispheric brain connectivity, 53, 55–56, 57, 58–59, 66, 68, 70–71, 72, 75, 86, 212
intuitive feeling, 46, 106, 107, 112, 126
language abilities and performance, 54, 57, 59, 60, 63–64, 72, 125, 181, 209–210
language processing, 41–42, 52, 53, 54–55, 56, 59, 67
language use, 59–60, 61, 67
memory, 41–42, 54, 72, 75, 77, 91, 107
mimicked and synchronized communication behaviors, 60, 62, 105, 186, 212
mood disturbance sensitivity, 98
navigation ability, 65, 125, 207–208
negative emotions, 85–87, 96–97
negative experience memories, 76, 94, 98
negativity bias, 43
nonverbal communication, 105, 108, 124, 125, 213
number processing, 46
object naming superiority, 53, 125, 181
orexin system expression to stress, 96–97
pain sensitivity, 6, 42, 84, 97, 98, 107, 109
pareidolia, 104
posttraumatic stress disorder, 85, 96, 99
problem-solving, 211–212
promiscuity, 134, 145
pupil dilation, 150, 190
rapport talk, 59, 60
reading into subtle comments, 70
response to viewing angry faces, 86, 87, 91
rest and relaxation, 114, 115
resting-state functional connectivity, 42, 43, 85, 94, 96, 97, 99, 103, 109, 114, 182
rewards and punishment responsiveness, 208
rumination, 42–43, 204
scent communication, 134–135, 149, 154
senses, 108–112, 126–127
sexual arousal, 135–136, 137
shopping behavior, 182
sight sensitivity, 110–112, 125
smell sensitivity, 108–109, 126–127, 187, 204
social abilities and strengths, 42, 43, 53, 56, 57–58, 75–76, 77, 83, 103, 104, 112, 125, 210, 213
social media use, 170, 182
spatial task solving, 46, 69
structurally dimorphic brain, 33, 35, 45
taste sensitivity, 109, 127, 187, 202, 204
teamwork, 212, 213
touch sensitivity, 6, 109
use of feeling words, 55
verbal fluency and memory, 45, 46, 55, 56, 64, 77, 107, 159
word processing, 52, 109, 125, 190
See also brain sex differences; children, female; estrogen; menopause; menstrual cycle; progesterone; sex hormones
fertility, increasing, 185
fetal brain development, survival information and, 186–187
flibanserin, 154
flirting behaviors, 146–147
fMRI, 19, 20–22
    See also fMRI studies
fMRI studies
    female testosterone levels, 91
    functional brain activity method, 22
    functional connectivity method, 22
    math performance, 46
    synthetic analysis method, 22–23
    visual imagery versus verbal cues, 76
food, 202–204
    female insula activation and, 203, 204
    female sensitivity, 202
    female sex hormones and, 203–204
    gender perceptions, 202, 204
    insula sex differences and, 203

sex hormone differences and, 203
See also eating disorders; smell; taste
FOXP2 gene, 51
functional magnetic reasoning imagery. *See* fMRI
fundamental attribution rule, 173
fusiform face area, female brain, 43, 67, 104, 149, 190, 196
G-Spot, 153
gender, sex versus, 8
gender communication, biological basis of, 11, 51–53
    See also gender communication differences
gender communication classes, 9–10, 13–14
    critiques, 14
    instructors and textbooks, 9–10, 14
    sociolinguistic approach, 9–10
gender communication differences, 73–74
    biological basis, 51–65
    body system differences and, 72–73
    brain blood flow and, 58–59
    brain connections and, 66–67
    brain structural differences and, 58
    conversation recall, 75–79
    corpus callosum and, 55–56
    early childhood, 59
    empathy, 67–68
    evolutionary explanations, 69–70
    female details and peripheral information, 74
    FOXP2 gene and, 51
    gray matter and, 54–55
    hippocampus and, 53–54, 72
    hormones and, 24–25, 57–58
    language differences and, 59–64
    limbic system differences and, 72
    male lack of detail and emotion, 73–74
    mental health and, 220
    oxytocin and, 58, 63, 107
    physical health and, 220
    self-disclosure, 60
    sex hormones and, 52, 56–57, 63, 64, 72–73
    spatial communication, 64–65
    touch and, 6, 7
    white matter and, 55
    See also brain sex differences; communication, female; communication, male; females; males
gender communication information, 9–10, 14, 51
gender communication research
methodology, 10–11, 15, 19–20
    critiques, 12–14
    historical data, 19
    interpretation in sociolinguistic, 10–11, 12
    observations, 19
    quality, 13
    researcher bias, 19
    self-reported data, 15
    societal observations, 19
    survey data, 19
gender discrimination, 206
genomic imprinting, 186–187
gift preferences
    female recipients, 160–161
    male recipients, 160
girls. *See* children, female
gray matter, 31, 32, 54–55, 57
    female, 45, 46–47, 54–55, 76, 106, 111, 149, 203
    information processing and, 54
    language processing and, 57
    male, 31, 54–55
    memory recall of language and, 76
    size of male versus female, 31, 54–55
gyrus regions, female resting state functional connectivity of, 114
hearing
    estrogen and, 110, 126, 190–191, 200
    female sensitivity, 109–110, 125, 126, 190–191, 200
    female versus male, 109–110
hippocampus, 32, 36, 42–43
    aging and, 200
    emotions and, 87
    estrogen and, 41, 54, 68, 72, 73, 83, 85, 86, 96
    face processing and, 97
    female, 54, 55, 68, 72, 73, 75–76, 85, 86, 87, 96, 98, 114, 155, 191, 216
    language and, 54
    locus coeruleus and, 72
    male, 54
    memory and, 54, 55, 72
    memory-language connection and, 54, 68, 72, 75
    progesterone and, 68
    relationships and, 54, 68
    sex hormones and, 91, 99
    stress and impairment of, 98
    testosterone and, 72
hobbies, 179–183
    adult gender differences, 181–182, 183
    early childhood gender differences,

179–181, 183
    sex hormones and, 179–180, 182
    shopping behavior gender differences, 181, 182
    testosterone and, 180
hormone levels, evaluating, 220
hormone replacement therapy. *See* hormone therapy
hormone research, 19, 24–25
hormone therapy, 153, 215–216
    biological female transitioning to male, 218–219
    biological male transitioning to female, 217
    depression in females and, 91
    estrogen patch, 217
    long-term effects, 220
    male sexual problems and, 217–218
    menopausal women and, 100, 216, 217
    postmenopausal women and, 216–217
    prostate cancer treatment, 218
    psychological effects, 219
    risks and side effects, 217–219
hormones. *See names of specific hormones*; hormone research; hormone therapy; sex hormones
hypothalamus, 33, 36, 89–90, 91, 96
immune system, brain and, 18
infants
    behavior of mothers with, 198
    body odors and bonding with mother, 187–188
    breastfeeding and bonding, 188
    evolution and female desire for, 184–185, 192
    fathers and, 185, 198–199
    female attention to faces, 187
    importance of touch, 4–5
    intrusive mothers and, 189
    mother facial perception ability and, 190
    need for bonding, 187, 188
    object tracking ability of male, 207
    positive emotional experience and survival, 185
    testosterone levels and later language performance, 57, 71, 73, 126, 210
inferior frontal gyrus, 97
inferior parietal lobe, 41, 64
infidelity, 132–133
information processing, 39, 56
insula, 94, 104, 106–107, 126, 149
    female empathy and, 106–107, 126
    female pain sensitivity and, 107
    food and sex differences and, 202–203, 204
    heightened sensory awareness and, 107
    intuitive feeling and, 106, 126–127
    sensory and emotional processing, 106, 126
    sensory motor coordination, 106
    smell and, 108, 126–127
    smelling potential mate and, 149
    sound and, 107
    taste and, 107, 127
intuitive feeling, female, 46, 106, 107, 112, 126
Iowa Gambling Task, 48
Jolie, Angelina, 157
language, females and
    abilities, 59, 125, 181–182, 210
    auditory connections and processing of, 66, 125, 190
    career skills, 210–211
    estrogen and, 54, 57, 68, 72, 73, 181, 210
    performance, 54, 57, 63–64, 72
    personal relational goals, 211
    processing, 41, 54, 55, 56, 59, 67
    self-disclosure, 60, 155
    task selective attention, 210
    use, 60, 61, 67
language, males and
    assertive, 62, 63, 209
    competitive style, 62, 63
    power and objects and, 211
    processing, 56, 58, 86
    self-disclosure to females, 63
    skills, 195
    speech disorders, 53
    testosterone and, 52–53, 57, 71, 73, 126, 164, 181, 195, 210
    use, 60
    visual connections for processing, 66
left middle temporal gyrus, 97, 175
left superior frontal gyrus (SFG), 84
limbic system, 41–42, 54, 72, 85, 104, 137, 152, 154–155
    female, 72, 85, 96, 104, 137, 152
    female stress and, 154–155
    male versus female, 72–73
    underperformance and lack of sexual desire, 137
    See also hippocampus
listening, 56, 60, 67–68
locus coeruleus (LC), 40, 72, 85–86, 95
    emotional memories and, 85–86
    emotional processing and, 95

sex differences, 85–86, 95
love
    as attachment, 157, 158
    as basic human need, 3–4
    relationship affection and, 162
    See also love addiction; love physiology
love addiction, 158–159
    dopamine and, 158
    oxytocin and, 158–159
    treatments, 159
love physiology, 157–159
    relationships and, 157–159, 162
    dopamine and, 157
    oxytocin and, 157, 158
    striatum and, 157–158
lying. *See* deception, relationship conversation
males
    action execution, 43
    big-picture focus, 69–70, 73, 74
    brain blood flow, 59
    brain size, 31, 39
    cardinal directions, 65, 207–208
    cognitive control, 44
    cognitive functioning, 40
    color blindness, 111
    communication style, 212, 213
    compartmentalized focus, 33, 41, 45, 54–55, 56, 59, 63, 67, 71, 166
    conflict management style, 165, 166
    conversation recall, 76, 77
    decision making, 56, 212, 213
    depression, 84, 87–88, 90, 94, 95
    emotion processing, 56, 58, 66–67, 86
    emotional regulation, 43, 44, 45, 69, 84
    focus, 54
    focus on spatial aspects, 47, 64
    general intelligence, 40
    genitalia excitement and sexual attraction, 150
    gift preferences, 160
    infidelity desires, 133
    intrahemispheric brain connectivity, 55–56, 58, 66, 121
    language and, 52–53, 56, 58, 60, 62–63, 86, 195, 211
    mental object rotation ability, 35, 41, 47, 64, 69, 70, 76, 208–209, 213
    motion ability, 160, 182, 199
    movement perception, 122
    number processing, 46
    object tracking, 122, 179, 207
    promiscuity, 134, 144
    report talk, 59, 60
    rest and relaxation, 113, 114–115, 182
    resting-state functional connectivity, 43
    retinal M-GCs, 182–183
    sense of direction, 41
    sex chromosomes, 29–30, 31
    shopping behavior, 181, 182
    social situation processing, 58
    spatial ability, 34, 35, 40, 41, 47, 64, 69, 70, 73, 76, 91, 121, 122–123, 160, 197, 199, 207, 208, 213
    spatial communication, 64–65, 123
    spatial-event memory, 64
    visual attention, 123
    visual connections for language processing, 66
    visual-event memory, 64, 69, 76
    word processing, 52, 76
    See also androgen; brain sex differences; children, male; hormone therapy; sex hormones; testosterone
mate, finding, 93
    sense of smell and, 149
mating differences, gender, 133–134
medial prefrontal cortex, 41, 94
mediodorsal nucleus of thalamus (MDN), 44, 84
melanocortins, attention and physiological desire functioning and, 137
memory, female, 41, 42, 54, 72
    autobiographical, 125
    emotional, 95
    episodic, 125
    faces and, 75, 77
    social cues and, 91
    social interactions and, 107
    verbal, 45, 46, 55
memory, male visual-event, 64, 69, 76
men. *See* males
menopause
    divorce and, 153
    emotional fluctuations and, 84, 85
    estrogen and, 84, 85, 90, 153, 200, 216
    muscle control and, 84
    relationship problem conversations during, 172–173
menstrual cycle
    caloric intake, 108, 204
    conflict resolution during follicular phase, 167
    creatine fluctuation, 90
    emotional fluctuations, 84
    estrogen levels, 139, 215
    female cognitive strategies and, 40
    fertility phase, 136

follicular phase, 140, 203
food cravings, 108, 139, 203–204
influence on males around female, 139–140
late follicular phase, 122
listening abilities and, 216
luteal phase, 185, 196, 203–204
midluteal phase, 87, 99
muscle control and, 84
orgasm and, 139
ovulation, 203
pregnancy and, 196
relationships and, 196–197
sexual motivation and, 139
stress sensitivity and, 99
synchronized with cohabitating females, 61, 95, 105, 196
synchronized headaches with cohabitating females, 61, 95, 105
See also estrogen
mental object rotation task ability
careers and, 209
female, 47, 69
male, 35, 41, 47, 64, 69, 70, 76, 208–209, 213
midbrain, 94
middle prefrontal cortex (mPFC), 95
mimicked and synchronized communication behaviors, 186, 212
couples and, 105
during gestation, 186
eye contact, 156
father-infant, 185, 198
female, 60, 62, 105, 186, 212
mother-newborn child, 188–189
in relationships, 156, 166
See also biobehavioral synchrony
mini-puberty, 53, 180, 194, 207
mirror neurons, 46–47, 110–111, 199
females versus males, 111
Monroe, Marilyn, 144
naltrexone, 203
needs, basic human, 3–7, 93
nervous system, 30–31
See also central nervous system; peripheral nervous system
neural circuits, 30, 35
neural messages, communication and, 24
neurons, 23–24, 30
See also mirror neurons
nonverbal communication
female children, 197
females, 76, 105, 108, 124, 125, 197, 213
gestures, 76

norepinephrine, 40
sexual arousal and, 137
nucleus accumbens (NAcc), 188–189, 200
occipital lobe, 94
offspring uncertainty
males and, 131–132, 141, 143, 150
paternity acknowledgment and, 132–133
opioids, lack of sexual desire and, 136
orbitofrontal cortex, 104
orexins, 96
orgasm, 135, 137–140, 141
emotional reappraisal and, 139
female, 138–139, 140
frequency and intensity, 138
male, 137–138
menstrual cycle and, 139–140
oxytocin and, 138
psychological factors, 138
relationship quality and, 138
overcrowding, stress and, 6
oxytocin, 165–166
affection infant touch and, 198
affectionate communication and, 100
biobehavioral synchrony and, 189
birth contractions and, 197
bonding and, 63
breastfeeding and, 197–198
childhood levels, 198
CNS neuromodulator, 58
communication and, 114
conversation recall and, 77
empathy and, 107
estrogen and, 68, 76, 107, 126, 182, 192, 197–198, 210
eye contact and, 61
fathers and infants and, 185
female conversation and, 61, 107, 210
females and, 58, 61, 68, 76, 77, 91, 107, 114, 137, 152
gender communication differences and, 58, 63, 107
human social cognition and, 63
love addiction and, 158
love and, 157
medications that reduce, 159
mothers and infants and, 185
orgasm and, 138
parent physical interaction with child and, 198
postpartum depression injections of, 192
relational conflict and, 165
relationships and, 155
sexual arousal/desire and, 137

socializing and, 58, 76, 89, 91, 182
stress reduction and, 152
talking and, 154
pain, female sensitivity to, 6, 42, 97, 98–99, 107, 109
    estrogen and, 36, 68, 84, 125–126
parabrachial nucleus, 32
pareidolia, 104
parietal area, 54
pay gap, gender, 205–206
periaqueductal gray (PAG), 86
perimenopause, 90, 99
peripheral nervous system, 18, 20, 30
Pitt, Brad, 157
postcentral gyrus, 97
posterior cingulate cortex, 104
postmenopause, hormonal changes during, 216
postpartum depression. *See* depression, postpartum
posttraumatic stress disorder, females and, 85, 96, 99
prefrontal cortex, 94, 103–104, 136
pregnancy, 185–187, 192
    age of mother, 187
    building social alliances during, 185
    contractions and oxytocin sensations, 197
    father in postpartum period, 192–193
    food cravings, 187
    healthy parent lifestyle and offspring DNA, 185–186
    hormonal changes during and after, 187, 197–199
    information passed from mother to fetus during, 120
    mother decreased brain volume, 186
    mother handgrip strength during, 187
    postpartum, 187–190
    season at time of conception, 187
    senses, 187
    serotonin and, 187
premenstrual dysphoric disorder, 90
primary visual cortex, 123
problem-solving, female, 211–212
progesterone, 34, 40, 68, 203, 204, 218
prolactin, 198
promiscuity
    female, 134, 145
    male, 134, 144
puberty, sex hormones during, 31, 52, 90, 99
pubic hair grooming, 147–148
pupil dilation, 87, 97
    females and infant distress, 190

    females and sexual arousal, 150
    males and sexual attraction, 150
rapport talk, 59, 60
recall, conversation, 75–79
    female, 75–76, 77–79
    improving, 77–79
    male, 76, 77–79
    sex physiology and, 75–76
    topic, 76–77
relationship maintenance, 152, 159–161, 162
    excitation transfer theory and, 161
    gift preferences, 160–161
relationship perception, 173–174
relationships, 152–159, 161–162
    affection, 152, 161
    communication, 3, 161–162
    core beliefs and values, 162
    females and, 41, 212–213
    love physiology and, 157–159
    mimicry and synchrony in, 156, 166
    oxytocin and, 155
    self-disclosure in, 162
    sex hormones and sexual desire and, 152–154
    sexual readiness and, 154–155
    touch in, 162
    See also conversations about problems, relationship; relationship maintenance
rest and relaxation, 113–115, 182
    females, 114, 115
    gender differences, 114–115
    males, 113, 114, 115, 182–183
    sex hormones and, 114–115
    See also resting-state functional connectivity (rsFC)
resting-state functional connectivity (rsFC), 42–43
    female, 42, 43, 85, 94, 96, 97, 99, 104, 109, 114
    female versus male, 42, 43
right insular cortex, 152
right lateral occipital cortex, 200
right superior temporal sulcus, 104
right temporal gyrus, 94
rumination, female, 42–43, 204
scent communication, female, 134–135, 149, 154
    See also chemosignals
senior living facilities, need for personal contact in, 5
serotonin, 87–89, 98, 154, 159
    lack of sexual desire and, 136
    pregnancy and, 187

serotonergic system, 87–88, 98
  sex hormones and, 89
sex, gender versus, 8
sex chromosomes, 29–30, 31
  serotonin and, 88
sex differences
  beginnings, 29–30
  fetal survival, 37
  general intelligence, 40–41
  information processing, 46–48
  on intelligence tests, 46
  sex hormones, 34–38
  See also androgen; brain sex differences; estrogen; females; males; testosterone
sex drive, 133, 135, 152–153, 159
sex hormones, 215–219
  artificial and gene pool, 215
  behavioral differences and, 52
  brain-area size and, 53
  brain development and, 31, 34–35, 39–40
  cognitive functioning and, 40
  emotions and, 91
  females, 216–217
  fetal development and, 34–35, 52, 121–122
  food preference differences and, 203–204
  gender communication differences and, 52–53, 56–57, 63, 64–65, 71–73, 220
  hippocampus and, 72, 91
  hobbies and, 179–180, 182
  hypothalamus and, 96
  language social understanding and, 56–58, 68
  males, 217–218
  mood and, 91
  motor coordination and, 34
  puberty and, 31, 52, 90, 99
  relational conflict and, 165–166
  rest and relaxation and, 114–115
  serotonergic system and, 89
  sex differences and, 34–36
  sexual desire in relationships and, 152–153
  spatial skills and, 52
  stress and, 96, 98–100
  verbal skills and, 52
  See also androgen; estrogen; progesterone; testosterone
sexual arousal, 134–137, 138–140, 154
  chemosignals and, 134–135
  emotional regulation and, 139
  female, 135–136, 137, 154–155
  male, 135, 154
sexual attention, 134–135
  body odors and, 134
  chemosignals and, 134–135
  sexual desire and, 135
  touch and, 134
  visual cues and, 134
sexual behaviors, 131–134, 140–141
  biological sexual differences and, 140–141
  double standard for men and women, 131
  gender mating differences, 133–134
  infidelity, 132–133
  See also offspring uncertainty; orgasm; sexual arousal; sexual attention
sexual desire, 133, 135, 136–137, 152–154
  anxiety/depression and, 138
  emotional regulation and, 139
  estradiol/estrogen and, 153, 204
  female lack of, 136–137, 153
  psychological factors for females, 138
  sex hormones in relationships and, 152–153
  sexual attention/arousal and, 135
  testosterone and, 133–134, 153
  treatments and therapies for low, 137, 153–154
sexual differences, biological, 140–141
sexual dysfunction, male, 153
sexual functioning, 136
sexual intimacy, male, 153
sexual mindfulness, 138
sexual needs, prioritizing, 135
sexual promiscuity
  females, 134, 145
  males, 134, 144
sexual readiness, relationships and, 154–155
  See also sexual arousal
sight
  color, 70, 77, 110, 111–112
  female retinal P-GCs and, 110, 125
  female versus male, 110–112
  male retinal M-GCs and, 123
  mirror neurons, 46–47, 110–111
smell, 108–109
  female versus male sense of, 108–109
  taste and, 109
  See also body odor; chemosignals
social information processing, female, 56
social learning, limitations of, 17
social media, 170, 173, 182
solitary confinement, effects of in jail/

prison, 4
solitary tract nucleus, 32
sound, insula and, 107
spatial abilities
    androgen and, 122
    congenital adrenal hyperplasia females, 122, 179, 181, 207, 209
    decrease, 91–92
    females, 46, 69
    line alignment and relations, 122
    male, 34, 35, 40, 41, 47, 64, 69, 70, 73, 76, 91, 121, 122–123, 160, 197, 199, 207, 208, 213
    male career choice and, 208
    male versus female, 122–123
    motion direction, 122
    reaction time to movement, 122
    visual acuity, 122
stress
    brain changes and, 83
    brain impairment and, 98
    cortisol and, 155
    depression and, 99–100, 219
    eating disorders and, 204
    empathy and, 95
    estrogen and, 90
    female versus male, 37, 94, 95–100
    female vulnerability to, 154–155
    gender brain differences, 93–95
    gender differences, 89–91, 100
    gender reaction differences, 96–98
    gender social awareness and, 95
    hypothalamus and, 89–90, 96
    male action/movement-related, 95
    overcrowding and, 6
    serotonergic system and, 98
    sex chromosome genes and, 93–94
    sex hormones and, 93–94, 98–100
    sleep deprivation and, 97
    social situations and, 95, 97
    testosterone levels and, 198–199
    See also stress reduction
stress reduction
    affectionate communication and, 93, 97, 100
    activities, 95
    cognitive reappraisal and distraction, 100
    communication and, 95
    father-child caregiving and, 198–199
    gender differences, 96–98
    hormone therapy and, 100
    oxytocin and, 152
    positive partner support and, 97–98
superior frontal gyrus, 188
superior temporal sulcus, 175
synapsis, 24
taste
    female sensitivity, 109, 127, 187, 202, 204
    female versus male sense of, 109
    insula and, 107
    smell and, 109
    See also food
teamwork, females and, 212, 213
temporal area, brain, 54
testosterone, 165, 217–219
    acne and, 134
    adult male versus adult female amount, 34, 63, 99, 121, 126, 133, 135, 143, 152, 181, 216
    aging and, 200, 201
    aggression and, 54, 62, 63, 72, 73, 106, 121, 180, 194–195
    as antidepressant, 89, 90
    antisocial behavior and, 63, 91
    antisocial cognition and, 63, 91, 121
    asocial behavior and, 63
    assertive language and, 62, 195
    big picture understanding and, 73
    caregiving and, 198
    cognitive functioning and, 40
    color hue differentiation and, 111
    color preference and, 112
    competition and, 54, 62, 63, 72, 121, 194–195, 198
    conversation behaviors and, 62
    decrease in, 91–92, 200, 201, 217
    eye contact and, 62
    father-infant touch and oxytocin and, 185
    fetal levels and toddler language performance and, 52, 56–57, 71, 126, 164, 181, 195
    fluctuating levels, 121
    gray matter decrease and, 57
    hippocampus and, 72
    hobbies and, 180–181
    hunting and, 123–124
    individualistic behavior and, 184
    infant levels and toddler language performance and, 57, 71, 73, 126, 210
    language style and, 63
    low father-infant mimicry and synchrony, 185
    low levels in males, 153, 217
    lower empathy and, 35, 106
    male brain and, 31, 39–40, 54, 72
    male children and, 194–195
    mating behaviors, 198

mother-infant touch and oxytocin and, 185
object rotation ability and, 209, 213
power and, 54, 63, 72, 73
puberty and, 31
relational conflict and, 165
rest and relaxation and, 113
self-oriented behavior and, 63, 182
sex drive and, 133, 135
sexual arousal/desire and, 133, 135
spatial ability and, 34, 35, 73, 91–92, 180, 209, 213
spatial cognition and women and, 217
Sry gene and, 34
status and, 54, 63, 72, 73
status-seeking behaviors and, 195
strength and, 121, 180
stress and, 198–199
as therapy for low female sex drive, 153
toy selection and, 180, 207
transformation into estradiol, 198
violent criminal behavior and, 96, 121
width-to-height face ratio and, 133
See also hormone therapy; sex hormones

thalamus, 44, 84, 94
touch, 4–7, 109, 162, 185
affective, 5
aging and, 5
amount, 6
as basic human need, 4–6
breastfeeding mothers and, 5
father and infant, 185
female sensitivity to, 6, 109
female versus male sense of, 109
gender communication differences, 7
importance of in relationships, 162
infants and, 4–5, 185
intentional healthy, 5
mother and infant, 185
orphanages and, 5
relationship uncertainty and, 170–171
toy play, 180–181
toy preferences/selection, 180, 207
uncertainty, relationship, 169–171
avoidance and, 169–170
criticism and, 169
eliminating, 170–171
negative behaviors and, 169
vagina, 140–141, 145
ventral frontal cortex, 64
ventromedial prefrontal cortex, 66
verbal fluency, female, 45, 55, 56, 63, 77, 108, 159

verbal memory, female, 45, 46, 55
visual-event memory, male, 64, 69, 76
Wernicke's area, 57
white matter, 32, 45–46, 55
    female, 46, 55
women. *See* females
word processing
    female, 52, 109, 125, 190
    male, 52, 76
workplace, 206–208, 211–212, 213
    advantages of having females in, 213
    advantages of having males in, 213
    biological influences, 206–208
    environmental responses and, 208–209
    gender communication applied in, 211–212
    See also pay gap, gender
X chromosome, 29–30, 88–89, 90, 111
Y chromosome, 29, 34, 89

ABOUT THE AUTHOR

Dr. Stephen Furlich has taught and researched communication at the university level for over twenty years. This includes teaching a variety of communication courses that place focus on the better understanding of oneself and others. His research projects and courses complement one another and lead into innovative directions.

He has always had an interest in understanding others beyond what is commonly understood. This entails reading and understanding research from a variety of disciplines. Taking that a step further, in every class taught and research project conducted he emphasizes the importance of applying knowledge gained in everyday life, both personally and professionally.

His communication paradigm is from a receiver's perspective. This places the emphasis on the listener to better understand from the speaker's perspectives, and as a speaker, emphasizing understanding from the listener's perspectives. Both of these become more challenging as differences increase between the speaker and listener.

He has become fascinated with the technological advancements in science that have enabled a better understanding of communication. Without these scientific advances, comprehending communication is quite limited. This line of research has inspired him to write this book so that he might bring together many different scientific studies and better understand the role of biology with gender communication differences.

Made in the USA
Middletown, DE
13 April 2021